From the Burning Archive

Jeff Rich

Copyright © 2022 Jeff Rich

All rights reserved.

ISBN:
ISBN-13: 978-0-6451592-2-6 (Print)
ISBN-13: 978-0-6451592-3-3 (E-Book)

A billion pages of etched life
In minutes, memos, letters -

The familiar writing of everyday,
Few metaphors, many more lists

Within a day, ten thousand years,
And more, gone, gone, gone.

The cord that held us to them,
A line of white ashen hearts.

Jeff Rich, "From the Burning Archive – the Beginning", in *Gathering Flowers of the Mind*

Contents

Part One. The Burning Archive 1

Part Two. Fire in the Voice 10

Part Three. Cultural Decay 75

Part Four. The Infinite Conversation 120

Part Five. Histories of Our Times 189

Part Six. Social Fragmentation 244

Part Seven. Unraveling Empires 329

Part One

The Burning Archive

Jeff Rich

The Burning Archive
August 2022

In 2015 I began writing a blog, *The Burning Archive*. It was my second blog. Between 2010 and 2014 I had secretly written *The Happy Pessimist* blog, largely concerning national politics in Australia. But *The Happy Pessimist* was cloaked in a pseudonym, Antonio Possevino, who was a sixteenth-century Jesuit diplomat, priest and author. I identified with Possevino, who became my digital avatar, because he also published tracts without his true name. So my first blog, *The Happy Pessimist*, was haunted by the prospect of the outing of its author. Its voice was muffled by fear of reprisals since that author had a day job as a minor government official subject to draconian speech codes that discouraged living in truth. When I began writing *The Burning Archive*, I defied those codes. I wrote in my own name, with no obfuscation of my occupation, and I released my voice and my mind to wander where they may.

The blog began in a period of deep personal crisis when freedom of speech and freedom of thought were essential, as I suppose they always are, to endurance through pain, suffering and defeat. Although at that time I did not know the poem by Kahlil Gilbran, "Defeat" (1918), it was as if I was in this blog screwing my courage to the sticking place and acting out Gilbran's final stanza.

> Defeat, my Defeat, my deathless courage,
> You and I shall laugh together with the storm,
> And together we shall dig graves for all that die in us,
> And we shall stand in the sun with a will,
> And we shall be dangerous.

The personal crisis was in itself related to my decision eighteen months earlier to close down my *Happy Pessimist* blog in fear. A public servant in Canberra had been sacked for a statement on social media. Governments of all stripes were controlling the communications of their servants, and suppressing the right to freedom of speech and freedom of thought of minor government officials. Major government officials who spoke in partisan ways in support of the government had nothing to fear. But lowly under-castellans such as me could threaten their careers by stating their mind in plain language. At that point I wanted to protect or even advance my career and obtain the rank long denied to me. So I decided to suppress my writing and seek favour in the court, but I was not successful. Then the recognition of this failure and the silent price I had paid provoked a major personal crisis.

So, *The Burning Archive* began. Although the fire began with personal crisis, the distressed emotions seeped only a little into the writing shared with the Ethernet of silenced screams. I had other outlets to express my inner torment: sessions with a psychologist; the love of my family; a series of black notebook journals, each titled poetically to evoke the soul-deepening experience I slowly made my way through; and my poetry and fictional writing. But I found my authorial persona on the blog, where I commented pessimistically on my sense of cultural or historical crisis, which I pointed to in the very name of the blog. The archive of our culture, with all its social memories and inherited institutions, was in flames. I had written poems before on this metaphor of the burning archive, and these poems were later published in 2021 in *Gathering Flowers of the Mind: Collected Poems, 1996-2020*. But I had not dared to share the image with the world. It was too intense, too painful, too precious. As poems, the image of the burning archive amplified my cries, and did not diffuse my pain. So by making the burning archive prosaic, the blog helped to map my way out of my personal crisis, and to turn a haunting poetic image into prose diagnosing a new time of troubles. From the start, I wrote with the idea that the blog could be an experimental art form, emerging in uncontrolled conditions, and a kind of digital *samizdat* in which the thoughts of people excluded from the published scene could describe, more truthfully than over-promoted authors, a culture on the brink of collapse. As I wrote on the first day, *The Burning Archive* would be "reflections and readings of today's political, social and gave a sermon.

He was unpractised as a public speaker before this time.

He was something of a courtier and yet an outsider, who tried but often failed to secure the sinecure he needed to sustain his status.

He only became a priest, when he abandoned hope of other offices, and sought an income.

His religiosity was not in doubt.

But he was a reformed soul, so the biography by John Stubbs labels him.[2]

He was reformed since he had converted from Catholicism, if ambivalently.

He was reformed since he gave up the life of a courtly ladies man to marry for love.

He was reformed too since he adopted the religious life late in life, and so anchored his writing in a discipline of communing with his flock.

Before then he was known more as a wit than a poet.

His renown is now for his poetry, especially for "No man is an island."

Among poets and the religious, he is known for his holy sonnets, of which one at least "Death, be not proud" speaks to our immortal fears.

Yet his poetry was passed around as private wit; perhaps only for money did he publish *Songs and Sonnets,* and then with reservations.

It was his sermons for which he was best known. They won renown and patrons for Donne. One sermon that praised the king, the king eagerly sought to publish and widen both Donne's fame and the king's prestige – the writer's long secret pact with power.

These sermons now continue to live in the luminarium, and a vast project of Oxford University Press that seeks to publish again every sermon's text, restored lovingly from Donne's own manuscripts. There is even a project that recreates in a digital and virtual world the

---

[2] John Stubbs, *John Donne: The Reformed Soul* (2007).

cultural orders, and my search for traditions in history, culture, and literature that I choose to preserve, so I might ward off an uneasy feeling of cultural collapse."

Today that uneasy feeling of cultural collapse, or at least senescence and sabotage of the West and other traditions, is a commonly expressed concern, certainly among more conservative social observers. Yet I had drawn the image from one of the founders of radical cultural Marxism. The poetic image inspiring the blog blew first from one of Walter Benjamin's theses on the philosophy of history. In this aphoristic text of fragments, the oddly mystical cultural Marxist imagined an Angel of History, blown forward by a firestorm of progress, yet looking back with tenderness at both the horror and the glory of the ruins. In those dog days of 2015, when I had no anticipation of any audience or any reception, I set out how I intuited the writing ahead:

> The burning archive is an image of human history, learning and heritage being destroyed through our own actions of forgetting and destruction. ... My blog is an extended meditation on both what is lost and what, despite the flames, is preserved, especially my most loved fragments of culture and literature. The blog is evolving into its own form of artwork, a new form of artwork made possible by the simple democratic tools of creativity in our digital age.

The advent of this archive in flames released my mind from an imprisoning magic ring of fire of my own making. For so long I had encased my spirit in an ill-chosen vocation: public servant, bureaucrat, and policy adviser. By choosing this path, I thought I walked the low road of the *vita activa*, and not the high road of the *vita contemplativa*.

For twenty years, while I led a mediocre career in government, I had kept my writing and intellectual life hidden. But it refused to be cowed. I wrote poetry. I began and never finished novels. I wrote essays for the drawer. I struggled with saying 'I am a writer', not 'I am a public servant'. I tried to make my working life as a policy bureaucrat a kind of intellectual vocation. I created a personal myth of the despised private intellectual, in which I, like Machiavelli, shared my thoughts privately with patrons, but remained unknown as a writer in the present. I believed, not without reason, because of my exposure to so many issues and so many people through government, that I knew more of the world than the journalists, academics, business flakes, advertising executives and NGO activists who make up our chattering classes. I tormented myself to believe my realm of knowledge, experience and thought was closeted and despised. It would only ever be known by some future archivist who might discover the genius of my boxed briefings a century on from now. My insights were privileged and secreted. I lived in a split world, experienced as a divided psyche, where I wrote for the Cabinet by day and for the drawer by night. This splitting of my psyche shackled my prose. I thought my commentaries had to be about the constructed practical and not the imagined real. I thought I had to control my topics to those in which I could authoritatively claim to be a subject matter expert—the practical policy judgments of governments. I thought I could not stray in public writings very far from the social consensus, capable of ready implementation, unlikely to provoke misunderstandings or conflict. I thought I had to choose between writing and bureaucracy, and that one path excluded the other. `Am I a writer or a bureaucrat?' I would ask this question, over and over, ever doubting the course I had taken. I believed that the only sign that writing was my vocation was by conventional publishing success, and that there was no way that an outcast such as myself would ever be admitted by a publisher to the world of commercial book sales. I thought my habit of withdrawing from the practical world to dream of unfinished novels, histories, poems, notebooks of aphorisms, intimations of madness, and diatribes about the treasonous clerks who I encountered day to day only proved my impotence as a writer and my incompetence as a bureaucrat. I thought that anything I wrote would bring social opprobrium on me, and that every action I took looked fearful, trembling, and pathetic to the alpha males and females who prowled the corridors of power.

But the personal crisis of 2015 dispelled the magical prison I had cast upon myself, and broke the hard casing of my vocational identity. In that long winter of 2015, I mended the split in my life between writer and bureaucrat, and began slowly to fire an integrated voice in the kiln of the burning archive. I stood among the flames, and found a way to walk out from the fire naked, renewed and empowered. I embraced my life as an outcast from two disordered regimes. I became dangerous.

I began to write on different topics and in different ways. History returned to my writing, after a long exile. I wrote about the books I read. I shared the troubled prophecies that previously I had cast in magical runes. I dared to write on anything and to disrespect any authority. I condemned experimental poetry and considered conservative political thought. I even predicted the victory of Donald Trump, at risk of mockery by the progressive crowd who still dominate the cultural and political institutions of Australia. I went back to old notes I had taken in my twenties about Derrida, Ponge and Blanchot, and speculated on mirrors. I shared my poetry. I doubted the wisdom of our rulers. I learned off the cuff, and did not try to hide it.

Rather to my surprise I found readers. Not many, but appreciative, and more than I had ever previously known. Now in August 2022 my blog has been viewed more than 16 000 times. These figures are trivial compared to the top tier of blogs, but, in the despair of 2015, when I began in the depths of a threefold crisis of career, psyche and culture, I did not expected more than 100 accidental views.

In early 2021 I found the blog started to transform. I decided to focus on bringing to publication my collected poems, which were published in June 2021 as *Gathering Flowers of the Mind: Collected Poems 1996-2020*. In April 2021 I launched a podcast, which I initially intended to name "The Tragic Sense of History", but then built around what was emerging now as my author platform, *The Burning Archive*. The podcast evolved into a regular show exploring history and culture. It grew from my reflections on the blog over six years, concentrating on abiding themes that I began to explore as hypotheses on this history of our times: imperial rivalry, political disorder, cultural decay and social fragmentation. Producing these spoken word essays on history each week led me to rethink the role of the blog in my writing. In September 2021 I began a new experiment, a kind of live journal where I noted from my black notebooks, my reading and other sources the fragments, inspirations and flowers of my mind, evoked in the title of my collected poems. Each Saturday morning I would gather these flowers and share them on my blog, in all their transience. From mid-2022, I began new experiments as my writing persona bloomed.

It seemed that my blog had returned to earlier fragmentary traditions, such as the live journal of that strange Russian intellectual Dmitri Galkovsky and the hand-written cahiers of Paul Valery. I saw shape and completeness in the extended writing project I had undertaken on *The Burning Archive* over six years. So I decided to gather and publish the texts of the blog as a book. I have excluded from this collection the poems I first published on my blog, and that are now available in print. I have also excluded most of the posts on politics or governing. These posts on politics will be published together with other essays and fragments in another book, *Thirteen Ways of Looking at a Bureaucrat*. Nearly all other posts are gathered, edited and now transformed in this collection of essays and fragments.

The writing of the blog is presented differently in this book. I have lightly edited the posts. There may be some repetition across the collection, but also common themes and evolving ideas will emerge for the reader in a way that may not be discovered in the screened and serial reading experience of the online blog. I have reduced many quotations in this book format, and gathered references to sources in footnotes, not hyperlinks. I have removed the images of each post, even though I enjoyed this form of play between text and image on the blog itself. The reader may turn to the online incarnation of these thoughts if they want to experience that shadow play. I have organised the collection into six parts, and within each part presented the posts in the order of their publication date. These six parts reflect some themes, abiding metaphors and enduring ideas.

In "Fire in the Voice" I have included the posts that show the slow development of my authorial persona, and the reflections I made on writing and its role in my emergence from the flames of my personal crisis. Here the post, "Craft, Voice and Fire" from May 2018 provides many of the keys to this section and the map of the journey I undertook in writing these texts.

In "Cultural Decay" I have gathered together cultural commentary and posts on my theme of cultural decay. These posts begin with a note on Mario Vargas Llosa, *Notes on the Death of Culture* (2015), and range across music, games, Jordan Petersen, travel, John Berryman, Bob Dylan and Emile Durkheim. They are all haunted by the fear of cultural collapse, and animated by the hope of rebirth.

The "The Infinite Conversation" contains posts on literature, other writers and the traditions of writing to which I belong. I took the metaphor of the infinite conversation from a misreading of the enigmatic French writer, Maurice Blanchot, although the trope of writing as emerging from dialogue with the ghosts of past writers or cultural figures is common, and appears in many forms in writers as different as Blanchot, Machiavelli, and Michael Oakeshott.

In "Histories of our Times" I have grouped my posts on that sub-category of literature, history. In the years after I left the university, I could not bear to read history at all for a few years. But I returned to the muse by reading Simon Schama, *Citizens*, on the French Revolution. Since then I have read widely, more in global history than my original sub-discipline. In these posts, I also write on history, even though I am not an accredited professional historian. It was a practice that would ultimately bloom in the Burning Archive podcast, which was dedicated to Faulkner's line that the past is not the dead, the past is not even past.

In "Social Fragmentation" I have gathered some posts on contemporary social issues, and my diagnosis that the societies of "the West" are under stress. In these posts, my writing is informed by my practice as a government official, in which I have sought ways to govern many social policy problems, including mental illness, violence, terrorism, trauma, and population ageing. But the posts are also animated by my own experiences of madness, alienation and isolation. There will be a wider selection of essays on policy issues in my collection, *Thirteen Ways of Looking at a Bureaucrat*.

In "Unraveling Empires" I have included my reflections on geopolitics and especially the unraveling of the American Empire. This theme is also prominent in "Histories of our Times", but I have included here the essays, prompted by the decisive shift in America's fate marked by Donald Trump's election in 2016. My interest in geopolitics grew over the years of the blog, and emerged as a central theme of my podcast from 2021.

There are posts that I have not included in this collection. There is a large group of posts on political events that I am publishing with other longer essays in *Thirteen Ways of Looking at a Bureaucrat*. A few posts were too ephemeral or too low quality for inclusion in this book. There were a few posts that I have discarded because they were too hasty predictions of political or social events. There were some posts where my writing, in retrospect, was too affected by the confusion of the times. On the whole, however, I have let the writing and the thoughts stand in all the errors, mixed with some truths, in which they were forged. Consistency, after all, is the enemy of intuited insight. Please enjoy my burning archive.

Jeff Rich

Part Two

Fire in the Voice

From the Burning Archive

Reclusive Samizdat.
13 October 2015

Today the artist, who lives in truth, has three obligations.
1. To live authentically within the ruins of our culture today.
2. To practise the ritual of writing solemnly, without regard for fame, fortune and the flickering nonsense of panel shows.
3. To be in the world as God's secretary, meticulous and devoted to something larger than your own life.

To live truly to each of these profound obligations requires the artist to withdraw both from the world and the relentless publicity machine of publishing. Today authenticity demands *samizdat*,[1] not marketable publications. It is by circulating words and thought outside the merchant machines that writing can find its way out of the dark wood in which it cries out for a saviour. No saviour will come, and each writer must risk an ocean of silence in response to truthful words.

Blanchot, for all his obscurities, prefigured the writer to come in his rigorous refusal, not of friendship, but of any promotion of the marketed figure of the writer. He did so from a place of high culture and secure publication. Today his heirs know the simplest act of pressing a button can secure the circulation of their ideas, but no guarantee of a response. To withhold a photo and a profile of the author of this obscure *samizdat* renews the author's sacred bond with Andrei Rubelev and a thousand anonymous icon painters.

---

[1] Samizdat (Russian: самиздат, lit. 'self-publishing') was a form of dissident activity in socialist Russia and Eastern Europe in which individuals produced underground publications, often by hand, and passed the documents from reader to reader.

Jeff Rich

Traditions beyond politics
29 December 2015

For much of my life I have thought about questions of politics and government. How can government respond to any one of dozens of social issues that have occupied my professional life? What can government do? How can a policy issue be presented to political decision-makers in a way that holds their attention, if briefly, and sustains their commitment, preferably with real decisions about people, money, rules and services, and not merely the empty word-pictures of abstract change, so beloved by the *consultocracy*.

Recent events in my life – and perhaps the broader world (these are difficult times when we must confront moral beliefs capable of terrorist murder) – have led me to doubt whether it is time to leave this field fallow for a few years. Our democratic governments are in a state of decay, with their administrative elites confused or treacherous about the purpose of democratic governing institutions. Managerialism has infected all institutions once served by a professional ethos. Political parties have lost all deep contact with vital social networks that might translate values into real political ideas, and have become patronage-ridden bureaucracies, over-stocked with networkers, advertisers and spinners, that turn political values into the degraded currency of brands. Universities lost their moral compass sometime after mass expansion and before turning education into an export industry. Their own forms of patronage persist despite mountains of managerialist rhetoric, and their sense of purpose to serve as wisdom for the state, as perhaps imagined by von Humboldt, was long lost.

It is a grim stocktake, and perhaps it leads to that other author of the ideals of intellectual life, Cardinal Newman. To him I should turn for inspiration, and in his fields of public reason on moral, religious, emotional and cultural life I may plant my next season's crops. So, I do find that a turn to other traditions of public and private thought are those that must sustain me over the years ahead.

Ich Habe Genung (I have had enough)
30 July 2016

A change of scene: music. If I have an aim in life, it is to leave behind something of beauty, and this search for transcendence does not take a religious form. I have known it in music, literature, thought, certain psychological states.

If I attain it, I imagine myself then singing Bach's Cantata *"Ich habe genung"* (*BWV* 82). It is exquisitely beautiful in its music, and its lyrics express a longing to leave the mortal body behind, to set aside this world of suffering after having achieved salvation, the embrace of Jesus, the attainment of transcendence. I secularise this longing and pursue it in writing and listening to music. Right now, as I write this post, Dietrich Fischer-Dieskau is singing this reconciliation of the body and spirit, and farewell to the world.

Some say that the music is similar to the *Erbarme Dich* ("Have mercy") from the St Matthew Passion. I know that aria for contralto and strings, and its haunting striving for mercy, from the long opening credits of the Tarkovsky film, *The Sacrifice*. The hero of the film, who is some kind of estranged artist or intellectual, sacrifices himself to save his family and the world from nuclear disaster. This film has always enthralled me, for reasons I can never quite fathom but I think come in part from its slowness and its draping of human tragedy across the stark interiors of modern culture.

But Bach is always the master of transcendent beauty in my mind, and Glenn Gould's 1981 recording of the Goldberg variations, in which he plays the variations at half the pace of his 1955 recording, and, on some tracks, audibly hums along eerily with his own playing inspired the following poem that is now published in Jeff Rich, *Gathering Flowers of the Mind: Collected Poems 1996-2020* (2021).

Jeff Rich

Gould's humming

In the first aria he begins to hum
This is the trace of true art and magic:
Ghostly.
At one with the music but different and beyond.
An *hors–texte* someone might say.
A moment's expression endures through recording,
this ghost of the artist,
unbidden, improvised, unscored,
not even beautiful,
but it becomes what I listen for each time:
To search again for the traces of the dead in our lives.

Going Sane Writing
28 July 2016

Adam Phillips says somewhere, perhaps in one of his intriguing essays, perhaps in an interview with the *Paris Review*, that writing is for him "an experiment in what your life might be like if you were to speak freely".

It is also a description he gives, in another way, to the process that goes on in the course of psychoanalysis and many other psychotherapies; for fifty minutes you can speak freely and know there is an audience to catch you, to cradle you, to correct you, to chase you to the deepest part of your self.

Phillips' essays are intriguing for three reasons: their style; the tacit knowledge of the psyche that he brings to them; and his own practice of writing.

The style reflects the pleasure that Phillips states as the only real purpose of his writing. Sentences roll on through enigmas, with never a hectoring voice or a pedantic explanation. Making beautiful sentences is the point of the exercises, and Phillips is true to the essay's exploratory and experimental genre, playing with and teasing out the silken strands of our stories with which we bind our inner lives. The simple play of his style is there in the title of *Going Sane*, pleading the paradoxical case that though insanity is well known, the course of developing into a sane person is not. His essays are, like Montaigne's, peppered with enigmatically selected quotations that point always to this strange artwork that we all practise: making sense of our lives. The epigraph that opens *Going Sane* is from Baudelaire's *Intimate Journals*: "if, by some mischance, people understood each other, they would never be able to reach agreement".

This deep, tacit knowledge of the strange workings of the psyche makes Phillip's essays worth reading, when an equivalent stylist's musings on fluff and fashion or the latest dilemmas of choice in politics are not. Though many of us have had experience of psychotherapy, much that is written about it does not register its subtle entanglement with the imagination. Here Phillips' sense of style makes him the best ambassador psychoanalysis has ever had. Confidences are not breached, but he does gently share the insights of years of listening to the enigmas and dilemmas of his patients, for whom, he says somewhere, life does not work. So it is for all of us from time to time.

This unique perspective is also seen in his practice of writing. It is not planned, except that he has a routine that he follows. He sets aside every Wednesday to write, while maintaining his other profession of therapist. He writes only what pleases him, and is not concerned to persuade or badger or entertain. He claims that the topic of each of his essays or talks is formed in response to and at the moment of the demand. It is, in its own way, his mirror of his patients talking out loud, not now as the patient but with a kind of free association of the mind of a very literate and cultured psychoanalyst.

It is this quality of his writing as a free experiment that I most admire; a release of the mind to think on the page; to think freely with compassionate attention to an audience, connected by an unspoken background belief that we do not share stories but do share the same endeavour to share stories; but without wanting to force himself into an invented image of the public or marketers. The advice on how to write, how to write to go sane, that began this post is a practice that I will bring to bear on my own writing, with a different professional background, requiring suspension of a whole different set of restrictions on speaking freely.

Gathering Flowers of the Mind

25 July 2016

This morning I pulled down from my bookshelf a cardboard box that contains a hundred or more index cards on which I had written in the 1980's and 1990's, back before personal computers, when I was a student. On each card I had transcribed a quotation drawn from my reading. This old habit is like gathering flowers for the mind, and the sewing together of wisdom or insight or simply perceptive observations from writers of the canon has long been a foundation of the essay genre.

Montaigne's essays after all are patchworks of the classical authors. I open the complete essays at a random page, and there in the first two paragraphs of "Of not Communicating One's Glory," I see Montaigne quoting a verse by Tasso, who I confess I do not know, and writing, "For as Cicero says, even those who combat it [the concern for reputation and glory] still want the books that they write about it to bear their name on the title page, and want to become glorious for having despised glory".

These cards remind me of what I have striven to be, a custodian of a cultural inheritance, a poet in destitute times, a prophet of the banished. I shuffle through the names – Arendt, Adorno, Heidegger, René Char, Foucault, Derrida, Benjamin, Beckett, Norman Brown, Barthes, Wallace Stevens, Weber, Schiller, Kafka and more. For years I reached for the titans in my mind; I sought to scale my mind's mountains, "cliffs of fall/ Frightful, sheer, no-man-fathomed" (Hopkins). Did it bring me anything but knowing I had sought the summit? These cards are my souvenirs, my pressed wildflowers of those long hours of walking into maelstroms of black thoughts and light-less uncertainty.

I find from Schiller's *Letters on Aesthetic Education* (letter 6):

> Everlastingly chained to a single little fragment of the whole, man himself develops into nothing but a fragment; everlastingly in his ear the monotonous sound of the wheel he turns, he never develops the harmony of his being, and instead of putting the stamp of his humanity upon his own nature, he becomes nothing more than the imprint of his occupation or of his knowledge.

So long I have sought transcendence of that petty imprint, the husk I have known I have lived in, with the disappointment of not finding a way to make a living in accordance with my deepest humanity, in this infinite conversation, whose ghosts and night whispers I have recorded on these cards. And this curse of being adrift in the world of work in a way that wars with my spirit I find annotated from Max Weber, *Protestant Ethic and the Spirit of Capitalism*:

> The Puritan wanted to work in a calling; we are forced to do so. For when asceticism was carried out of monastic cells into everyday life, and began to dominate worldly morality, it did its part in building the tremendous cosmos of the modern economic order. This order is now bound to the technical and economic conditions of machine production which today determine the lives of all the individuals who are born into this mechanism, not only those directly concerned with economic acquisition,

with irresistible force. Perhaps it will so determine them until
the last ton of fossilised coal is burned. In Baxter's view the care
for external goods should only lie on the shoulders of the saint
like a "light cloak, which can be thrown aside at any moment."
But fate decreed that the cloak should become a housing as hard
as steel [or an iron cage].

There I find myself and my struggles again in the summoning of the irresistible force that took me far from the life of the mind and the way of life I most love. There in the hint of dark prophecy – 'when the last ton of fossilised coal is burned' – I see my own troubled relationship with our times, driven by both an ethic of responsibility to act in the world, not merely to paint word pictures of it, and a deep unease with the people and preoccupations of corporations and contemporary governments.

I read Arendt's musing on whether political traditions exert their force most powerfully on human minds when the living force of the tradition has died, and people can no longer even think to rebel against it. And I wonder how I can be a vessel for a more vital tradition, a tradition of political thought that honours the ordinary virtues of governing well, if only I allow all that I have been to flow through me and become all that I might be.

And then, at last, I remember Mikhail Bakhtin, and his sense of the carnivalesque and the dialogic, and his words, from *Speech Genres and other essays,* may best complete this glimpse of recovery of the imagination and of the narrative of my life:

> There is neither a first word nor a last word. The contexts of dialogue are without limit. They extend into the deepest past and the most distant future. Even meanings born in dialogues of the remotest past will never be finally grasped once and for all, for they will always be renewed in later dialogue. At any present moment of the dialogue there are great masses of forgotten meanings, but these will be recalled again at a given moment in the dialogue's later course when it will be given new life. For nothing is absolutely dead: every meaning will someday have its homecoming festival.

When will be my homecoming festival? Beyond the flames and ash of the burning archive?

Allusiveness
11 August 2016

When I used to play World of Warcraft – happy nights, even if not the best for my writing – I would name all of my characters by an allusion. So, I named a night elf priest, Paracelself (Paracelsus was taken); another character, Minnerva, and two historical figures wandered through Azeroth, False Dmitri, the pretender tsar of early 17th century Russia, and Possevino, the Jesuit priest whose mission to Moscow in 1582 encountered Tsar Ivan IV (*groznyi*), as he wailed in grief at the murder of his son. I even created a guild, Allusions of Azeroth, to gather my names and legends together. I played the game as a form of literary invention, with these tokens of belonging to an infinite conversation wandering the alternative universe in search of seeking itself.

So too, in both reading and writing, I enjoy the webs of significance that allusions weave. Memorising poetry heightens this pleasure, and fills my head with echoes and notes of humanity's great incantations. The more poems you know by heart, the more common the pleasure. So yesterday, as I learnt by heart Shelley's *Ozymandias*, I found the source of one of Fernández-Armesto's chapter titles in *Civilizations*, 'lone and level sands'. Fernández-Armesto delights in his allusions, defying his tormented editors, but showing greater respect to his readers.

Allusiveness is a more light-footed dance than dull pedantry, which prefers to bore, rather than banter. It is more than ceaseless quotation, and requires a more versatile repertoire. Reading Bloom's *Anatomy of Influence*, I discover a typology of this lifeblood of literature, borrowed in turn from Hollander's *Figure of Echo* (itself an allusion):

> Hollander avoids distinguishing between intended and what I might call unruly allusions, and divides allusion in Milton and after into five types of echo: acoustical, allegorical, schematic, metaphorical, and metaleptic, illuminating this last mode with a marvelous excursus upon Angus Fletcher's trope of transumption, which I tend to call the Galileo syndrome.

This last mode means the use of a figure of speech in a new context – and is this not a favoured device in entitling a blog post? – and shows how allusion need not only be the preserve of the erudite and the bookish. It is a game we all can play. It is life in literature. It is the great chain of being revealed in language.

Coming Back Late from the Hyacinth Garden
August 2016

Is there a muse more poorly treated in modern culture than Clio?

We forget. We lose the art of telling the stories of history in all their intricacy. We seek to judge and condemn, identify and parade, rather than understand and look at the ruins with curiosity. We raid the same old valley of stories from Western civilization over and over, like George Martin ransacking the War of the Roses, and neglect the greener fields on the other side of the valley. Even the names of Clio and her sister Muses have become brands for more commerce, more advertising awards.

Sure there are exceptions. Inga Clendinnen and Felipe Fernández-Armesto are just two historians who write in a way that does celebrate Clio. But perhaps we should not be surprised. Life, even in the *mythos*, did not turn out so well for Clio. After offending the goddess of love, she was passed off in some loveless marriage to some mortal king. Her only son wounded and died, and from his blood sprang perhaps this muse's greatest gift to the world.

So whose spirit are the old couple grieving for in the garden pavilion of Böcklin's painting, *In der Gartenlaube* (1891)?

A list of 21 books that shaped me
2 August 2016

This list may never end, or so the green dream of the solitary reader goes.

1. A book of modern verse whose name I cannot recall but it was from this fawn paperback that I first absorbed, reading and hearing verses as a child, the taste for modernism.

2. A *Teach Yourself Russian* book, from which, though I never got much past da and nyet, I created a vision of an Other land in my memory.

3. *Wisden*. From its statistics and spirit of English summer wistfulness, I elaborated a now defunct philosophy of sport.

4. A now forgotten historical young adult fiction or chivalric romance of the crusades that gave me a love of history.

5. Russell Braddon's *Year of the Angry Rabbit* (1964) which I confused with a political world of apocalyptic possibility and corrupted cynicism.

6. Trollope's *Palliser* novels that gave me a preternatural sense of political and bureaucratic life, but left me for a long time a denizen of the nineteenth century.

7. *Anna Karenina*, the first great novel I read in my teen years, in a Penguin paperback edition that had a cover illustration of a magically impossible, for me, scene of aristocratic skaters in winter Moscow or St Petersburg.

8. Alfred Jarry's *Père Ubu*, which I heard, but did not read, on ABC Radio National's *Radio Helicon*, back when there were true arts programs on the radio. Its energy of pre-WWI cultural breakdown and artistic rebellion returned me to the twentieth century.

9. Foucault's *Madness and Civilisation*, for reasons I have elaborated on elsewhere on this blog (see "Madness and History").

10. E.P. Thompson, *The Making of the English Working Class*, out of whose tradition of rescuing the poor stockinger from the condescension of posterity I conceived in rootless error my failed early academic research career that sought to recover the lived experience of the workers of nineteenth century Australia.

11. Anthony Giddens, *Central Problems in Social Theory*, which took me to giddy heights of abstraction but still taught a sophisticated discipline in conceiving and perceiving social phenomenon. Blessedly, it also inoculated me against the academic vice of Marxist nostalgia.

12. Max Weber, *Protestant Ethic and the Spirit of Capitalism*, that showed me both the uncanny power of ideas and how even a sociologist can write to seek salvation from personal torment.

13. Thomas Bernhard, *The Loser, The Lime Works, Concrete, Wittgenstein's Nephew,* and others. Of all the great post-1945 modernist authors who I discovered through the recommendations of critics, Bernhard intrigued me most, with his musical, obsessive rants by intellectual outsiders.

14. Proust, *In Search of Lost Time*. I still feel like Proust, on a search for redemption through art or culture (beauty is truth, truth beauty, that is all there is to know and all that ye need to know on this earth) – and to escape the force of self-defiling habit that is among the banal

evils of the world.

15. Szymborska's *View with a Grain of Sand*, which made me realise that I could write poetry again.

16. *A Book of Luminous Things: an International Anthology of Poetry*, edited by Czeslaw Milosz, which sustained my spirit and mind through many dark years of disconsolate wandering through the outer corridors of power.

17. *The Tempest*, as imagined through Greenaway's film, *Prospero's Books*, which reanimated my enchantments and made me spurn my own Milan and find again my precious books in my own solitary isle.

18. Simon Schama, *Citizens: A Chronicle of the French Revolution*, which brought me back again into history, and cured me of the latent violence of political radicalism.

19 Felipe Fernández-Armesto, *Millenium: A History of our Last Thousand Years* that introduced me to global history and made me in mid-life an explorer again.

20. W.G. "Max" Sebald, *The Rings of Saturn* that mesmerised me with its melancholic mental events, and made me rethink whether I need ever write within the shackles of a genre again.

21. Roger Scruton, *The Uses of Pessimism* that revealed to me the conservative disposition I had long cloaked in discontent with what life had dealt to me.

Emily's Enigma

29 September 2016

The enigma of Emily Dickinson for me is how she shows that the very act of writing - conceived to include the recording of that writing in some simple enduring way, if only, as she did, by sewing pages of preserved poems, together into small handmade booklets – is publication enough. Everything that may happen after that moment – when the writing on the page is given to the world – is not part of the creative process, and is incidental to the purpose of the poet. Of course, recognition in all its forms is longed for – whether that be prizes or sales or just likes on a blog. But recognition can carry a burden that makes the writing less free.

I am temperamentally reclusive, like Emily, and her example has always strengthened me to write as I will, not as the crowd calls for. So, each time I press these keys and make a thing that endures in the world, despite any fears I may hold, Emily sits at my back and quietly whispers her incantations of possibility.

This morning I discovered Emily Dickinson's poem 709 in which she writes that "Publication – is the Auction/ Of the Mind of Man – Poverty – be justifying/ For so foul a thing." Dickinson's enigmatic model inspires me to keep writing, if in private, "But reduce no Human Spirit/ To Disgrace of Price."

An Awakening

23 September 2016

I have over the last two months been going through the program of creative recovery set out in Julia Cameron's *The Artist's Way: a course in discovering and recovering your creative self*. It is a program that I have begun before but not persisted with in the way that I am this time. And it is making a difference. Now I am sharing my creativity more openly, and this blog is the result. Now my creativity is appreciated – thank you, dear readers and likers of the internet.

And now I treat myself and my creativity more gently – small steps, beautiful moments, not big paralysing overhauls. It is like the poem I wrote, "Simple Steps", and it is satisfying to know that the life you want is within reach if you take simple, small steps.

I am in week 8 of the program, which focuses on recovering a sense of strength. Cameron urges the recovering artist to do the simple things each day because there is always one action you can take each day to support your creativity. Along the way she quotes a line from the American poet, influenced by Zen Buddhism, Theodore Roethke. The line "you learn by going where you have to go."

I looked up the whole poem from which this line is taken, "The Waking." I found a tribute to my awakening sense of strength. I discovered a beautiful, meditative villanelle that celebrates everyday awakening.

John Donne's Sermons and the Blogging Tradition
31 March 2021 and 15 September 2016

Today, 31 March, the Anglican and Lutheran denominations celebrate the feast day for John Donne, the metaphysical poet and reluctant priest who died in 1631. In honour of this intriguing figure, whose poetry and prose I wish to read more, I am reposting a post from September 2016. It speaks of the enduring relevance today of Donne's sermons from 400 years ago.

***

Twice every Sunday for 16 years from 1615 to 1631 John Donne acoustics and the appearance of Donne giving his lectures at St Paul's cathedral.[3]

Within the sermons, it is Donne's practice, and his discipline that registers most with me. He spoke with subtlety before the storms of romantic confession. The sermon itself is a genre that I do not know, and may have become a dead form. His sermons are offered as bible study, and I barely know a single text from that book.

A sermon begins with a text, and so goes on to draw the lesson that John Donne chose. His model inspires me to begin essays anew. Yet can I know in my civil tongue the sounds of his holy words?

They say – the critics – that he was a master of paradox, using it to strip well-known certainties to replace them with deeper faiths. It was a device he trained in as a young poet, with Renaissance conceit, even though Montaigne knew it as a fencer's trick. In the sermons he traveled through his own perplexed spirit, accompanied by learning and wit. Did his sermons promulgate faith, or did they exhibit doubt?

Today, I can search through these prose puzzles by date, occasion, location, audience and source text.

His last sermon was delivered in the beginning of Lent 1631 and was titled "Death's Duel or a consolation to the soule against the dying Life and living death of the body." It was styled his own funeral sermon, delivered a few days before his death, and having been spoken, left the audience the impression that the speaker now had nothing left to do but to die.

His texts themselves escape my comprehension. Faith, religion, the Renaissance mind, the biblical texts, and the archaic literary references all stand as hurdles for me to know them.

Yet his model urges me on to write my own secular sermons each week.

To secure an office in which the duty is only to speak of the creation of the meaning of the soul in both its eternal search and its daily duties.

No temporary things, but yes polemic and the engagement of all

---

[3] http://www.luminarium.org, and https://vpcp.chass.ncsu.edu/.

parts of the mind and spirit.
So I commit to secular sermons of the spirit of our times.

The Nobility of Poetry and a Normal Life
7 October 2016

Yesterday I visited the State Library of Victoria and there I read from the *Collected Poetry and Prose of Wallace Stevens*.

Wallace Stevens is perhaps my most loved American poet, and certainly an influence on me – his diction, his mix of abstraction with the most remarkable particulars of the beautiful world, his romance of the self, his playfulness with the treasure-hoards of the things of this world and the words that name them.

I have at home both an old copy of his *Selected Poems*, which I bought in my early twenties from the now shut second-hand bookshop near the University of Melbourne, and a more recent edition of his *Collected Poems*. At one point this year I had the mad plan to only read from these *Collected Poems* and one other book, *Parzival* by von Eschenbach. Curiosity, thankfully, overwhelmed this puritanical plan. I learned by heart some years ago "The Idea of Order at Key West". Its line that "there never was a world for her/ Except the one she sang and singing, made" is talismanic for me. I might even pin it with some suited image, and display it on the pin-board that sits beside my desk.

Stevens also seemed a role model for me. His life as an insurance executive grounded him in something outside his imagination, and did not defeat his poetic venture. So much of the superfluous romance or self-defeating *sturm und drang* of writing is unnecessary – belonging to circles, issuing manifestos, rebelling against the world. In refuge from the tempest, the greatest art and the purest imagination arises from a quiet, normal life.

Still, I had never read any of Wallace Stevens' prose. Yesterday I dipped into the first of his essays in *The Necessary Angel: Essays on Reality and the Imagination* (1951), which I have just now discovered is available online in full on archive.org. One essay from the collection, "The Noble Rider and the Sound of Words", proceeds from a discussion of a metaphor used by Plato to evoke the imagination at work: a noble rider of a chariot in the sky. Towards the end of the essay, Stevens asserts the importance of nobility for poetry, not grandiloquent nobility, but a nobility that sits at the base the call to write poems. In so doing he reanimates contemporary poetry with the dignity of free imagination. He writes that:

> There is no element more conspicuously absent from contemporary poetry than nobility. There is no element that poets have sought after, more curiously and more piously, certain of its obscure existence. Its voice is one of the inarticulate voices which it is their business to overhear and to record.[4]

This is a paradoxical idea, that nobility is an *inarticulate* voice, which the poet must search for and rescue from shadows of obscurity. Nobility is more commonly seen, if I may use a pastiche of current pseudo-intellectual discourse, as a site of privileged cultural power. I shake off such trite slogans, but Stevens' idea connects more deeply to the striving I feel when I write poetry, a striving to find some kind of nobility in this life. Stevens goes on to elaborate what I may be feeling in those moments. He writes:

> For the sensitive poet, conscious of negations, nothing is more difficult than the affirmations of nobility and yet there is nothing that he requires of himself more persistently, since in them and in their kind, alone, are to be found those sanctions that are the reasons for his being and for that occasional ecstasy or ecstatic freedom of the mind, which is his special privilege.

I think I am discovering, I hope not too late, that the pursuit of the ecstatic freedom of the mind, that complete and utter freedom, is

---

[4] Stevens, *The Necessary Angel*, (1951) p. 664.

indeed a special privilege, and a privilege that can confer nobility on, and be claimed justly within, the most ordinary and normal of suburban lives. In the late poem, 'A quiet normal life', Stevens wrote: "Here in his house and in his room,/In his chair the most tranquil thought grew peaked".[5] So he urged in this tranquil, suburban life, "May all our candles" - and our archives - "blaze with artifice".

Sponges, metamorphoses and psyche
23 April 2017

After a morning during which I searched my ravaged memory for the concealed door to my troubles, I opened an old box which contained five old, forgotten notebooks of mine. Their black covers and red spines revealed nothing to me of when I last used them to gather observations, thoughts, fragments of lines, like a dark sponge wiping up the mess of my mental life.

I opened the first notebook of the pile, and flicked through the pages. Quickly I dated it to the months or years around 1999. There I have noted the words spoken by Steve Bracks, a former Premier of Victoria, on election night in 1999, when he defeated the apparently invincible, more despised, but more enduring figure of Jeff Kennett, the preceding Premier of Victoria: "Bracks: 'a victory for decency, honour, compassion". Beside it, I have scrawled thoughts that record my state of mind:

> The joy of seeing a tyrant brought to his knees. The reminder that government is not execution. A child's eyes pleading for

---

[5] *The Collected Poems of Wallace Stevens: the corrected edition* (2nd Vintage Books edition, 2015), p. 553.

mercy in the midst of horror. A reminder that there can be a reward for waiting and persistence. The heroism of enduring.

They are not surprising thoughts, except I am struck today with the sense then that the dramas of even minor provincial politics still held for me this fascination to find ordinary virtues – "the heroism of enduring" – in my struggles as a lowly under-castellan. But these residues of reactions to old news are not the most surprising finding in this notebook. There in the early pages I have written:

> Francis Ponge wrote this (or something like this) *"an artist has one duty to set up a workshop and to bring in the world for repair as he finds it in pieces."* So the experience, day to day, is transcribed and out of intuition, some poetry found.

Ponge was one of the many French writers who I came to know through my strange search for an artistic identity through the works of Jacques Derrida and Michel Foucault. I was in my 20's and at university, and my first sally into the world of adult identity had failed dismally, when I had sought election as a student politician and failed. I never really belonged to that world in any case, and my true affiliation was with the worlds of dream, madness, transgression and outlandish thought, or so I fitfully thought then. It was this world that welcomed me as an outcast from reason, familial life and all practical careers, which I believed myself then to be exiled from.

Through them, and the ultimately futile attempt to think like them and not like myself, I discovered Ponge, but also Leiris, Blanchot, Bataille, René Char, Beckett (in a new way), Artaud, and the truly enigmatic Raymond Roussel. I tried but could not really understand the philosophy, but I completely absorbed the idea of consecrating my life through an unique and idiosyncratic practice of writing. Just now I picked up Leiris, *Manhood* from my shelf, with its frightening, disturbing image of the naked Judith holding a knife and the severed head of Holofernes, from Lucas Cranach's *Judith and Lucretia*. I read from the prologue these words, which spoke to me then and still do today:

> My chief activity is literature, a term greatly disparaged today.

... anyone who likes to think with a pen in his hand is a writer. The few books I have published have won me no fame. I do not complain of this, any more than I brag of it, for I feel the same distaste for the "popular author' genre as for that of the 'neglected poet'. [6]

Unlike Leiris or Bataille, to whom Leiris dedicated his self-inquiry, or Bataille's friend Blanchot, I never gathered on my shelves the works of Francis Ponge. Where I learnt of Ponge's aphorism that "the artist brings into his workshop items of the world to repair one at a time", I do not know. A cursory internet search cannot conceal the sloppiness of my literary scholarship in that notebook, penned at a time of desperation, when I did not know how to continue being what I was, a literary man, and still succeed in the world.

All I remember of reading Ponge is struggling to find my way through Derrida's essay *Signponge* – and wondering what it was that provoked such an extraordinary text. I think now, as I read more of Ponge's attention to the thing itself, simple things, ordinary things, re-imagined with puns, dad jokes, word play, that it was simplicity itself that so infuriated Derrida, and made him turn the pun of Ponge's name into an *attack* on any aspiration to find meaning in things themselves, outside the endless commentary of *différance*.[7]

> At the same time I would deliberately set aside the too difficult question announced by this word; it escapes any frontal approach, and the thing [Ponge's name, the thing that is not a thing, and yet is declared in Derrida's sentence] that I am going to talk about obliges me to reconsider *mimesis* through and through, as an open-ended question, but also as a miniscule vanishing point at the already sunlit abyssal depths of the *mimosa*.

The aggressive brio of the scholar. Shots fired at the podium. Words as weapons.

---

[6] Michel Leiris, *Manhood: a journey from childhood into the fierce order of virility* (1963, tr. 1984; trans. Richard Howard), p 4.

[7] Derrida, *Signponge* (1976, trans 1984), p. 4.

Derrida's words no longer fascinate me. But through Ponge I discover things that can renew poetry. I read also that Ponge became a recluse in his later life. In this fate, which he shared with Blanchot, I see my own. The writer who is a recluse looks like Narcissus into the pool and hopes to see his Psyche's echo.

It reminds me of the poem, 'Dream Life", I published in *ars poetica* IV in May 1997, a couple of years before I penned my thoughts in this notebook, at a time when I hoped to escape the dreariness of a life in servitude as a lowly under-castellan to a minor provincial government, an escape which I have never been able to effect. In the first stanza of the poem I wrote, "In that small moment dream takes/ to fly from memory and become/ the nagging image of forgetfulness/ the muted clank of psyche's hold/ I can turn too well in bed/ and learn the pains of comfort".

The poem evoked the painting of Arthur Boyd *Nebuchadnezzar's Dream of a Tree*, a kind of metamorphosis by dream, and in the first line of Derrida's *Psyche: Inventions of the other, I discover this question*: "What else am I going to be able to invent?" It leads us back to Ponge.

Metamorphosis

By Francis Ponge

You can twist at the foot of the stems
The elastic of your heart
It is not like chenille
That you will know the flowers
When more than one sign
Your Rush to Happiness

...

He shuddered and jumped
Joined the butterflies ...

Jeff Rich

Strange Salt

7 April 2017

> All I've suffered, and all the suffering I've caused, might have arisen from the lack of a little salt in my brain. (Robert Lowell)

I have been reading Kay Redfield Jamison, *Robert Lowell, Setting the River on Fire: a Study of Genius, Mania and Character*. It is a lusciously detailed, clinically informed study of Lowell's bipolar disorder, its treatments and the endurance of his writing through the many crises his madness bestowed on him.

In the late 60's Lowell began to take lithium for his illness. Lithium, this strange and ancient salt, would change Lowell's experience of illness and mania. For the next 15 years the frequent attacks of mania would subside. These attacks had harrowed Lowell's soul and left him with a constant fear of the recurrence of mania. Jamison insightfully compares the trauma of mania or other psychotic episodes to the trauma of war. After lithium, Lowell could live through a late peace.

There is a debate about the quality of Lowell's poetry in these years of lesser strife and torment. Jamison takes the view that the lithium gave Lowell more years to write without the ravages of madness. Jamison can speak with authority. She has known herself those manias and the frightful falls from the mountains of the mind, and has written a wonderful account of her own descent as a psychiatrist into her personal bipolar hell. I share her view, knowing in my own life how a little pill can school an errant mind.

Surely, poetry, literature, art do not demand the sacrifice of the poet, writer, artist, or prophet to the destructive gods of madness. Surely, we can shift the inner circles of body and mind, just as we remake nature with culture, which at base is part of nature. Surely, we can make this small offering of a little salt to appease the gods of destruction.

From the Burning Archive

Error is in Control
2 May 2017

The mind errs. My mind errs.

The mind slips from its own grasp.

The mind believes the clouds that surround it are summoned by its will.

The mind, my errant mind, this proud mind, the mind we share in confusion, lives by one illusion.

The mind calls this illusion, control.

Knowledge does not dispel this illusion.

Even though it claims to.

There is no enlightenment from this illusion.

Except in madness.

Kindness too, the humble gift of the unhinged, dissolves the clouds.

Then, in the time left to us, we see the madness of the day.

Its beauty. Its fear.

In that final abandon, we forgive control.

We stoop.

We live in a freedom we can never control.

Adam Phillips, In Writing
5 June 2017

> Writing needn't be a world domination project… but just the attempt to find enough people who are interested in what matters to you. (Adam Phillips)

This quotation comes from Adam Phillips' latest collection, *In Writing*. How timely I should stumble on this remark – I have begun to ask: what values guide my writing and what matters to me in writing?

These questions came to me in therapy, and Phillips' practice of writing is a model for my own. It appears I can find company by "going sane writing".

Thank you, dear few readers, for being interested in what matters to me.

Waste Books and Epigrams
4 June 2017

> The excuses we make to ourselves when we want to do something are excellent material for soliloquies, for they are rarely made except when we are alone, and are very often made aloud. (George Lichtenberg [1742-99], *The Waste Books*)

I collected from the local library *The Notebooks of Robert Frost*, which features on its cover an emblematic photograph of the aged poet writing in his Vermont home in 1958, as if he were painting at an easel.

The notebooks stretch from the 1890's to the 1970's, spanning a life's adventure in writing that is surely both too majestic and too humble to be known as a career. The notebooks contain all manner of writing, reflection, experiment, and, as suits their form, annotations. *Notebook 20* dates from 1929, and begins: "These are not monologues but my part in a conversation in which the other part is more or less implied".[8]

The thought reminds me of Maurice Blanchot's idea of the infinite conversation, which I imagine as the eternal, enigmatic survival of solitary murmurs of great words that sustain the connection between

---

[8] *The Notebooks of Robert Frost* (2010), p 267.

the dead and the living. That is why I write: to be part of this infinite conversation; to attend to the fading murmurs of this conversation; to rescue the words that are at risk of ashen destruction in the burning archive. That is why I write, and why I devote so much time, despite no show of social success or fame or even much of an audience, to this life in literature.

It comes with a moral imperative, an ordinary virtue of dignity and grace in defeat, evoked in Herbert's "Envoy of Mr Cogito":

> repeat old incantations of humanity fables and legends
> because this is how you will attain the good you will not attain
> repeat great words repeat them stubbornly
> like those crossing the desert who perished in the sand

To be an old, gray, wizened and solitary man, like Frost in his Vermont home, yet still to repeat these old incantations is my path of redemption.

Strange, though, that all we write is so perishable, so vulnerable to fire and neglect, and yet these impermanent notebooks endure. It is a paradox that these words survive beyond death when they are ephemeral, a temporary incantation against the chaos of the world, in which the poet-priest marks the lost place of truth and beauty in the world as if in a disappearing rite. These are words consigned to "waste books"; spells thrown in flames and mould, not inscribed defiantly in stone like the original epigrams.

The introduction to Frost's *Notebooks* compares them to the *Waste Books* of George Lichtenberg. From this pile of waste arose an author, but only after death. Lichtenberg, the aphorist celebrated as great only posthumously, emerged out of these scraps of notes, ideas, drafts, quotations, and the ordinary observations of life. The temporary words of waste books became in time monuments of soul-making.

Is the blog the new waste book? It is somewhere else surely. It does not have the privacy of personal experiment, but nor does it have the polish and mirage of publication. Still, it seeks to endure beyond its act of writing, just as Frost kept and preserved his notebooks. He dated them. He organised them. He secured them against loss and destruction, and bequeathed them to those who wish to take part in the infinite conversation.

So too this blog finds its way to endure, even if it is always written in a first draft, with little plan or attempt to impress a brand. I pen the words, and cast them adrift on the digital ocean. This ordinary, modern *samizdat* lets me accomplish form without dragging me down in organisation. Perhaps the lesser forms are those that endure the most?[9] As Frost wrote:

> Fortunately too no forms are more engrossing, gratifying, comforting, staying than those lesser ones we throw off, like vortex rings of smoke, all our individual enterprise and needing nobody's cooperation; a basket, a garden, a room, an idea, a picture, a poem.

And a blog (even if, or perhaps especially if, that blog has few readers, no great name) is surely such a comforting solitary form, as defined by Blanchot.[10]

> The work is solitary: that does not mean that it remains incommunicable, that it lacks a reader. But the person who reads it enters into that affirmation of the solitude of the work, just as the one who writes it belongs to the risk of solitude.

---

[9] Robert Frost, Letter to *The Amherst Student*, quoted in *Notebooks*, p xv.

[10] Maurice Blanchot, "The Essential Solitude" in *The Gaze of Orpheus*, p 64.

From the Burning Archive

Self-Portrait in a Time of Hunger
12 November 2017

The storm of progress now threatens to burn the remaining archives of human memory. In an infinite set of information, no tradition holds fast. Where then does the Orphean writer look, if not like this angel towards the past, while being blown irresistibly forward by a fire storm? (This blogger, July 2015, his first post of *The Burning Archive*)

Today and tomorrow I am fasting prior to a medical procedure, a probe into my bowels for malignant growths. Much though I would like to find a topic external to my mere self, my inattentive mind keeps circling back to images of food. I walk into the kitchen to make a cup of black tea, and I crave the ripe black Hass avocados. I remind myself that I cannot snack on the salted dry biscuits. I turn quickly away from the crisp, radiant pink lady apples.

With no topic held steadily in mind, and ever diminishing concentration, I skitter about and look back over the topics of this blog. It has voiced poems, and been visited by Dr Cogito. It has been graced with the presence of Symborska, Keats, John Clare, Wallace Stevens, Zbigniew Herbert, Emily Dickinson, Anna Akhmatova, Joyce and more. This blog has emulated Adam Phillips in venturing a form of essay on the life that I lead and the alternatives that I might imagine into being through writing. It has more secretly followed Valéry in his *Cahiers*, improvising connections and committing myself to an artwork as a form of provisional self-creation. It has gathered the fallen blooms of thought from a personal canon, stretching across Proust, Kafka, Havel, Rilke, Benjamin, Fukuyama, Fernández-Armesto, John Gray (the pessimist, not the fantasist), Blanchot and Sebald.

I have contemplated madness, the history of suicide, the tragedies of history, play, sacred violence, bureaucracy, governing, trauma, terror, child sexual abuse, sanity, memory, music, literature and more.

Jeff Rich

Certain images – the archive in flames – have recurred as uncanny repetitions. But others have sprung from nowhere and surprised me. There were times when a mere phrase – the disappearance of stories from the world – took hold of me, and found its way to some new thought. Other times I have dared to voice my dissent with the world that I have found in my day job, even if I cannot believe these obscure *samizdat* will make much, if any, difference. Still, I can aspire to live in truth and to practise the ordinary virtues – dignity, compassion, the life of the mind. And what is culture if not an unenclosed field in which we are all free to sow our gifts?

The stats page of my wordpress tells me that I have now, after nearly two and a half years writing this blog, written 164 posts. These posts have enjoyed, at this moment, 1317 views and 773 visitors. To each of you, viewers and visitors, I say thank you. Despite my hunger I affirm that this project will continue, whatever strange artwork it may in some future time be known as, if it is not forgotten entirely.

It is the convex mirror in which I write my soul.

... The soul establishes itself.
But how far can it swim out through the eyes
And still return safely to its nest? The surface
Of the mirror being convex, the distance increases
Significantly; that is, enough to make the point
That the soul is a captive, treated humanely, kept
In suspension, unable to advance much farther

Than your look as it intercepts the picture.

(from John Ashbery, "Self-Portrait in a Convex Mirror")

Reflections on 2017

10 December 2017

The year is drawing to a close, and while it is yet weeks from New Year, the office Christmas party season is in full swing, and my mind is turning to an upcoming holiday. I am approaching the end of my current assignment and am going into my annual leave without knowing what I will do or who I will be working with next year. It seems I am very much in internal exile in the minor provincial bureaucracy on which I depend for my livelihood.

I have a crushing sense of defeat in what I suppose I may still call a career. All my qualities seem unwanted, and I can only suppose that the consultocrats and courtiers who run my Castle have decided rightly that I will never be a loyal follower to them. I need to begin to look elsewhere, and to find hope and purpose in more nourishing lands.

So, it occurs to me this morning that one way I can reconnect with a sense of strength is to reflect on this year through the lens of my blog. In many eyes it has been a dark year, but events of the world and events in the life of the mind have different rhythms.

So today let me recap the topics of my posts this year, and next week allow me to reflect on the themes and stories of the year.

In January, I had returned from a trip to Vietnam and Cambodia during which I reread *After Tamerlane* by John Darwin.

It led to a post on the unraveling of empires "adrift in the great historical tides of convergence and divergence" that defeat beliefs in any unitary imperial order, as we see today, when America declines into narcissistic tantrums and China re-dreams the One Road of Tamerlane.

A post on massacres in history discovered a precedent for Islamic foreign fighters in Syria in the exodus of youthful enthusiasts for Hellenic and Christian culture to the Greek war of independence.

Among these fighters was the original literary psychopath – mad, bad and dangerous to know – Lord Byron.

Then my failure to read *Don Quixote*, led me to reflect on reading ambitions, and the sheer impossibility to realise them all in our media-saturated world. But the attempt led me to pose the paradox: "In our madness is our truest dignity?"

By the end of the month, by now returned to work, I began my series "Thirteen ways of looking at a bureaucrat" (to be published in a separate book), inspired by Wallace Stevens' poem with the same number of perspectives on a blackbird. I described this series as "an elegy for a kind of life of the mind that has died around me. I sing my sad songs and hope the gods will resurrect this tradition. But the odds on that seem to grow slimmer by the day".

In February, I wrote posts in response to stanzas I through to V of Stevens' poem, each with a new subtitle: I Vigilance amidst Stillness; II The Three-eyed Raven; III The Craft of the Cameo Actor; IV In Unity is Death; and V The Beauty of the Bureaucrat.

In March, I completed the series, 'Thirteen Ways of Looking at a Bureaucrat', with VI Through Barbaric Glass Darkly; VII At the Feet of Thin Men; VIII Involved in What I Know; IX Servants of Utopias; X Flight in Green Light; XI People who Live in Glass Coaches; XII The Thaw, the Flight; XIII The Long Waits of Winter. I felt the last few posts were rushed, more lapidary, more gnomic. I have since collected all 14 posts together, and may yet expand into a short book. But I am so wary of the publication industry; I may simply self-publish.

In April, I turned to more literary and cultural themes. In that month I was intensely preparing a secret government report on violence and mental illness, and what, if anything could be done, to prevent acts like the Bourke Street vehicular homicide, which occurred in February 2017. I needed relief in beauty.

Literature and scholarship were refuges since I posted on Beckett's *Unnameable*, Kay Redfield Jamison's biography of Robert Lowell, Felipe Fernández-Armesto's *A foot in the river: why our lives change and the limits of evolution*, Andrew Scull's *Madness in Civilization: a cultural history of insanity*, and W.G. Sebald's sentences.

Most poetically of all, I ventured a kind of cultural autobiography in the post, "Sponges, metamorphoses and psyche", in which I reached more deeply into my personal and cultural repertoire, while remaining detached and curious about what I found there. Here also I republished my first published poem – *Dream Life*, first published in *ars poetica* in May 1997, one year after the birth of my first child.

In May, I experimented with writing posts late at night in bed in response to the daily prompt on wordpress and fragments composed on my daily commute. It was, I confess, a search for readers.

I reposted a series of older posts from my blog, like six asides about culture (and Havel), and going sane writing, which was prompted by a role model of sorts, the British psychoanalyst and essayist, Adam Phillips.

I curated more of my content, linking to an essay and conference paper I wrote on "Why is alcohol policy difficult?" This paper I presented to a conference of public health scholarly zealots. At least one person came up to me after my talk and expressed appreciation for what I said. But it was a drop in the ocean of public health zealotry.

I reflected on Hannah Arendt and her philosophy of natality, which:

> spoke to me as an outcast. Where our podcast literary critic embraced Arendt's status as a refugee to castigate the world; I saw in her a determination to love the world as an outcast, to see it clearly, and yet to make new beginnings and to disclose your self to the world. That is what human freedom is for Arendt. Not to remake the world; but to give birth to new things in a world that is precious, bounded, beyond our control and yet the only one we can ever know.

I appreciated Kenneth Slessor's poem, "Five Bells", linking to a beautiful radiophonic performance, and continuing the thoughts on natality: "To endure you must begin. To survive you must write without success... Only for those five bells".

In June, I returned to something of a more stable pattern. I reflected on Robert Frost's practice of poetry and the form of the blog in "Waste Books and Epigrams." I wrote an essay "On Humility" prompted by one of my favourite quotes by Jung and by still more humiliations and rebuffs at work. I posted the complete paper that I had presented to a conference on children's voices and the history of emotions. The paper was about how the Royal Commission into Institutional Responses to Child Sexual Abuse created a new way of feeling about trauma. I will return to this paper, and my reflections on this inquiry in the tradition of truth and reconciliation commissions, over coming months, since I am committed to writing a long essay on the significance of this public event. I castigated the Nobel Prize for literature for awarding Bob Dylan the prize. I explored the powerful metaphor of the infinite conversation, which emerged for me as an important theme for my writing, my recovery and my psychotherapy.

In July, I published two poems of mine – "The state of politics", and "Nouriel's shoes". In August, I turned back to themes of politics. I was struggling to find a new place for myself, and began to reach out to the powerful men who I knew as mentors, if not as patrons. I wrote some starting hypotheses for a planned essay on *Republics in Distress*:

> So, in our distressed republics, a committed life will only destroy itself if it tries to break the wheel of our decadent politics. Rather, in each of our lives, we should turn to the simple actions that preserve, protect and nourish for renewal in a better time a more virtuous politics.

I wrote on my long held view about the restrictions of freedom of speech and freedom of thought for public servants. Then I wrote a darker piece, 'The Death of the Soul', prompted by debates in the press about the decay of culture and decline of religion, in which I asked: "How then do we live in these dark, destructive times, haunted by terror and our own comforts?"

In September, while I researched lone actor terrorist attacks, I reflected on the return of sacred violence, and this was a kind of dissent against comforting progressive notions of the causes and responses to terrorism. I commented indirectly on the debate on destruction of monuments to historical figures who are no longer as widely esteemed. Here I said:

> There is enough war in history; we do not need history wars and culture wars that both consecrate and desecrate public memory. We need rather to practise humility in asserting and nurturing our mercurial identities, while kindly forgiving, if not forgetting, the sins that lie in all of our pasts.

And I posted more poems, with the best being "Dr Cogito brings his mind to heel". In October, I wrote about sorrow in response to my aged mother's declining health and cognition; the Red Nostalgia I observed at a lecture on the centenary of Red October, the Russian Revolution; and the meaning for me of Keats' poem, "When I have fears".

In November, I returned to reflections on major cultural figures with "Conrad's Darkness", "Forgetting Foucault", and "Self-portrait in a time of hunger", which was a kind of premonition of this review of my own work. This last post contained some reflections on my enduring purpose and abiding concerns. Lastly, in December, I wrote "On revenge", stirred by images of Captain Ahab, and this long recapitulation of the year.

Such has been my year. Reviewing my words, my reading, my images from the year has given me new strength. The verdicts of courtiers and consultocrats should not bother me. They bring nothing to the infinite conversation. I will survive beyond their defeat of me. I will walk unburnt from the flaming archive.

Jeff Rich

A thousand thanks
1 April 2018

Some time in the last couple of weeks the counter on my wordpress visitor stats clocked over one thousand. So this is a short post to say thank you to all those readers.

When I commenced this blog back in July 2015 – nearly three years ago – I did not imagine I could reach such an audience, modest though it is – very much in the small long tail of the distribution of blogging site stats. I had written a blog previously, but had done so anonymously. That blog – *the happy pessimist* – was about politics, and my read of political events in Australia. It was part medicine, part poison for me. I vented there and nursed grievances. I responded to the strange years of political crisis in Australia from the fall of Kevin Rudd to the fall of Tony Abbott. It rarely found readers, except an occasional, enthusiastic anarchist who egged me on in my more poisonous state of mind. I kept it going for maybe three years, and then took it down in fear of reprisals against public servants speaking their mind. I downloaded all my posts and put them into a *Scrivener* file. Maybe one day I will use them again somehow. But I never put my name or any clearly identifying information to my posts. It was all done under the avatar of Antonio Possevino – a Jesuit priest and diplomat of the 16th century, who himself published a number of political tracts under pseudonyms.

This blog, *The Burning Archive*, marked a new path for me, and a new kind of personal courage. I wrote not about my daily worlds of politics and policy, but my night journeys through culture and symbols. And from early on I wrote in my own name. I began the blog in the depths of a personal crisis, and it took a couple of months before I resumed regular postings. Initially I posted mainly on historical and large political topics. But after a while I freed myself to write on culture, literature, writing, my personal story and, of course, poetry. I probed my losses to bear them with more dignity. I explored the unique paths my life has traveled, without concern to compare myself with others. I rediscovered my life of the mind and found at last courage to speak in my own voice.

It was one of these more personal adventures of my own mind that was shared by other bloggers and began to gain me followers and readers. This was a lesson to me – speak with vulnerability and authenticity, not behind masks of authority and power.

To all you readers who have visited me on this journey: thank you. An especially big thank you to Daniel Paul Marshall, whose comments and affirmations of the value of my writing have been especially kind and helpful for me. The strength you have given me will help me continue with this blog, and share more of my writing with the world. I plan to publish three books of poetry shortly, and have commenced work on an essay on the ordinary virtues of governing well. Three years ago, I could not imagine this day. I have walked through the fires of the *Burning Archive,* and stand before my readers naked, unburnt and transformed.

Craft, Voice and Fire
27 May 2018

We all know poetry isn't a craft that you can just turn on and off. It has to strike fire somewhere, and truth, maybe unpleasant truth about yourself, may be the thing that does that. (Robert Lowell[11])

---

[11] From a letter quoted in Kay Redfield Jamison, *Setting the River on Fire: A Study of Genius, Mania, and Character* (2017).

Jeff Rich

It has taken me a long time to know assurance in the seasons of my writing. For a long time I was burdened by shame. I could not disclose to anyone the true scope and matter of the words that set my soul on fire. I lived with chronic disappointment that I could not meet one or other standard of productivity, fluency, discipline or focus as a writer. Projects would come and go, speaking of Michelangelo, and I would punish myself with drunkenness, depression and dedication to a false calling, my life as a bureaucrat.

The shame lay in the fragility of my mind, and the fear that I would repeat my genetic destiny of manic-depression. Every abandoned draft, every incompletely scanned poem, every half-cocked political essay gave me more concern that madness lay at my feet, and that one day I would be compelled to kneel, to scrape, and to pick up in my shaking hands the curse of my fate. I too would live life as a neglected ruin, hidden away from the hard minds of the world, known only to some too-busy mind-doctor who would medicate me into submission.

The company of cold skulls that I kept by night, in whom I vested the frenzy and invention of madness, never spoke with the orderly and rational fellow who made his way with some forced ease through the corridors of power by day. I would pretend to an insider's knowledge and a comfort with power, and conceal my chaotic inner life. But the great powerful patrons always suspected something was amiss. They described it as a kind of unworldliness, and so it was. They could see that I always shrunk from negotiating conflicts with people, and preferred the imaginative flight of words.

I believed that I had to make a choice, and I could not set both my lives down together to share a meal. I needed a break to follow another path. But life never gave me a break. In the year my first child was born, I published my first poem, and began a writing course. But this was no time to throw away an identity that paid the mortgage. Still, becoming a parent in my thirties freed me to withdraw from the world of power, to shelter against the tempests that I feared, and live more hours each week for what truly mattered.

But still I kept my writing secret. Through my forties I established more regular habits: each Sunday I would show up to write, even if often the products were anguished rants about money and career, and dissatisfaction with this writing self who struggled to stick at any piece of art for more than a couple of weeks. I also experienced at work a great stretch of productive contribution and esteem, shaping alcohol and drug and mental health policy, which led me to dream that I could yet play a leadership role in the bureaucracy, and lead a life of the mind on issues of deep importance to me. But still I lead this double-helix life, in which my workaday world never spoke with the true ambitions of my imagination. I began a blog – the happy pessimist – in which I wrote under the pseudonym of Antonio Possevino about the world of politics and government; but I kept it secret.

And my madness made me suspect my mind, and shroud its feverish scribbles in shame. I felt like Robert Lowell,[12] that:

> Sometimes, my mind is a rocked and dangerous bell; I climb the spiral stairs to my own music, each step more poignantly oracular, something inhuman always rising in me.

Yet in this decade I also finally accepted medical treatment for my long-standing depression. Regular torments were dampened down, and I found a new freedom and comfortable habit of writing. And I published an e-book of my poems on Smashwords, and then later on Kindle Direct Publishing (later revised and included in *Gathering Flowers of the Mind: Collected Poems 1996-2020*). This initial book of poems – *After the Pills* – explored the difficult knowledge that we are not masters of our minds. I wrote in the preface:

> Whichever genre I have selected, my writing has explored the difficult relationship I have with my self. Know thyself is the old adage, and most romantic and post-romantic, modern and post-modern stories of the artist celebrate the depth of self-awareness, the inherent capability, and the assurance of the self who bears the pen into the battles of self-definition. This self of mine who I

---

[12] Quoted in Jamison, *Setting the River on Fire*.

encounter in the traditions of the lyric, however, seems altogether too slippery, enigmatic and treacherous for such stories.

The poems also explored the troubling truth that, for reasons even medicine is not sure of, this little pill or mirtazapine could transform my life and give me assurance of my mind in a way that no reason, no philosophy, no counsel, no mere mental event could. How could this pill release the craft of writing and the voice of the poet from the destructive fires of madness?

> For me the self is a more inherently limited and weak thing, and I remain spellbound by how different my experience of life is as a result of the daily ingestion of one small pill. The pill works away on the biochemistry of my brain in ways that I cannot comprehend, and yet I sit and observe how it has made a life once riven by months of darkness and doubt into an enjoyable and productive routine.

Still, though the routines of my writing became more firmly established, I told absolutely no-one outside of my family of my poems. By my fifties, my mind collapsed under the psychological strain of concealing my true vocation, out of shame and out of a desire to protect a false professional identity. Then my professional career crumbled. I was humiliated, scapegoated and isolated. I made mistakes driven by a desire to enact a fantasy of inclusion amongst the powerful that had comforted me since childhood. This crisis provoked a deep depression. I began titling my journals to self-mythologise this dark night of the soul: *The Wilderness Book*; *The Fearless Walk through the Flames*; *The Prophet Redeemed*; *The Pilgrim Returns to the Road*; *The Return to the Great Forest*. I began my most successful course of psychotherapy, which gave me a new course through life, away from the vast shipwreck of my career.

I walked through this destructive fire, and left behind the ruins transformed and redeemed. I had become the Unburnt One, the Father of Dragons, and the fires that surrounded me no longer threatened my songs. And, out of this fire, came *The Burning Archive*.

Here I learned the seasons of my mind. Here I found the register with which to sing about both my underworld and my adventures of the spring. Here I learned to be comfortable in my own unburnt skin. Here I settled into my craft and my form. Here I learned that I could walk with the truly great "who wore at their hearts the fire's centre" (Spender) – my companions in the infinite conversation – and leave behind my cravings for power, status, and recognition.

The Floating Life Within
4 November 2018

In the 1980s or 1990s I wrote down, on an index card, this observation from Robert Musil, *The Man Without Qualities:*
> An essay is not the provisional or incidental expression of a conviction that might on a more favorable occasion be elevated to the status of truth or that might just as easily be recognized as error … an essay is the unique and unalterable form that a man's inner life assumes in a decisive thought … There have been quite a number of such essayists and masters of the floating life within, but there would be no point in naming them. Their domain lies between religion and knowledge, between example and doctrine, between *amor intellectualis* and poetry; they are saints with and without religion, and sometimes too they are simply men who have gone out on an adventure and lost their way.

Musil died poor, forgotten and exiled in the calamity of second world war Europe. His *Man without Qualities*, which had been his work for the two decades, lay ever-revised, sprawling and unfinished at the time of his death. His fragmentary tale of cultural decay survived, through the random miracles of cultural legacies, to inspire my own essay adventures through the floating life within.

Self-Portrait at 55 (Reflections on 2018)
9 December 2018

The year is drawing to a close, so time to begin reflecting on what the year's stream of images, texts and events meant to me. Where has this year left me, and what has it left for me to say?

I am ending the year in a bit of a slump, one of those periodic recessions of belief in my thoughts and courage in my voice. Bold declarations of judgment are not coming to mind. I have retreated into the timidity of retweeting. "This too will pass" I say to myself, although with the chorus of my madness singing, "and this too will return".

I have reached an age and a stage in my working career when I no longer expect worldly success. I am overlooked and disregarded, neglected, isolated and forgotten. The strange peripatetic life I have made through so many issues of policy has only marked me out as a monstrosity in the world of executive courtiers. The progressive princelings of the court see me, I suspect, as unworldly, and as a complaining survival of another era. Untimely meditations, indeed.

Outwardly, I have been conferred with a status in the bureaucracy that I have not held before – for a time a senior executive, and, more still, the trustee of an independent review. It is an honour for an exile, and it is as an exile from my times that I must live out, or so I fear, the last ten to fifteen years of my working life; if not an ordered exile, then a voluntary exile that I want to embrace, though with regrets. I am like

Li Po, who the emperor Xuanzong suspected of supporting the An Shi rebellion, being sent into exile in Yehlang, where he would live out the last years of his poetic life.

Zazen on Ching-t'ing Mountain (Li Po, 702-762)

The birds have vanished down the sky.
Now the last cloud drains away.
We sit together, the mountain and me,
Until only the mountain remains

And is not exile the true destiny of those who "speak truth to power"? In truth, power does not care so much for speakers of truth, who only mar power's vengeful reforms of reality. Power indulges courtiers and clowns, not sages and poets. The world in which I make my career has seemingly grown more hostile to me this year. Government institutions have developed a culture to which I no longer wish to belong, and yet I cannot renounce my attachment to the values and the people they have lost. Its organisations are led by brats and bullies, and all the decent people, and as many people over 50 as possible, have been pushed aside. In the minor provincial government in which I am but a lowly under-castellan, a party and a government are in power that scorn intellectual tradition and constitutional convention, and practise a ruthless form of modern populist client politics. Their marketing machine has been affirmed by the electoral calculus in the most stunning way. "Four more years", their supporters shout triumphantly, and I shudder knowing that what will come is more partisanship, more patronage, more pranks, and more vandalism of institutions. So, internal exile it will be. I try to comfort myself that the best works of political philosophy have been born from the ordeal of prison cells and the wandering of exile. The task before me next year is to realise this dream, and to comfort myself with the lines from Pound's *Canto LXXXI* that I featured in my post "Cantos from a cage":

What thou lovest well remains, the rest is dross
What thou lov'st well shall not be reft from thee
What thou lov'st well is thy true heritage.

Jeff Rich

Ambiguous Loss (Reflections on 2018)
December 2018

I am listening to the *On Being* podcast that features this week a conversation with Pauline Boss on the meaning of ambiguous loss and how there is a myth of closure in our cultures of impatient striving and ceaseless ambition. There does not need to be an end to grief or to loss. We have to and we do live with loss and grief, without end, and should really stop pressuring ourselves to close off the sadness, the mourning, and the endless search to make sense of our losses. We need to learn "to be comfortable with what we cannot solve".

Strangely, I attuned to ambiguous loss after listening to two contrasting podcasts in the morning. The first was an interview with a former politician, Victor Perton, who has made out of the ruins of his parliamentary career a new business of optimism. He has written a book, *The Case for Optimism*, and everyday tweets out an optimistic thought. I once wrote a blog called the *Happy Pessimist* (now taken down, but the text saved to my private collection) with a twitter handle of the sad optimist, so you would not think I would take well to Mr Perton's ruthlessly Panglossian view of the world. There is, of course, some truth to his view of matters – we do, after all, enjoy such extraordinary affluence and access to so much knowledge and so many means of self-flowering. Yet the *Case for Optimism* shuts out the sadness of ambiguous loss, and tries to shame it. How can you be sad and grieving on this sunny day with a smartphone in your hand, when somewhere in China a billion people have been lifted out of poverty?

The other, contrasting podcast I listened to was an episode of *Poetry off the Shelf* on Gerard Manley Hopkins. It is 100 years since the publication of his poems, which in turn were published 20 years after his death by the now forgotten Poet Laureate Robert Bridges. Uncannily, during the week, I was reading Hopkins, and posted his poem, *"The times are nightfall, look their light grows less"*. He is one of my favourite writers, and like other beloved writers of my strange fate, such as the good Emily Dickinson, he was barely known in his lifetime. The sound-world, the old Anglo-Saxon internal rhymes in the line, the archaic invention of the word-land – all these marks of his poetry created a world of magic – captured beautifully in an old sound recording by Cyril Cusack – but Hopkins' religious sensibility did not sing to me in my younger years. Still, he is a poet I have known since childhood, from an old paperback edition held by my mother, bought perhaps in her university days, and so inseparable for me from the grief and ambiguous loss of her death this year.

But a few years back, during my long dark night of the soul, I discovered the *terrible sonnets* – which Hopkins shared with no-one, and that Bridges only discovered as tear-soaked drafts after Gerard's death. Then Hopkins' rhapsodic, mad sadness struck me as a bell. Then I learned by heart the terrible sonnet, *"No worst there is none. Pitched past pitch of grief"* and wandered the streets of Fitzroy as a broken man while whispering the sonnets *sotto voce*, beneath my rebellion against reason.

One line from this dark sonnet – "O the mind, mind has mountains; cliffs of fall/ Frightful, sheer, no-man-fathomed" – is the rejoinder to every Panglossian optimist like Victor Perton. It is the cry from the mad depths where dwell those who do not deny ambiguous loss, who do not yield to strict ambition's orders to present a sunny facade of positive, optimistic plans to the world.

This year has known ambiguous loss, and, at times, I have stood with the "sad heart of Ruth when, sick for home, she stood in tears amid the alien corn" (Keats, "Ode to a Nightingale"). My mother died in February, after some years of slow disappearance from memory and sentences due to dementia. Late in the year, my partner's brother's partner died a shocking early death, brought on by a brain tumour that seized her from the midst of vibrant art. And the world of culture and politics has grown more alien to me. Increasingly, I see a world sinking in its over-production, and the beauty I seek in the world is disappearing in battles and ruins and screaming matches between urban gangs played out against a "melancholy, long withdrawing roar, retreating, to the breath of the night-wind, down the vast edges drear and naked shingles of the world" (Matthew Arnold, *Dover Beach*).

But the world is getting better, they say, and I cannot deny my life is comfortable, peaceful and with few troubles. Steven Pinker, with his cheery American salesmanship, chimes in with the facts and graphs that prove, even to me, that the Enlightenment is a land of triumph and achievement that has made our lives a temple of progress. Still, I think with Roger Scruton:

> The Enlightenment has been with us for two to three centuries, but so too has been the resistance to it. There are poets who have responded to Enlightenment as a kind of light-pollution, from which pockets of darkness must be salvaged in order that we can see the stars. Arnold was one of them, T.S. Eliot another, Rilke a third. Such artists acknowledge loss, but refuse to mourn it, doing what they can to hold things in place while looking to the future.[13]

To dwell in culture and history, to walk these long corridors of the lost beloved meanings of the dead and the living, reminds me every moment of the sadness of our losses and the beauty of our striving to hold onto those things that we cherish. It is to be constantly under threat of being overwhelmed by the next wave of time and human creativity. But it is also to plunge bravely into the surge and power of the next wave. Loss and tears in alien corn, but not paralysis in mourning.

---

[13] Roger Scruton, "A Valediction Forbidding Mourning, but Admitting Loss", *How to be a Conservative* (2014).

Jeff Rich

Fragments Reflecting on 2018
30 December 2018

This year has had no coherent themes for me, and perhaps that is why I have struggled to write posts with a clearly signposted judgment on 2018. Only now it occurred to me that it has been a year of fragments and broken off story lines. So, the form of the fragment may be my refuge, aging modernist that I am.

"Walk with grief like an old friend / Listen to what he says" I read this yesterday in a poem by Rumi. I have walked with grief most of this year: my mother's death, the decay of the institutions of government in which I wander like like a bereaved stranger, the loneliness of my intellectual life, divorced from like-mindedness. But have I listened well to grief, my old friend? It tells me about my losses, and all that I did not have, although I do not know if others do. The comfort of a family home. Memories of a happy childhood. But have I shed tears for these absences? Or is grief's lesson to me to be thankful for who I am, and not sorry for who I was not?

Turning away from the world. In the last few days I have been reading William Dalrymple's *From the Holy Mountain: a journey in the shadow of Byzantium* (1998). It describes with uncanny foresight the world of escalating cultural conflict in the former Byzantine world, and the slow extinction of Eastern Christian life in its homelands. As Dalrymple's narrative of travel and contending faiths unfolds, I imagine myself to be a monk turning my back on the world and its spiteful illusions. I see a path to enlightenment: in simple habits, and in the consecration of one's life to beauty, truth and that which was one holds divine, even within a secular imagination. The world that I inhabit in my workaday life, the bureaucracy of a failing liberal democracy, has grown more bitter and more ashen to me this year. Its best traditions are trashed, and any dreams of renewal are fading. Its leaders are hollow men and women. I still plan to write my work of both faith and dissent, *The Ordinary Virtues of Governing Well*, and imagine that this *samizdat* may last beyond me, like Confucian

teachings in a kingdom that had abandoned the virtuous life in its government. But I wonder also if next year I do not need to turn away from the political world, and find the kind of institution that cares for the texts I want to give to the world.

A world in disarray. I have no pretence any longer that I could govern events in our disintegrating world, and even my long-held confidence in interpreting or predicting political events has been shattered by my misreading of events close to home. I am in the same valley as billions of citizens who watch the high summits with both horror and a growing gratitude that 'Heaven is high and the emperor is far away'. The daily outrage of liberal journalists at Trump's latest offence against virtue only frustrates me. It is up to Americans, in the end, to reassert decent values for their republic, and every *faux pas* from the White House does not need to be broadcast to the world as a sign of the end of days. The retrenchment of the American Empire is, I believe, a good thing, and will only mean that this emperor is even further away from we who wish to escape him. But the advocates of liberal hegemony react to every event with shrill nonsense – "how dare Trump withdraw troops from the Middle East and so give a victory to Turkey, Russia and Iran!" – all of which have real interests in this region, unlike those of faraway America. I am more scared by the hysterical nonsense spoken about Russia and China on Capitol Hill than I am by any efforts by Putin to secure Crimea and borders with Europe or by Xi Jinping's assertion of China's ancient claims to the South China Sea. After all, any realist would recognise these territories belong to these great states. I have begun to read Richard Haass, *A World in Disarray: American Foreign Policy and the crisis of the old order*, and I expect we will see some dramatic events in the next year that see the *unravelling of the American empire*, which it coyly calls the global rules-based order. An escalating trade war? Cyber attacks? Trump reneging on America's debts and China calling in its chips? The growth of a Democratic war faction in Washington? A left-liberal coup backed by the deep state in America? The collapse of the United Kingdom? A small proxy war? The resurgence of Islamic extremism?

As this older order collapses, I must seek to create better visions of a good life that can outlast the derangement of the West in my small corner of the South Pacific.

Rules for living. This year I read Jordan Peterson, *12 Rules for Life: an antidote to chaos*. I read it needing an antidote to the chaos of feeling I experienced in the wake of my mother's death. It had a profound effect on me. Initially, I was tentative since I had heard Peterson's name through controversies about culture wars. I soon discovered that Peterson has been maliciously misrepresented by so much of the progressive press. His deepest message to our disordered times – paradoxically, given the lens of political controversy through which many commentators see his work – is that ***the psychological is not political***. Our culture has suffered through the viral penetration of the 60's radical slogan that the personal is political. This is not to deny that these movements have led to improvements in the circumstances of many lives. But it has poisoned how we talk to strangers about governing. We don't, not anymore; except to issue hisses of denunciation. Peterson reminds us: he without sin may cast the first stone. There is a lot of wisdom in Peterson's teachings. They point me to the pilgrimage to the sites of true meaning in my life that I can begin; now that I have turned my back on the delusions of the political world.

Reflections on 2019

29 December 2019

2019 has been a barren year. My writing projects have not developed as I would like. I have made progress with *Ivan's Singer*, but I have not been finishing the sections according to schedule. I think it is still viable for me to finish next year this Sebald-like novel about Ivar the Terrible and my own encounters with the terrifying monstrosity of power. I am 80 per cent there, but also need to do some editing. I curated my poetry editions, but stumbled on the technical process of self-publication and preparation of the covers and book file. I have kept going with *Ordinary Virtues*, but written too little this year.

I have had few imaginative ideas. I have written a few fresh poems this year, but not many and not regularly. It has been a year more of fulfilling promises to myself to complete the ideas born in the past. Over these last six months I do feel some turning in my thinking about the history, politics, and government; but I am not yet sure where those thoughts will go. I am hesitating on the threshold of the *renunciation of the political world*, but do not yet have the courage to step forward into an unknown domain.

The pace, range and fecundity of this blog have been constrained. I have reposted old blog entries in July and August in celebration of 11 years with Wordpress. I have written a series of posts reflecting on the ordinary virtues of governing well, which will appear in a later volume of my essays on politics and governing, *Thirteen Ways of Looking at a Bureaucrat*:

- *Do we repair our republics with big ideas or ordinary virtues?*, in which I challenged my old mentor Terry Moran's recipe for a new Labor Government;
- *On human frailty in governing*, in which I reflected on the meaning of the "unexpected" Labor loss in the Australian election, and commented that "If governing elites are to repair the breach of authority with ordinary people, they must accept, and indeed love, human frailty";
- *To govern does not equal to change* in which I questioned the progressivist authoritarian instinct that the goal of politics is to change other people; and
- *The impeachment of the republic* in which I reflected on the attempt by bureaucrats to usurp Presidential authority in the USA.

The more creative entries were my travel posts stimulated by my travels through Europe in May and June. These began with *Encountering Fernando Pessoa in Lisbon*, but were not quite finished, as completely as I would have liked.

I have wondered at times as I sat at my desk on a Sunday morning if I would ever write anything again, or if my ideas would ever reach an audience. The last six months, since my return from the European trip to arrive in my own circles of hell at work, have been dominated by stress, insecurity, threats to my wellbeing, broken sleep, and the distress of being ostracised. This burden will be lifted next year, and I promise: my long walk through the desert will end in Timbuktu.

The Kaleidoscope of 2020: Year in Review

16 December 2020

A tradition that I have embraced on this blog over the last few years has been to write year-in-review posts in December.

In 2019 I reflected on *walking through the desert, notes on my reading, the democratic rebuff to progressives,* and *walking through the circles of hell.*

In 2018 I reflected on *ambiguous loss,* the *year in history, (not) belonging,* and *fragments;* but it was a year with no coherent theme for me.

In 2017, the year I began this tradition on the blog, and where I set the expectation of coherent themes for my written life, I reflected on *cultural decay and political institutions* (an enduring and insistent theme), a *multi-polar world,* the *end of history revisited,* a recap of my blooming writings of that year, and *persistence, terror and Das Schloss.* This last post expressed with uncanny foresight the dilemma I face today:

> Now at the end of a year in which I have tried to live in truth, to write my own thoughts as authentically as I can and to act in the

world in a way that approaches my values, I still stand as an outcast beyond the reaches of *Das Schloss*. Which way do I walk next year? To the Castle and back, or do I turn my back on this great civil dream, and wander alone like a grey wolf into the Great Dark Forest?

The more things change, the more they stay the same? In truth, this post from three years ago speaks to my personal challenge of that moment, and the deep tides of culture, institution, history and archetype that run through decades of my story. This text generates an infinitely repeating fractal of my mind.

This year I thought I would approach my tradition a little differently, and write and update fragmentary texts reflecting on the year in review all in one consolidated, expanding post – the kaleidoscope of 2020.

And so it begins…. [to be continued, fractally]

Viral Meltdown

How could the year in review not begin with the pandemic and the virus? Since January I have followed the story of coronavirus and the subsequent viral meltdown of our elites and institutions. The coda on the year is the miracle of a vaccine developed, tested, manufactured, ratified and distributed all within ten or eleven months – not ten or more years. And yet there is a bitter note underneath this coda; since the public health zealots, the Great Reset boosters, the lockdown looters want to say their bad rules are better than this good cure.

The big story of the year is not the virus but the failed response of the governing elites, as Niall Ferguson has consistently argued through the year. His *Doom: the politics of catastrophe* will be the book to read in May 2021 – let us hope it does not come too late. And I have lived in the eye of this storm this year, an unwilling and dissenting accomplice in a catastrophic failure of governing. At times I have thought about writing a book to recount this failure, but will instead absorb my lesson, and strike out in a different direction, clearly separated from the incompetent oligarchic generals of "Build Back Better".

Yet – even though constrained by the soft authoritarianism and the post-democratic shackles on free speech and, still worse, on free thought – I have written and reflected on the viral meltdown throughout the year on this blog. It began in March with my posts on *The Plague Year*, *The Great Seclusion* and *Plague Notes*. On March 19 in "The Plague Year", I wrote:

> This crisis will have large effects on the economy, society and the culture. It will break some leaders in all those fields, and will make others. It is in large part a crisis of governing, and over the months of its unfolding I may return to that. But will this crisis also lead to events and adaptations of the decaying culture. Will we turn from constant consumerism, flippant influencers and corrupt, complacent elites? Will our culture regenerate? Will the onset of a biological event – the outbreak of a pathogenic RNA virus – lead to a transvaluation of all values?

At the end of the year I do not think anything so "transformative" as a transvaluation of all values has or will occur, but perhaps I struck a truer note on March 29 when I speculated that the "slow viral transformation of our characters induced by this global retreat may be the most fertile seed planted by this crisis". However, toxic seeds of bitter weeds have also been planted this year.

In April amidst the difficulty of lockdown, social isolation and fearful panic, I turned to poems (to be published in full in a later collection), and in 'Lockdown' I wrote:

> Do they countenance their own folly
> When the whole world screamed at a mouse
> When our leaders fitted people to a sigmoid curve
> Flattened the uncertainty of death
> Relived the Spanish flu from their textbooks
> First as tragedy, and then as farce

Then in the maelstrom of the Australian response to coronavirus, on May 9 I saw through the will to power in the *diktats* of the public health officials – *Public Health Rulez, OK?* – that wove one of my spiritual ancestors, Sir Thomas Browne, into a hope for a different and more humble response:

> So, we may hope that the quieter practitioners of true medicine might come to the fore before too long, and this brief Puritanical Commonwealth of Lockdown may come to the end. As Sir Thomas Browne said, 'We all labour against our own cure, for death is the cure of all disease'.

Not till late July did I return to the theme, when I compared the viral meltdown of our elites to the failures of the European aristocrats in the Crimean War in *A very modern Charge of the Light Brigade*.

In August, the "shock and awe" of the disproportionate response of my minor failing provincial government, in which I am but a lowly under-castellan, led me to a reflection on *The Failure of Institutions in the Pandemic Crisis*, which sought in Yuval Levin and Patrick Dineen possible ways out, and pinned hope on an ethic of institution-building to treat the virus of institutional decay. In September I wrote *Captain Ahab and Lockdown in Melbourne*. In October I signed the Great Barrington Declaration – refusing to live the lies of the political commissars of my own institution – and stated my belief that we had to move *From here to immunity: charting COVID from pandemic to endemic*.

And then I turned my mind and my heart to living in freedom and truth. I acted as if no longer shackled by the broken rules of our failed institutions. In 2021, there will be life after lockdown; there will be restoration of deeper values, not the Great Reset of the Viral Meltdown.

Fragments from the diary

Throughout the year I have kept a diary in an A5 black notebook of 200 pages or so. I have followed this practice for quite some years now, and give each notebook a title. This year's notebooks were titled, "The view from Thucydides Tower" (January 2020 to November 2020) and "Live not by Lies" (from November 2020).

Jeff Rich

Over the last two days I have read through these *cahiers,* and noted down some of the abiding personal themes (abandonment, the search for affiliation, deep pessimism about the state of the world, frustration with the corrupted institutions of government) and the interpretations I made of the events of this year of isolation and home imprisonment in the Puritanical Commonwealth of Lockdown.

Here are some fragments from the diary that strike me today as worth sharing.

12 January 2020 ... *Suicide by democracy – elites become professionalised and mercenary to play the democratic game, and in doing so destroy the self-governing ethic and virtues of democracy.*

24 January 2020 ... *All becomes nothing. All falls into desuetude. We are but sere leaves, falling through an ashen sky.*

28 January ... *I am now an abandoned Cassandra. My way of life is forgotten among the powerful.*

4 February ... [A quotation heard on a podcast] *"What is important is not to report what you see, but to see what you see."*

13 February ... *Plague and disasters are an insult to the control of the liberal imagination, the power of the liberal world view.... The collapse of the liberal centre is the collapse of a political cartel.*

3 March ... *I have returned from Bali with a determination to live my life as I will, to reshape some habits and patterns, to do more of what I want and to build a healthier, more expressive, stronger, more responsible and impactful life.*

7 March ... *my latest poetry series concept, the sleep machine... [is] a metaphor for the augmentation of the self by society/culture – how we are born frail, imperfect – not self-realisation, but self-compensation, submission or acceptance of the weakness of the human animal; but by submission, living in the augmentation of tradition, knowledge, culture, the infinite conversation, then dreams return, culture is fulfilled, consciousness is heightened, responsibility takes hold.*

22 March ... *Hard to focus on anything other than coronavirus – in the midst of a great social crisis, a great crisis of authority. The regime of merchant elites and their craven clerk mercenaries is crumbling. I have been*

criticising it for years now, and have hoped that my words could break apart this decaying old ship – but that was always an illusion, and an over-rating of my individual power. Could it be that this crisis might create an opening for my voice, my ideas for another way of governing? Maybe, but there are bad scenarios too. Sunset is not always followed by sunrise in the dark rhythms of history.

3 April … *Suicide by public health – the earnest group-think of public health officials who put a whole society at risk to protect their inadequately robust, resilient health care system from being exposed.*

16 April … *Suicide by public health – the world has stumbled into a vast medical and social experiment that makes the Stanford Prison experiment look ethical*

25 July … *Abandon the progressive intelligentsia, and be the old dignified eagle soaring over the mountain alone.*

6 August … *I am cursed to be like Cassandra, cursed by my prophetic pessimism. My thought seizes a world in decay, but can it communicate anything better? Or is the hard message that we must put our hope in other things: love of family, culture, tradition and abandon the worldly State?*

9 August … *Work from home has created the perfect conditions for a cabal takeover, and the complete defeat of institutions.*

16 November … *I can't do it alone, and yet I have never found allies in my dissidence, never cultivated followers in my path, so solitary, so hardened. I fall into the black hole and am condemned to dwell there with only my jailer and the ghosts of my mind. I preach to the birds.*

29 November … *Borges: 'literature is nought but guided dreaming, anyway'.*

11 December … *I feel I am living through a fight between progressive totalitarianism and the real purposes of life – that I am like the dissidents of Eastern Europe in the 70's and 80's. And I am so appalled by the suppression of free speech, the denigration of characters, the ostracism perpetrated by Big Tech, Big Media and the mercenary elite. I think about Frank Knopfelmacher and his moral courage – how he was mocked and pilloried and slandered – and yet he stood for a moral truth against a self-deluding and morally corrupt elite.*

"If you rely on other people's approval, you become their prisoner," Lao Tsu.

These diary fragments from a bitter year show my archive burnt into a handful of ash, but also the seeds to plant in that fertile ash.

The freedom of internal exile

So much of this year I have struggled with the moral crisis of how to endure and to live well through a corrupt, decaying, failing and abusive regime. I do not mean just the errant minor provincial government in which I serve as lowly under-castellan. I mean the wider institutional regime of our now post-democratic society, riven with political and cultural decay.

In recent days, I have been returning to the concept of the Chinese recluse, *yinshi*, and my own thoughts from May 2019, eighteen months ago, "*On the Renunciation of the Political World*". Temperamentally, I do not have the attributes of a fighter, negotiator or general. I incline to the *vita contemplativa*, not the *vita activa*. I look out on the strife of the world as a scholar viewing a lake, not a strategist plotting a battlefield, rather like the scholar viewing a lake in the artwork of Kanō Tan'yū (1602-1674).

And yet, I do not choose a quiet life easily – not when I see the tectonic grinding of collapsing empires; not when I see republics in distress and democracies in the throes of death; not when I see lies and soft totalitarianism entrenched amongst our new Red Guard elites. Throughout this year I have struggled with how to live in truth and to lead a moral life amidst the crises of 2020: the pandemic and the poor response of our elites to governing the virus; the social unrest of the American colour revolution; the constitutional crises of the dominant imperial power; the appalling lockdowns, border closures, breaches of medical ethics, abuses of power and catastrophic policy and administrative failures in Australia. Outraged by the injustice, the incompetence and the derangement, I wish I could be like Vaclav Havel and convene a new Civic Forum and bring signatures to a new Charter 77.

Yet, I know I do not have that fate. I do not have those attributes. I do not have those strengths for that battle. I accept my fate as an internal exile in this distressed republic. I stand solitary by the great lake of the infinite conversation, and look out to the great trees on the shore, and hope to plant one seed.

> This tree was growing before the forest was born.
> If you guess its age, it's twice as old.
> Its roots met the changes of hills and ravines,
> its leaves were altered by wind and frost.
> Everyone laughs at its outer decay,
> failing to appreciate the colorful patterns within.
> Its bark may have peeled away,
> but there is only truth inside.
>
> (Hanshan, 9th century)

The year of fear

2020 has been the year of the Great Fear. This Fear has locked us down in safety. This Fear has opened the gate to soft totalitarianism. This Fear has sabotaged the freedom, responsibility, associations and independent thought of hundreds of millions of citizens. This Fear has shed the decrepit liberal skin of the post-democratic reptile our elites have become.

The Great Fear has been more infectious than the novel coronavirus, SARS-COV-2. Yet no-one has calculated its R (reproduction) number. No statistician has modeled its consequences. No epidemiologist has rules of a new normal to dictate so we may stand up from our cowering corners. The Great Fear most likely has been more deadly than the virus – in suicides, substance abuse, mental illness, doctor visits avoided. It has inflicted more misery and more lonely deaths – terrified old people dying alone as rulers scream at their carers to stay away – because staying apart keeps us together in power.

The Great Fear found other spectres than strands of RNA virus. Racism was one. Police violence another. Russian collusion. Trump's "coup" against democracy. The power of the wicked Four Olds.

Thousands marched the streets to tear down their Fears. Thousands desecrated statues and relics of the past – from Robert E. Lee to Abraham Lincoln, even that former slave, soldier and war prisoner, Miguel de Cervantes – to calm their Fears. Some Red Guards even raised their fists in a power salute and shouted in the faces of innocent bystanders to share the cleansing Fears of 2020.

The Great Fear has been the crisis/opportunity for the svengalis of the Great Reset. All the humdrum local leaders of the world jumped on shouting at the dragon far beyond the city gates. They realised they could pose as heroes on the city walls, as long as the poor plebeians who sheltered in their quarters could never see the reality of the danger posed by the dragon. From the walls they and their media collaborators shouted every day about tests, cases and the horror stories from overseas, most often that calamity of the media's construction, Trump's America. The exceptional became normalised. Bizarre and rare complications were shouted from the rooftops. The true comparisons - apparent if people opened their eyes - were not made plain. And the Great Lies – this "unprecedented" event, this 100 year pandemic, this modern narcissistic version of the Black Death – laid the groundwork for the Little Dictators who want to remake the world by public health orders. Now Klaus Schwab and his globalist sycophants want to entrench their wealth and status as the Elect through the terrors of the Great Reset. Push this button to cede all control to experts.

As we stand on the cusp of 2021, the Great Fear has not yet receded. London is living in the new Puritanical Commonwealth of Lockdown. We are all told we must hide behind masks. Our tweets are censored. Our searches are watched. Our votes are miscounted. Our laws are twisted. Everyday at work the compliant tell me how strange it is that there are people out there who do not respect the rules; how grateful they are that the public enforce the rules against their neighbours on behalf of the authorities; how terrified they are that we may not keep a record of zero cases. Fear looks like it will try to rule our lives again in 2021; and I can only embrace my fate and resist. To see through the lies of the Great Fear has been the greatest gift of 2020.

> Do not be afraid; our fate
> Cannot be taken from us; it is a gift.
>
> (Dante, *Inferno*)

Dream. Life. Recovery.
23 January 2021

For several years in my early thirties, I attended a dream group with the Jungian psychotherapist, Peter O'Connor. Peter, who is now retired, was a gifted therapist who for many years from the late 1970's held the torch in Melbourne for a humanistic psychology with insights from myth and poetry. He was a rebel against the rat-observers and statistical behaviouralists who were dominant back then. Peter had built a public profile by writing on the mid-life crisis, and had written a book, *Dreams and the search for meaning* (1986), which I had read as part of my self-driven diagnosis of distress and recovery from the traumas of life.

It must have been this little book on dreams that led me to call Peter O'Connor's rooms and ask to participate in the dream group. Peter interviewed me in his rooms in a late Victorian mansion on Glenferrie Road, Hawthorn, where I recall he had small statues both of Shiva in the form of Nataraja, the divine dancer, and of Asclepius, the ancient Greek god of healers. We clicked, or so I felt, because of a common quest to search for meaning in both the traditions of literature and myth and the fallen petals of my mind, of which the most delicate and fragile were my dreams.

Jeff Rich

I had pursued an intellectual interest in dreams for many years, reading Freud's *Interpretation of Dreams*, Jung, and many humanistic and existential psychologists. Among the writings of those existential thinkers of the psyche was the text of the remarkable Swiss peer of Jung, Ludwig Binswanger, *Dream and Existence (1930)*, that I discovered in my then obsessive search through the early writings of Michel Foucault. From my mid-to-late-20's I explored dreams further and began to keep a dream diary. The frequency of my conscientious recording of my unconscious was highest in these years of my late 20's and early 30's, after I had left my university life and abandoned my aspiration to become a history professor, or in truth a writer in disguise, when I was still struggling with my right-sized, ill-fitted clothes as a bureaucrat. The dreams worked mercurially as part of my therapeutic journey, and I became convinced they were the royal road to my recovery. Back then in the early 1990's, I had sought therapy from a clinical psychologist, Ivan Milton, who later became a Buddhist monk, initially to help me cease smoking, then to overcome the procrastination and blocks that were preventing me completing my doctoral thesis, and then lastly to make meaning from the broader, but more murkily identified, concerns of depression, anxiety, father absence and uncertain purpose. In the course of this therapeutic alliance, from which I emerged so much stronger, so much freer, I had some profoundly important dreams that I still recall vividly.

I still have that book in which for years I recorded my dreams, palely, without ornament, imitating the model set by Jung himself in his *Red Book*. I called it, "*The Book of Soul I*". There in that book, which I described as "a meticulous gesture to dignify and deepen my soul", I discover tonight, after leafing through this personal archive, my notes from the first dream that I shared with Peter O'Connor's dream group in late 1994.

Dream – The bloodied, poisoned fish

I am in the water, like a lake or ocean but with one walled concreted edge where I am supporting myself. Rising out up from the water is a poisoned, bloodied fish hanging from a large hook, like a meat hook. The front half of its body drops down, as if it were unfolding. It drenches in blood, like a gush of tears, or shit. Like a shower bag being released. It hangs there a while and then is slowly drawn away over the water. It hangs above the water in the distance, and sharks leap up on their tails in the water to bite at the fish.

My notes say: "The first dream I shared with the group had great force. Peter and the group felt it was an archetypal dream. Its core symbol remains perplexing to me."

Dreams are gifts of the underworld. Can we, imitators of Orpheus, ever truly look back and explain these gifts or the world from which they come? We can only be thankful for these gifts and embroider their meanings into the texts of our lives. We can be thankful for when the gods bestow dreams on our memories. For many years, I slept without recalling dreaming, almost certainly – I think now – because of the interruptions to sleep from snoring and sleep apnea. But over the last year, as a result of the improvement of my sleep through a CPAP machine, the dreams have begun to resume and emerge from the clouded horizon of morning. Thankful for this renewal of imagination after a long shriven winter, I took down from my shelf the other day, after being prompted to remember the dream group on my camping holiday at the beach at Lorne, another book which I used to deepen my soul, James Hillmann, *The Dream and the Underworld*.

From that book I noted two quotations with which I will end this post. In the first, Hillman asserts the primacy of night over day, dream over reality, image over fact.[14]

> The image has been my starting point for the archetypal re-visioning of psychology… To start with the image in depth psychology is to begin in the mythical underworld, so this book provides the mythical perspective to our psychology of the image. The claim that images come first is to say that dreams are the primary givens and that all daylight consciousness begins in the night and bears its shadows.

And lastly, in his epigraph, Hillman summons Jung, rather like

---

[14] James Hillmann, *The Dream and the Underworld* (1979), p. 5.

Dante calling on Virgil to guide Dante through the circles of Hell, and warns us how serious is the approach to recovery through dreams:

> The dread and resistance which every natural human being experiences when it comes to delving too deeply into himself is, at bottom, the fear of the journey into Hades.[15]

---

[15] C.G. Jung, "Psychology and Alchemy", *Collected Works*, v. 12, p. 439.

From the Burning Archive

PART THREE

CULTURAL DECAY

Jeff Rich

Notes on the Death of Culture
21 October 2015 and 4 August 2016

Mario Vargas Llosa reviews, in the overture to this work, *Notes on the Death of Culture* (2015) four influential essays on the traumatic descent into death of culture, as he says, in the meaning traditionally ascribed to that term.

First, he reviews T.S. Eliot, *Notes Towards a Definition of Culture* (1948), in which Eliot anticipated today's burning archive. Eliot wrote:

> I see no reason why the decay of culture should not proceed much further, and why we may not even anticipate a period, of some duration, of which it will be possible to say that it will have *no* culture.

Then, he distances himself from George Steiner, *Bluebeard's Castle* (1971), a late reply to Eliot, haunted by the complicity of high culture with the holocaust. Steiner spoke uncertainly of the loss of the culture of the word, so personally precious to him, but now fading before the image, pop music, number and science. Steiner: "Already a dominant proportion of poetry, of religious thought, of art, has receded from personal immediacy into the keeping of the specialist". Now the keeper and his archive burn.

Third, Guy Debord, *The Society of the Spectacle* (1967), provides propositions that Mario Vargas Llosa incorporates into his own, and indeed the subtitle of his book, essays on spectacle and society. Mario Vargas Llosa judges Proposition 47 prescient: "the real consumer becomes a consumer of illusions".

Fourth, Vargas Llosa comments on two contemporary reflections on the emergence of a global democratic, market consumer or pop culture, Lipovetsky and Serroy *Culture-World: response to a disoriented world* (2008) and Frederic Martel's *Mainstream* (2010). These works provide the counterpoint to Mario Vargas Llosa's final judgment. These works celebrate the "creative industries" – a ghastly term of culture bureaucrats that Mario Vargas Llosa rightly leaves in quotation marks – dedicated above all to mass production and commercial market success. *Notes on the Death of Culture* does not host the same celebration.

While these latter authors celebrate with post-modern brio the commercial transvaluation of all values, Mario Vargas Llosa reasserts Eliot's prophecy as a fact of today's life.

> The great majority of humanity does not engage with, produce or appreciate any form of culture other than what used to be considered by cultured people, disparagingly, as mere popular pastimes, with no links to the intellectual, artistic and literary activities that were once at the heart of culture. This former culture is now dead, although it survives in small social enclaves, without any influence on the mainstream. The essential difference between the culture of the past and the entertainment of today is that the products of the former sought to transcend mere present time, to endure, to stay alive for future generations, while the products of the latter are made to be consumed instantly and disappear, like cake or popcorn.[16]

This death of culture creates a great trauma among the few isolated and devoted souls who keep their archives, write their sonnets, and study the word. It is a trauma that can only be healed by writing to defy death, through entering into Blanchot's infinite conversation.

---

[16] Mario Vargas Llosa, *Notes on the Death of Culture: Essays on Spectacle and Society* (2016), p. 20.

Jeff Rich

The Extinction of Meaning
11 October 2015

    The solitary writer dwells in an oppressive fear; that the line of culture, the traditions, the teachings that his or her labors seek to preserve against the decay of all human institutions, this thread of meaning, which he or she has painstakingly recovered from the past and braided with the personal traumas that inspire any writer, this way of being will not live beyond his or her death.
    All solitary writers fear becoming the last of their kind, and after the arrogant brashness of youth, it is mourning for the imminent death of words that keeps more words coming. I insist on these statements, with all their confusions and ambiguities, and I set the bier afloat on the current, before then shooting a flaming arrow to extinguish its last untouchable meaning. We know languages are disappearing from the world, but we cannot for long contemplate the flames in the libraries and the infinite profusion of novelties that together overwhelm any tradition's attempt to preserve meaning. We utter our own unique death rites, and slide unnoticed into the infinitude of commentary.

A New Dark Age
17 January 2016

    It is a dark age when learning is despised; when violence prowls our streets; when the cherished teachings of our wisest culture falls disused and forgotten. Apocalypses are not fashionable, though innovation and disruption are. We celebrate the piracy of wanton wealth and mock the traditionalists who sit in their cells and speak alone with their gods in the poems without which they could not love.

In the ruins of the crises of the tenth century, Western European culture was born and indeed so was the glory of Kievan Rus. Monasticism, a resurgent faith and a reform of the church, a flowering Renaissance, the emergence of order in modern government, law, conscience, mysticism and on it goes. Who will speak like Abelard and Héloïse across the centuries in this new dark age?

On a Requiem
30 August 2016

This morning I listened to an old CD recording I had of György Ligeti's *Requiem*, which transported me through floating clouds of sound back to my love of avant-garde music.

Ligeti was a Hungarian composer who fled the communist regime, and pursued his development of new musical techniques in Austria. The Requiem dates from 1965, and together with several other excerpts from Ligeti's music was featured in Kubrick's *2001: A Space Odyssey*. To me it resembles a chorus of the city of the dead, reeling in horror at the destruction of culture during the horrible first fifty years of the twentieth century. The chorus sings from the chaos, the ruin and the wandering ghosts of a great fallen city.

Through techniques I cannot really explain, and certainly I can not reproduce, Ligeti composed music that is strangely mobile, as if it comes not from one source or place, but is alive in the air, moving to and from many places in a desperate clambering to beauty in flight from horror. I recall in the late 1980's I attended a concert conducted by Pierre Boulez at the Sydney Opera House. The ensemble performed one of Ligeti's chamber works, and my abiding memory of the concert, other than walking past David Malouf at interval, was how Ligeti's music seemed to move all around the concert chamber, and worked its way through wormholes in the physical soundscape that no other music does.

Back then, when I was a graduate student, I was committed to the avant-garde, and, in some ways, I still have something of that post-romantic belief that the true artist transcends the structures of culture bequeathed them so that a terrible new beauty will be born. This was Ligeti's philosophy. He said in an interview once with the *Vienna Review* (as I recall, though my notes are lost or the link is broken, amateur scholar that I am):

> When I think of the avant-garde, I have this image in my head: I am sitting in an airplane, the sky is blue and I see a landscape. And then the plane flies into a cloud: everything is grey-white. At first the grey seems interesting if you compare it to the earlier landscape, but soon becomes monotonous. I then fly out of the cloud and again see the landscape, which has completely changed in the meantime…. I believe we have flown into such a cloud of high entropy and great disorder…. The instant I emerge out of the cloud, I see, and this is being very critical, that the music we wrote was in fact rather ugly.

I am not sure anymore if I will ever emerge from the cloud – or is it smoke and ash? But, at least for today, Ligeti's music reminded me that beauty can be born, despite terror, and without changing everything, changing it utterly.

From the Burning Archive

Five Reasons Games Add to Culture
25 August 2016

> Play is a uniquely adaptive act, not subordinate to some other adaptive act, but with a special function of its own in human experience. (Johann Huizinga)

As well as being a serious student of literature and history, and the occasional listener to melancholy and sometimes merely strange music, I play computer games, most especially, over the last 10 years, *World of Warcraft*. Or at least I do play them now, and over the last week have returned to playing *World of Warcraft*. Before then I went through a long stretch of 4 to 5 years during which time I played this game only spasmodically and with a sense of shame and embarrassment. I was concerned that I played too compulsively, and that the long hours in these imagined worlds deprived me of time to write and to read and to imagine.

I also wondered if I could marry my identity as a man of culture who performed a serious job in government with the night time playful avatar who prowled forests and dungeons as a night elf. Gamer and poet and governor? That is a bit odd, surely.

But over the last week I have realised those different identities can co-exist well, and that, in a way, I am more happy and more fulfilled when I do play games. Returning to *World of Warcraft* has been a kind of personal and artistic recovery. It returns a sense of play and adventure to my life.

I realise now that over the last five years I had made the playing of this game an embarrassed secret, yet another addiction to overcome, yet another part of me to hide away in secrecy and surround with shame. My creative instinct to play was suppressed and put to shame in my silent self; and so I lost something important, and suffered, if not for these reasons alone, periods of deep depression.

Gaming and culture can wed, both within my personal life and within the wider culture. I am not saying that I like everything about gamer culture – a lot of which is male youthful exuberance. But I am saying that any strong culture has a strong element of play.

These reflections bring to mind the medieval historian and cultural theorist of the earlier twentieth century, Johannes Huizinga. On the cusp of the Second World War – in no less serious a time of dire catastrophe, if in the neutral territory of Switzerland – he wrote *Homo Ludens: a study of the play element in culture* (1938; tr. German 1944; tr. English 1949). There he asserted that humans need to be understood not only as the wise animals (*homo sapiens*), nor makers and producers in a remorseless economy (*homo faber*), but as *Homo Ludens*, Humans the Player.

Huizinga identifies five characteristics of play, and it is these five traits that make my list for this week – five reasons games and, more broadly, play add to culture.

1. Play is free, and is, in fact, freedom. So by playing games we enlarge our personal freedom, and enrich our culture with that freedom.

2. Play is not "ordinary" or "real" life. By giving us a second life, games and their virtual reality bring into being the play of freedom, and the creation of culture. They make any ordinary life richer – they are the double realm.

3. Play is distinct from "ordinary" life, both as to locality and duration. Play and games are not escapes, so much as the separateness, not of the sacred, but of the playful.

4. Play creates order, is order. Play demands order absolute and supreme. And in order is the beautiful. Or, after Foucault from *Madness and Civilization*, where there is *oeuvre*, there is not madness, but free expression of each person's terrible strangeness. In playing games you are still subject to the supreme fiction; and the experience of playing the game is to reach for that order, not to dissolve into futility and abandonment.

5. Play is connected with no material interest, and no profit can be gained from it. And equally all can play – there are no gatekeepers

to play, only different orders of the game.
Let us all enjoy both play and culture.

Berryman and the Unpredictability of Dream Songs
3 August 2016

There is a remarkable video somewhere on the internet that shows a television interview with John Berryman, the American poet, that was filmed, if I remember correctly, a few hours or days before he committed suicide in 1972. He was wholly non-compliant with any TV producer directions or assumed rules of how to appear before a camera. When I watched this survivor from the archive, I was struck by the implausibility of such a thing in today's media. Despite all our demotic trash talk about our drives and our seeming candour about mental illness, it seems to me, that madness is more off-screen than ever before. Human distinctiveness and the discomfort of people who speak awkwardly and differ erratically are edited out from our ubiquitous screens. We need to listen again to the Dream Songs of John Berryman.

Jeff Rich

Six Asides about Vaclav Havel
27 September 2016

In 1984 Vaclav Havel reflected in an essay titled "Six Asides about Culture" on the second culture emerging in from the difficult conditions of post-totalitarian Czechoslovakia, more broadly Soviet Eastern Europe and Russia. Inspired by his example, with a similar desert of meaning about me, I offer my own six asides about culture.

I. Culture forms chaotically from spirit.

Havel begins his essay, or talk, "Six asides about Culture" with some speculation that tomorrow he might write his best ever literary work, or then again he might never write another word again. Culture escapes determinants. It has the quality of life, and not the predictable attributes of an economist's spreadsheet. So, Havel writes, the future of a culture is open to freedom and the spirit. In Communist Czechoslovakia this message was one of possibility. The "second culture" – that formed against the grain of the official culture of the regime among dissidents, in private life, shared covertly through *samizdat* – could bloom. It could also die. It could also wither on the vine in a dull compromise with the regime, perhaps as so much contemporary culture in the West has since done. But its future rested in the spirits of those who carried forward their projects, however small. Havel had been asked to speculate on the future development of this culture. In a characteristic feint, he left the future in the hands of all who read him:

> When even a single author... cannot foresee his literary future, how can anyone foresee what the overall development of culture will be?.... The secrets of a culture's future are a reflection of the very secrets of the human spirit.[17]

---

[17] Havel, "Six Asides about Culture", *Living in Truth*, pp. 123-4.

II. The living community has an "irrepressible cultural hunger."

To believe in this credo was an act of faith, and a will to survive the repression of the regime in communist Eastern Europe. That regime fought its own people, and made the conditions of participation in culture enormously difficult. For many it compromised and brutalized lives. Roger Scruton speaks of meeting many "stokers" in Czechoslovakia who were punished by the regime by placement in the meaningless and demeaning job to stoke a furnace or an engine, rather than to work in their chosen and trained field, whether that was science or philosophy or carpentry. We do not have the same repression today, except the strange repression imposed by marketing and the commercial operations of the production of culture. Where Havel looked out and saw hope and survival for the second culture in *samizdat*, theatre, young people crossing the country to attend a concert that may not even be allowed to be staged, I see hope for a new second culture, unshackled from endless compromised selling, in blogging, alt-lit and the aesthetics of play.

III. Thought – free thought, not luxurious thought – involves sacrifice.

Havel wanted to free the thought of the dissidents from two locked doors – first, the obligation to be a martyr in person, since he knew very well the real suffering endured by those who opposed the regime; and second, the condescension of the liberal West, who pitied and belittled the second culture with the icons of martyrdom. Here Havel saw a truth about the Western culture that many still do not see:

> as I follow from a distance various individual actions and social upheavals in the 'free world', I am not at all sure that they are inevitably characterized by penetrating thought. I fear that far too often the idea comes limping behind the enthusiasm. And might that just not be because for the most part no great price need be paid for that enthusiasm? Are thought and sacrifice really so mutually exclusive? Might not sacrifice, under some circumstances, be simply the consequence of a thought, its proof,

or conversely, its moving force.[18]

IV. Culture – and within it, of preeminent importance to me, writing – conforms to no mould.

Culture outgrows its mould, whether that be cast by five-year plans, drawn by the ideologically pure, or carved by the demands of the market. "If there is anything essentially foreign to culture", writes Havel, "it is the uniform". Culture and writing need to be what they are. Put aside any judgments of their worthiness, their marketability, their relevance to the times.

> A great many people can peck at a typewriter and, fortunately, no one can stop them. But for that reason, even in *samizdat*, there will always be countless bad books or poems for every important book. If anything there will be more bad ones than in the days of printing because, even in the most liberated times, printing is still a more complicated process than typing. But even if, objectively, there were some possibility of selection, who could claim the right to exercise it? Who among us would dare to say that he can unerringly distinguish something of value – even though it may still be nascent, unfamiliar, as yet only potential – from its counterfeit? *Who among us can know what may seem today to be marginal graphomania might not one day appear to our descendants as the most substantial thing written in our time?*[19]

V. Culture does not divide into political allegiances

There is no more reason to celebrate some art as independent, alternative or progressive, just because it aligns with some form of political idea. What counts for culture is not political preferences, but the pursuit of "autonomous free humanity." The first culture in Havel's essay was that of the Communist regime. Just like today's mainstream and subsidised alternative culture (all the fringe festivals as well as the opera companies) this first culture belonged to "what is permitted, subsidized or at least tolerated, an area that naturally tends

---

[18] Havel, *Living in Truth*, p. 126 – my emphasis.
[19] Havel, *Living in Truth*, p. 129.

to attract more of those who, for reasons of advantage, are willing to compromise their truth." Like Havel, I choose the heirs of the second culture, "an area constituted through self-help, which is the refuge, voluntary or enforced, of those who refuse all compromise (regardless of how overtly 'political' or 'non-political' their work is)".

VI *The creation of culture is an intrinsic good in itself.*

It does not matter whether an act of culture is created in the first or second orders, in the mainstream media or on an alternative literature blog, in a bestseller or a *samizdat*. If it is authentic, it is valuable in itself. Belonging to one or other culture matters little, rather like the ceaseless badges of identity that are constantly pressed upon us. "Every meaningful cultural act," Havel writes, "wherever it takes place – is unquestionably good in and of itself simply because it offers something to someone." He asks:

> Does not the bare fact that a work of art has meant something to someone – even if only for a moment, perhaps to a single person – already somehow change, however, minutely, the overall condition for the better?

This idea that the cultural act is a free gift takes us back to the human spirit. So Havel concludes his six asides on culture:

> Is not precisely some 'impulse to move' – again in that deeper existential sense – the primordial intent of everything that really belongs to culture? After all, that is precisely the mark of every good work of culture: it sets our drowsy souls and our lazy hearts 'moving.'! And can we separate the awakening human soul from what it always, already is – an awakening human community?

Vale Vaclav Havel. As was written on a banner photograph displayed after his death at the National Museum of Prague, overlooking Wencelas Square – Havel forever.

Jeff Rich

Wasting Time on Conceptual Poetry
27 October 2016

I borrowed from my local public library *Postmodern American Poetry: a Norton Anthology* (2nd edition), edited by Paul Hoover. I am not quite sure what was the impulse that led me to this step; perhaps it was a feeling that I had little real sense of what was up in the current poetry scene, and that I should give some attention to the profuse ideas about writing that my contemporaries have given voice to. It was a kind of anxiety of no influence, and a fear that my own writing practice is cut so adrift from the songs of others that they can only die solitary and alone.

If that was my intention, I soon found myself confirmed in shunning the poetics of these postmodern poets, which went by a bevy of terms I read for the first time in the anthology's introduction in place of a manifesto – terms like proceduralism, uncreative writing, language poetry, Newlipo, cyberpoetry, Flarf, post-language lyrics and conceptual poetry. The last term, the anthologist proclaimed, is what represented The New, which is a new form of the incarnation of the sacred, tinged with revolutionary politics.

Of course, I was familiar with terms like post-modernism, and found in the introduction some old and familiar practitioners of slippery academic prophecy, in miscast runes, like Frederic Jameson. Jameson is quoted approvingly as the announcer of the postmodern which the anthologist declares the reigning style of this era and of its culture: "It is safest to grasp the concept of the postmodern as an attempt to think about the present historically in an age that has forgotten how to think historically in the first place." This rather gnomic piece of circular self-deception comes from Jameson's 1991 treatise, *Postmodernism, or the Cultural Logic of Late Capitalism*, which reassures its revolutionary readers of its prophetic truth with that little adjective, `late', slipped in before `capitalism'. Made of the same cloth are the *faux* prophecies and drunken manifestos of various kinds of Revolutionary, Post-Modern and New Poetry. Jameson seems temperamentally unable to admit that the literary critic simply has not bothered to look around the university, or even outside its fevered halls, for some people who do think historically.

But this is very much a common infection among the conceptual poets. I learned from the anthology that Kenneth Goldsmith is the reigning arch-priest among these poets. Goldsmith practices a self-declared form of uncreative writing. His notable works include word-for-word (or approximation of verisimilitude) reproductions of a newspaper, a report on terror, and a transcript of each word he has spoken over a period of a week, in all their quotidian inanity. They are entirely uninteresting. They are only known because of the self-promotions that they serve. Indeed at UbuWeb (ubu.com) he is his own custodian of digital permanence and trustee of the *avant-garde* as forever *chic*, sadly for me appropriating Jarry's Père Ubu and presenting Beckett as a model for sunglasses.

Goldsmith has recently lost the mantle of the New and the Radical by reading, with significant but minor alterations, the autopsy report of an African-American man shot by the police. This act quite understandably offended many people involved in the Black Lives Matter movement, and although there is a persecutory leftism in the tone of the criticism, it is a sign that idle word games and *enfant terrible* poses for publicity are no match for deeply felt emotions.

Goldsmith's radicalism is generously supported by an academic position at an American University where he teaches his brand of poetic practice with such courses as "Wasting Time on the Internet". Here he practices a form of mid-Western American shuckster fakery that promises to his students that "this class will focus on the alchemical recuperation of aimless surfing into substantial works of literature". He destroys poetic practice and turns it into an entertainment-driven series of stunts. Conceptual poetry is nothing more than that, a series of media stunts that leaves nothing behind.

Still, Goldsmith clings to a stage persona of the great artist. His uncreative writing does not practice a humble craft, but like a thousand avant-gardists before him, offers a masterpiece of dada in the wish to be known as a great artist. It is American consumerism's darkest hour, when it has turned people, who are paid to teach poetry and to guard the culture, into exponents of an uncreative writing that advocates that lists of on-line purchases and browser histories "be churned into compelling works of identity-based literature".

Unsurprisingly, such a busker of the New has a poor understanding of history. He is quoted towards the end of the introduction as writing in a debate on the current state of poetry:

> Any notion of history has been leveled by the internet. Now, it's all fodder for the remix and recreation of works of art: free-floating toolboxes and strategies unmoored from context of historicity… All types of proposed linear historical trajectories have been scrambled and discredited by the tidal wave of digitality, which has crept up on us and so completely saturated our culture that we, although deeply immersed in it, have no idea what hit us. In the face of the digital, postmodernism is the quaint last gasp of modernism.[20]

His interlocutor in this false debate between the New and the Old Slow poetry is Dale Smith, who advocates a slow poetry, which dwells, like this blog, in the mysterious image created by Walter Benjamin's philosophy of history.

> We're surrounded by the past in the form of digitized archives. I understand that. But Benjamin's notion of history is rooted in a sense of the catastrophic failures of history in the twentieth century, too. Paradise is a dream – a true liberating force (an impossibility?) – that is rooted in a meaningful search for images. We are surrounded by artifacts, endless fodder for remixing as you say. But how do we proceed with this material in respect to the catastrophe? Are we really free to ignore the contexts and situations produced by these images?[21]

I share Smith's belief in a slow poetry, without his longing for a radically changed paradise. Conceptual poetry, such as that practised

---

[20] Goldsmith quoted from "The Tortoise and the Hare" (2009).

[21] Dale Smith quoted from from "The Tortoise and the Hare" (2009)

by Goldsmith in the cursed tradition of Andy Warhol, is a series o empty gestures. It is hand-waving that venerates the career of the artist, and neglects the suffering about which the poet ought to give testimony. History is not kind to artists who try to turn her into a funhouse for their happenings. It is the private lyric voice, who is not acclaimed as New or Radical or Shocking in its own time, that is the true, lasting voice of poetry.

Mr Dylan's Bad Language
16 June 2017

I like to check out the winners of the Nobel Prize for Literature. In our highly literate world, the world of books is so vast that any pointers to quality *oeuvres* that speak of different histories is welcome. It is how I discovered Symborska, Tranströmer, Milosz and others.

You can imagine my shock then, late last year, when the Nobel Committee declared the 2016 winner to be the over-celebrated bard of the 60's, Bob Dylan.

Shock rapidly grew to serious doubts about the Nobel's claim to award distinctions, and then to questioning about what such fickle prizes mean about the culture. It was not the first unconventional choice by the Swedish Academy. The year before a Russian-Belorussian journalist, Svetlana Alexievich, won the prize; but at least her deep testimonies of the experiences of the post-communist Soviet States were unequivocally her own work, and she showed up to accept the prize.

Mr Dylan struck out on both counts. He did not go to his award ceremony. He had other commitments, a schedule full of the kind of unbreakable commitments made by aging rock celebrities. A rather sheepish American ambassador appeared in his stead, and duly read what she had to say, in the diplomatic tradition of lying for one's country, was Mr Dylan's speech.

But it gets worse. The Committee insisted that to claim the prize, and the substantial money attached, Mr Dylan must give an acceptance speech. So he did, a mere couple of days before the deadline, after when he would have, if he had failed to gave his speech, lost his cheque. But the aging rolling stone or traveling wilbury could not make it to Sweden; he posted his speech to YouTube, a 30 minute ramble about the great literary traditions from which he sprang, including *Moby Dick*.

Perhaps this is innovation? Perhaps it is the undying rebellion of the 60's songster? Perhaps it is a sly parody of formality from which he chooses to stand apart. Or, perhaps, it is lazy, arrogant and incompetent contempt.

On investigation, it appears Mr Dylan was not capable of giving an authentic account of his literary craft, and too narcissistic to believe he would be found out for his failure. His speech contained dozens of sentences cribbed like a lackadaisical student directly from *Spark Notes*, that well known den of scholarly scoundrels. Andrea Pitzer at *Slate* makes the case, complete with laid out comparisons between Mr Dylan's *ars poetica* and the Spark Notes texts on that US high school text, *Moby Dick*. Pitzer puts the compelling question: is the current Nobel Laureate the very model of a not very literary plagiarist?

So what does this mean for the culture? What does it tell us about the destructive flames of contemporary life that threaten to burn to the ground our precious archive of memory, history, tradition, literature and culture? I fear it is another sign of the death of culture. I fear it is a sign of a new bourgeois stupidity that we do not yet know how to fight, as Flaubert did in another age.

But perhaps I could presume to ask, if only when speaking to the twisting nether, that the Nobel Committee take the prize back from Mr Dylan's slack and begging hands. It is time for the culture to mutiny against Mr Dylan's bad language.

From the Burning Archive

The Death of the Soul
27 August 2017

In *The Australian* this weekend Greg Sheridan, the conservative and perceptive foreign affairs journalist, comments on the decline of religion and its impact on Western liberal mores. He restores Nietzsche's parable of the madman, who proclaims to an indifferent crowd that God is dead, and then revokes his claim, but still sees a dark prophecy:

> Finally he threw his lantern on the ground so that it broke into pieces and went out. 'I come too early', he then said; 'my time is not yet. This tremendous event is still on its way, wandering; it has not yet reached the ears of men. Lightning and thunder need time; the light of the stars needs time; deeds need time, even after they are done, in order to be seen and heard. This deed is still more remote to them than the remotest stars – and yet they have done it themselves!' (Nietzsche, *The Gay Science*, s. 125)

Sheridan's article, entitled "Is God Dead?", poses the question of whether that time has indeed now come. He sees the failing vital signs of the Christian God all around him. The last *Census* in Australia found that only a small majority identified as a Christian, and a third of the population professed no religion. Sheridan sees an assault on the Church, brought on by its own weaknesses, including above all its tragic failure to respond to child sexual abuse. But this attack grows ever more shrill, until it chases the Church from the public square, ignorant of the thousand acts of kindness, humility and compassion in hospices, in churches, on the streets that make us a society, not a market. The assault of the progressive world on the institutions of traditional morality has grown more venomous, Sheridan implies, when liberalism or progressive modernity forgets the deep reservoir of holy water from which we all drink. Religion, which once was a spiritual foundation for liberal and progressive beliefs, has become a discriminatory and embarrassing constraint on the dreams of efflorescent identity, beloved by our society of consumption.

Against this forgetting, Sheridan poses the Churches' long history of charity, of education, of nurturing the very foundations of the culture, which this blog watches mournfully dying in flames. Sheridan refers to the work of Larry Siedentrop, *Inventing the individual: the origins of Western liberalism*. Siedentrop traces to the monasteries of the Middle Ages a birth of an alternative way of living, or in Sheridan's words "an early expression of human freedom". "People chose to be monks," Sheridan writes, "and therefore to have a life beyond that dictated by circumstances of birth and family." By conserving their symbols, music, texts and religious objects and sacralising their lives in a cherished institution bonded by rules of tradition, they were midwives to a great and vital culture.

Without knowing Siedentrop's book, the thought resembles my reflections on our impending dark ages, and the reasons for hope in these times. Nietzsche's madman had also asked his liberal crowd, thoughtlessly wiping the blood from the dagger plunged in the heart of God:

> What festivals of atonement, what holy games will we have to invent for ourselves? Is the magnitude of this deed not too great for us? Do we not ourselves have to become gods merely to appear worthy of it? (*The Gay Science*, s. 125)

Festivals of atonement indeed. Is this a way of describing the modern parades of virtue signalling and spasms of shaming of the people who are uncomfortable with ready-to-wear sexual and political identities? And these festivals of atonement have created a new authoritarianism, as we know from the rainbow guards who police sentiment itself in the new politics of identities.

Identity politics troubles Sheridan, as it troubles me, despite my thoughts being made from a different, more secular cloth. Identity politics reflects "a certain moral panic at the existential emptiness of atheism", and this panic drives the new liberal authoritarianism:

> Everyone must genuflect to the same secular pieties.... Nothing is more powerful in Western politics now, and in the long run more destructive, than identity politics. This sells itself as a

means to empower and to help disadvantaged minorities. But everyone wants a slice of identity politics.[22]

Donald Trump is as much a manifestation of identity politics as the campaign for gay marriage – it is the demand of resentful American whites demanding their identity politics too. The public square has descended into the melée at Charlottesville; one side shouting 'black lives matter', the other shouting back 'white lives matter'. Neither side speak to each other's reasons. The significance of this polarisation of politics to Sheridan's broader argument is that the aims of Christian citizenship, even secular humanist citizenship are abandoned to fissiparous identity. This path is "a dreadful wrong turn for Western civilisation" because it dissolves the soul in modern culture. It leads to "perverse worship of power for its own sake" and "antisocial self-absorption". This leads, I think, to Sheridan's deepest observation, which echoes that of Philip Rieff: therapy has replaced religion. Certainly in my life therapists are greater teachers than priests. But rampant post-modern consumerism does not drive the same existential search for meaning that was the goal of the great humanist psychologists. Rather, as Sheridan writes, "Now, in our postmodern times, even self has been supplanted by brand. Soul to self to brand is a steep decline in what it means to be a human being".

Sheridan, of course, is not the first to see this withering of the soul, this paradoxical abandonment of the depths for the shallow celebration of trinkets and baubles. In *Brothers Karamazov*, Dostoevsky wrote, "But what will become of men then?' I asked him, 'without God and immortal life? All things are permitted then, they can do what they like?" We have lived 137 years under the shadow of that question. Perhaps that long century is no worse than the millenniums before them. Religion has, after all, been an ark of grievance as much as a cowl of faith. Sacred violence lies at the heart of what it means to be human. But for at least some of those 137 years, the archive of our culture was not burning. How then do we live in these dark, destructive times, haunted by terror and our own comforts? How do

---

[22]Greg Sheridan, *The Australian*, 26 August 2017.

we live well in the face of such losses, we who have never had a religious belief, but have consoled ourselves in the word-hoards of our culture? How do we write the Benedictine rule for our times?

Fragments on Tradition

25 March 2018

Today's cultures are both disintegrating and proliferating. Any writer has close to hand the near infinite profusion of symbolic thought spawned by every culture across history. These treasures are there to be used with the simplicity of an internet search. But their readiness-to-hand does not by itself make them vital traditions; they can also be but cut-and-paste decorations of the modern soul in torment. The human symbolic inheritance can become a storm of misunderstanding, not a guide to life. The writer is dazed and confused amid this super-abundant cultural inheritance; but the writer has no guide, no anchor, no institution of belonging, and standard of selection. No tradition holds, except that salvaged in flight from ruins.

***

There is a paradox at the heart of today's culture. We live in the most broadly educated societies ever, and yet our culture is imploding. Education has been prostituted to the pursuit of income and status, and lost connection with its true value, the transmission of our most valued traditions so that our characters may extinguish our petty selves.

***

And yet traditions survive. Deepak Chopra teaches deep fulfillment to millions with Sanskrit mantras inherited from the *Vedas*, knowledge itself. Nordic noir, like *Midnight Sun*, shows the songs of the *noadi* of the Saami of the Arctic Circle, Sápmi and their persistent power in defining an undercurrent of spiritual law beneath the corruption of modern life. And a million bloggers, like me, like you, burst through the gates of the publishing industry, with its custodians of taste, status and commercial success, and call out their songs from their lonely hovels as they travel through the celestial internet on their long night journeys.

***

In *The Uses of Pessimism*, Roger Scruton wrote:

> The true history of the modern artist is the story told by the great modernists themselves. It is the story told by T. S. Eliot in his essays and the *Four Quartets*, by Ezra Pound in the *Cantos*, by Schoenberg in his critical writings and in *Moses und Aron*, by Rilke in the *Sonnets to Orpheus* and by Valéry in *Le cimetière marin*. And it sees the goal of the modern artist not as a break with tradition, but as a recapturing of tradition, in circumstances for which the artistic legacy has made little or no provision.

I would put this differently because I do not believe tradition can be both captured and vital. When captured, it becomes a marker of success and status. All tradition truly needs is to be inherited, practised and handed on. Tradition is not recaptured. It is sung again.

***

Modern artists have a difficult obligation. They inherit plural traditions, and yet carry none of them whole, hear none of them pure. Modern artists must spend years in the wilderness finding the traditions to which they have an elective affinity, and then find a way to practise this uniquely defined tradition in a way that does not compromise authenticity. This is difficult in a world ruled by celebrity and commerce. And then the hardest task of all. The tradition that is not one must be shared – through words uttered into the vast empty silence of the internet – in the cherished dream that someone else in the world may speak these songs too. That is the work of the infinite conversation.

Jeff Rich

Reflections on the emergence of Jordan B. Peterson
22 July 2018

#1 – One recent Jordan B. Peterson podcast featured his appearance at the Aspen Ideas Festival. His interlocutor begins by asking a genuinely interesting question. How does he understand his rise through the culture, not only to prominence but to a remarkable kind of phenomenon?

There are many tiresome commentaries on how Dr Peterson is the leader of the intellectual dark web, an unwitting ally of the alt-right and conservatives, and some strange response to Trump's America (because, of course, the world's culture really does centre on the narcissistic politics of Washington). These accounts may reassure progressive activists that the Peterson phenomenon is "nothing new"; but Peterson has a more engaging thought.

His reflection is that technological change – the emergence of youtubing, podcasting and blogging – has created new possibilities in the culture.

> For the first time in history the spoken word has the same reach as the written word, and not only that, no lag to publication and no barrier to entry. That is a major technological revolution, that is a Gutenberg Revolution. This is a game-changer.

#2 – These new possibilities for participation in high level culture have been launched into the world starved of truly sustaining culture by its mediocre gatekeeper elites. The mainstream media have turned their talent – what used to be known as reporters – into the star attractions, who pimp themselves endlessly on fluffy talk and panel shows, and so offer their audience a false celebrity culture, not a culture of education and development. The universities have betrayed their purpose in games of virtue-signalling, and commercialisation of education. The culture channels of television are little more than pop music shows. Gone are the days of my youth when Sunday afternoon and evening programming regularly featured some real substantial high culture. As Peterson says in this podcast,

> The narrow bandwidth of television has made us think we are stupider than we are, and so people have a real hunger for deep intellectual dialogue and that can be met with these new technologies and that has revolutionary significance.

#3 "The personal is political" was one of the chants of the 60s, 70s and beyond. It is an idea that created new possibilities of social policy, but that has frozen into a kind of new totalitarianism of identity politics today. One of Peterson's deepest insights into the errors of the left is that they like to think, at least today, that everything is political. In truth, Peterson says everything is at its most fundamental level psychological. His emergence is explained by his attention to this deeper level of experience.

#4 "The case for growing up is not made well," says Peterson during a talk with Melbourne radio 3AW host, Neil Mitchell. Our culture has sung insistently since the 1960s, "Forever young, I want to be forever young". Yet our societies are aged like never before. To read the *12 Rules for Life* is to accept the call to responsibility and to maturation. It is to put order into the chaos of youth and rebellion and endless yearning for a new boundary to transgress. It is a message for everyone older than 21, and that, after all, is most of us.

The Abyss and Cultural Rebirth
26 August 2018

> It is by going down into the abyss that we recover the treasures of life. Where you stumble, there lies your treasure. (Joseph Campbell)

Jeff Rich

> He who fights with monsters should look to it that he himself does not become a monster. And if you gaze long into an abyss, the abyss also gazes into you. (Friedrich Nietzsche, *Beyond Good and Evil*, Aphorism 146)

We are surrounded by the ruins of our cultures.

Our cities crumble. All the marbled statuary has been pulled to the ground.

Crowds jeer the few remaining priests, and expel them outside the city walls.

Broken, bitter and barren, they flee the flames of the burning archive, carrying in plastic sacks the last books of their lives.

The crowds chase the priests to the beach, and set fire to the libraries and homes they escaped from.

Beyond the flames, beyond the borders of the besieged coastal city, surge the dark abyssal waters.

It is there that these lame priests must dive in search of the treasures that may renew us.

Hidden in tangled seaweed, in a cave beneath the swirling whirlpool, so it is said, the last prophet deposited his five books of wisdom.

No-one alive has read these books, although the last priests have caught glimpses, now and then in their meditations, of the Lost Tradition.

The priests paint their faces with ash, and then make their escape by boat from the stones and fire of the angry crowd.

They row towards the whirlpool to recover the Lost Tradition of the Great Prophet.

But the surging waters seize their boats, and into the maw of the ocean died their dreamy days.

All lost. To prayers, to prayers. All lost.

And in the ashen city, surrounded by dross and the shrieks of the panicked crowd, there sat one darkened priest who stayed in the gloom of his basement.

He lights a candle, and begins to write the sixth book of wisdom.

From the Burning Archive

How Game of Thrones re-enchants world
14 April 2019

There are three points of view from which a writer can be considered: he may be considered as a storyteller, as a teacher, and as an enchanter. A major writer combines these three – storyteller, teacher, enchanter – but it is the enchanter in him that predominates and makes him a major writer. (Vladimir Nabokov, *Lectures on Literature*)

The world stands on the threshold of the (possibly) final revelations of a cluster of stories that since 1996 have, like a magical spell, re-enchanted our decadent cultural world – the *Song of Fire and Ice*, George R. Martin's *Game of Thrones* series of long, gritty fantasy novels.

I am, like tens of millions around the world, anticipating the screening tomorrow of the first episode in the final season of *Game of Thrones*. It is an unusual cultural event, and worth reflecting on. Here the world is waiting breathlessly on the storyteller's final story. How will it end? How will all the threads come together? What in the prophecies was misdirection and what contained truth? How will Fire and Ice at last come together or extinguish each other in their final Song? How remarkable is it that after 23 years we are still entranced and uncertain about the answers to these questions?

It is more remarkable still when we consider the extraordinary way in which these final stories are being revealed to the world. George R. Martin, after all, still has not finished writing his books – or at least so we understand. There is some speculation that *Winds of Winter* is in the can, waiting to cash in on the vastly greater sales generated by the audience of the television drama. Then there is the seventh book, *A Dream of Spring*, which one can only hope the world will not have to wait for another eight years – the likely interval between *Dance of Dragons* in 2011 and *Winds of Winter* maybe in 2019 – before reading how Martin himself in prose ends this *Song of Fire and Ice*. Three seasons of the HBO series will anticipate the story, certainly under Martin's guidance, but not through his execution. The storyteller's staff has been shared across forms and among Martin, Benioff and Weiss. How will the story change when only Martin holds the staff, and he has merely his narrative and his prose, not the magic of film, to weave his enchantment?

I came to the *Game of Thrones* phenomenon quite late and quite sceptically. It was perhaps after the third season had screened and I was persuaded finally to give it a go. It took more than one episode, two or three maybe, but the stories began to cast their spell. Then I read the books, and listened to the podcasts by fans and amateur scholars of this modern literature, and joined in the sociable speculations on what might happen next. I would not say, as perhaps some fans believe, that Game of Thrones books belong in canon of the greatest literature or counsel of the deepest psychology. The superb acting of the television drama does provide a subtlety of soul and range of emotion that I did not always find in the text. Still, these books took me into a re-enchanted world in which glimmer magic, dragons, brothers raised from the dead, a female khan of the steppe - Khaleesi – who is reborn in fire, red priestesses who see into the soul, prophecies of promised princes, astrolabes in citadels of scholarship, and swords that destroy our deepest fears, all these spells spoke of a deeper experience of perception, culture and imagination.

Game of Thrones has re-enchanted the world with its gritty fantasy that is rooted in the darker twists of human history and the disenchanted observation of our prosperous, power-ridden, fragmented, threatened world. We all do see ourselves as powerless pawns, sheltering behind the wall, waiting for the impending winter catastrophe of climate change. We all dream we might be freed from the endless turning wheel that the Stormborn Daenerys would break, and we might find ourselves ruled by a prince in the disguise of a bastard. We all hope to find some magic or some faith with which to redeem our troubled lives. We all still dream of stories that can comfort us after the terrors of our culture's long dark night of the soul.

The poetry of travel
5 May 2019

> We travel, some of us forever, to seek other states, other lives, other souls. (Anaïs Nin)

In less than two weeks I will go on a trip to Europe with my partner, the first time we have travelled overseas (as we say in the great island of Australia) alone after nearly thirty years together. A couple of years ago we traveled to Vietnam and Cambodia with our children, and over 15 years ago I traveled alone (in an organised group tour) to China, Mongolia and Russia on the Trans-Siberian/Mongolian railway. It will be perhaps the greatest exploratory adventure of my life. I never had the money or the freedom from cares and illness to travel as a young man or student, and before I knew it children, money worries and responsibilities pegged me down.

And perhaps also a belief that it was not for me – a strange belief this one, mixed from fear and anxiety and social humiliation. The abiding image that has haunted me: the outcast; who stands in the rain and looks through the glass windows into the restaurants where the young, beautiful and connected are celebrating their lives.

Now I will know the joy of exploring, of walking into foreign cities, with all their built beauty that yet persists through the necessary ugliness of modern life, and finding my way through their streets and culture, at once strange and familiar. Each day will be free of the usual routine of responsibility, and will be created through the encounter of my mind and the world.

Still, I feel I am going into exile. There is no assurance that I know where I will return to in my job. All I know is I am unwanted from the courtiers who rule today.

But on this trip, I will bring a small soft notebook and aim to write each day notes, and sometimes a poem about my travels. In this way I will seek above all to touch the face of the world.

In a fine and old anthology of poems, *A book of luminous things: an international anthology of poetry*, edited by Czelaw Milosz, I found this morning this poem by Po Chu-I or Bai Juyi that spoke to how I want to respond to both my exile and my odyssey.

Madly Singing in the Mountains (Bai Juyi, 772-846)

> There is no one among men that has not a special failing;
> And my failing consists in writing verses.
> I have broken away from the thousand ties of life;
> But this infirmity still remains behind.
> Each time that I look at a fine landscape,
> Each time that I meet a loved friend,
> I raise my voice and recite a stanza of poetry
> And marvel as though a God had crossed my path.
> Ever since the day I was banished to Hsu-yang
> Half my time I have lived among the hills.
> And often, when I have finished a new poem,
> Alone I climb the road to the Eastern Rock.
> I lean my body on the banks of white Stone;
> I pull down with my hands a green cassia branch.
> My mad singing startles the valleys and hills;
> The apes and birds all come to peep.
> Fearing to become a laughing-stock to the world,
> I choose a place that is unfrequented by men.

From the Burning Archive

The Return of the Prodigal Son
10 November 2019

> What matters at this stage is the construction of local forms of community within which civility and the intellectual and moral life can be sustained through the new dark ages that are already upon us. And if the tradition of the virtues was able to survive the horrors of the last dark ages, we are not entirely without grounds for hope. This time however the barbarians are not waiting behind the frontiers; they have already been governing us for quite some time. And it is our lack of consciousness of this that constitutes part of our predicament. We are waiting not for Godot, but for another – doubtless very different – St. Benedict. (Alasdair MacIntyre, *After Virtue*)

I discovered this quotation from the Scottish moral philosopher, Alasdair MacIntyre, this week in an unexpected place, a commentary in the pugnacious pages of *Quadrant* from the author of *The Benedictine Option*, Rod Dreher. This commentary, which roams across Zygmunt Bauman and other enigmatic reflections on our dissolving culture, responds to the plangent question in Dreher's soul: "Do we have the courage to turn our backs to this world, as St Benedict did, and seek Christ where he may be found in these calamitous times?"[23]

And Dreher quotes MacIntyre, who himself converted to Catholicism in his fifties and wrote his enduring works in response to that crisis and conversion. Unlike MacIntyre or Dreher, I can never claim to respond to the gloomy catastrophe of our disintegrating culture from the viewpoint of a Christian tradition. It is simply not my path, which has rather been through the classics of literary, historical and cultural modernism of the 20th century. This blog has its roots not in the hallowed and fallen angels of a lost paradise, but in Walter Benjamin's strange parable and Paul Klee's painting a New Angel,

---

[23] Rod Dreher, *The Christian Way Forward In A Time Of Crisis* (2019).

which caught the ambivalent tragedy of real, not sacred, history.

Yet I was struck by the resonance between Dreher's question and MacIntyre's 1981 words. I have long been aware of MacIntyre's book, from my days in the University of Melbourne Library in the 1980's, but I have never read it in full. Yet mysteriusly, ignorant until now of MacIntyre's and Dreher's idea of the Benedictine option, I have occasionally evoked the monastic tradition as a response of virtue in troubled times. In January 2016, I posted similar thoughts on a "New Dark Age": who will speak like Abelard and Héloïse across the centuries in this new dark age?

I do not know where to find this community of virtue in our time of cultural fragmentation, decay and disorder. I can only evoke images of it, such as in my story of sorts, "The Abyss and Cultural Rebirth". And yesterday I had a long conversation with my daughter on this very dilemma: are we ruined; is our culture so decayed, so driven by consumerist folly and digital delusion that there is no hope; and where might we turn for grounds of hope, signs of rebirth, acts of virtue amid the horror of Ragnarök? Where is virtue in these dark times?

My personal dilemma is that while I hold dear what I lovest well – in the hope that it will not be reft from thee – I have no circle, no monastic community, no discipline of tradition, no Benedictine rule of order to dedicate myself to when I withdraw from this world, and seek to join the infinite conversation. I am like Saint Antony, but finding seclusion in the simple life of the suburbs and seeking salvation in the infinite conversation, which surrounds me in this internet-spun and book-lined study. In those modest rules of order, I find grounds for hope, and intimations of my own infinitude.

Perhaps I must find my way to another coincidence. Rod Dreher (on his blog on *The American Conservative),* whose thoughts emerge from traditions so different from mine, recounted his recent visit to the Hermitage in St Petersburg, where he went to venerate the great Rembrandt painting, *The Return of the Prodigal Son*. I made the same pilgrimage in June this year, and I bought a large print reproduction of this painting, which hangs now proudly over my antipodean library.

Dreher remarks that Sir Kenneth Clark – who in 1969 produced the magnificent BBC series, *Civilisation* – appraised this Rembrandt as the greatest painting ever. In the 1970's I watched Clark's series as a growing child, even then aspiring to belong to the infinite conversation, and now a reproduction of this great artwork sits in my room showing me a way to forgiveness, acceptance and some light in these dark times. Does it represent how we might renew our culture?

The Red Guards are Coming
9 June 2020

Since posting "Is America reliving the 1917 revolution?" a few days ago I have noticed numerous other commentators make similar comparisons between this induced insurrection and earlier revolutionary prequels. Just to be clear, in my mind, "revolutionary" is stripped of all romanticism, and is viewed with an historian's tragic sense of life.

The admirable thinkers at *The Duran* posted a long video discussion, "America's Neoliberal October Revolution" in which Peter Lavelle of *CrossTalk on RT* made the critical observation that when an elite loses all confidence to rule, then authority can collapse very quickly. Alex Christoforou and Alexander Mercouris extended the comparison and identified the similarity in street tactics and propaganda between the current disorders and the colour revolutions. Franklin Foer at the left-wing *Atlantic* makes the same comparison in celebration, while tweeting in support of the protesters: "What's happening in the streets—and with officials refusing to cooperate—is a lot like the revolutions that toppled dictators in Serbia, Ukraine, and

Tunisia". Jonathon Turley, the distinguished, courageous and independently-minded legal scholar, who was brave enough to testify against the Democrat impeachment curse, has written a compelling piece on *The Hill*, "Can this American version of the French Revolution bring change?" Turley speculates that this movement for reform may become a Revolutionary tragedy. Turley writes:

> Welcome to the American version of the French Revolution. The horrible killing of George Floyd sparked an important focus on race relations and justice in this country. However, it is being lost to an emerging radicalism that challenges people to prove their faith by endorsing farce. Politicians and commentators are outdoing each other to demonstrate fealty to this new order by attacking key institutions and values. Politicians are calling to defund the police and commentators are calling for censorship. Most moderate voices seem to be fading under escalating demands.[24]

I am deeply troubled by events in recent weeks. There are troubling coincidences: riots on the street; propaganda for the revolution taking over the media; open advocacy of the overthrow of a democratically elected president; sabotage of the institutions of public order like the police ("All power to the Soviets"); the intellectual corruption of professors and media identities (even a magazine like *Slate*) who advocate rebellion and the legitimacy of political violence; reactivation of the impeachment rhetoric of the Democrats; and now, most troubling of all the emergence from the swamp of former generals and security state operatives who claim Trump is 'dividing the nation', 'breaching the constitution', 'risking national security', and... you fill in the blanks.

Now I observe a troubling resemblance between these still theatrical disorders and the more violent mass action of China's Cultural Revolution. In the early 1960's, after Mao's disastrous Great Leap Forward and Kruschev's 1956 condemnation of Stalinism, the

---

[24] Jonathon Turley, "Can This American Version Of The French Revolution Bring Change?" *The Hill*, 2020.

leadership of the Chinese Communist Party began to edge Mao out from his dominant position. Threatened by this elite power struggle, Mao mobilised his favoured factional leaders and channeled the zealotry of young people in a frenzy of ideological possesion that aimed to "Bombard the Headquarters". The campaign aimed to denigrate Mao's enemies as traitors in a "nationwide civil war". Many names were used: rightists, capitalist-roaders, counter-revolutionary elements, representatives of the Four Olds. Today new toxic terms are used: fascist, nationalist, Trump supporter, racist. New counter-truths emerged, just as today some ephemeral leaders of a frantic crowd might declaim that "Silence is Violence," or that the evidence of our lying eyes betrays us, that the scenes we witness – looting, burning buildings, destruction of monuments, throwing projectiles, beating people prone on the street, even the shooting and death of David Dorn, which streamed live on Facebook, just like the infamous New Zealand terrorist attack – all these apparent outrages are not violence, but rather "largely peaceful protests".

In the Cultural Revolution bands of students came together and formed a militia to harass all forms of culture, other than party propaganda. They burned down the house, as we might say today, and denounced all things old. They tortured, humiliated and publicly shamed teachers, professors, bureaucrats or anyone who wanted to lead an orderly life. They admitted on their knees their brokenness and their white privilege, with an *auto-da-fé* cap on their heads, and slogan-bearing placard hung around their necks. The great film, *Farewell My Concubine*, portrayed the horror, devastation, vandalism and terror of this period in the most intense, beautiful way. The cultural and intellectual heritage of China was under siege, and almost went under.

Let there be no doubt: the Red Guards are coming for us again today. They are bringing terror. Kneeling may bring for some demeaned categories of persons a symbolic, cultural bullet in the back of the head; for some it may induce real violence and victimisation. I am genuinely afraid that spectres of the past are haunting our societies. I grew up amid leftist authoritarianism; I knew great combatants of this scourge like Frank Knopfelmacher; and I read deeply in its history, traditions and iconography. I can feel the chill of these undead in my spine today. But I cannot let fear freeze me or force me into compliance with this latest wave of militant millenarianism. I can and will remember the importance of courage for all other virtues. With courage comes the ability to live in truth, as Vaclav Havel said.

Perhaps the most important and inspiring words I have noticed in recent times on twitter – before I deleted the sewer pipe from my phone in an act of self-protection – were tweeted out by the admirable Rod Dreher. It is an essay – "Live not by Lies" – written by Alexander Solzhenitsyn as a *samizdat* in 1974. Solzhenitsyn wrote:

> When violence intrudes into peaceful life, its face glows with self-confidence, as if it were carrying a banner and shouting: 'I am violence. Run away, make way for me—I will crush you'. But violence quickly grows old. And it has lost confidence in itself, and in order to maintain a respectable face it summons falsehood as its ally—since violence lays its ponderous paw not every day and not on every shoulder. It demands from us only obedience to lies and daily participation in lies—all loyalty lies in that.[25]

And then Solzhenitsyn provides important advice for us to resist the Red Guards in our writing, our workplaces, our schools, our streets, our culture, our hearts and our minds.

> So in our timidity, let each of us make a choice: Whether consciously, to remain a servant of falsehood—of course, it is not out of inclination, but to feed one's family, that one raises his children in the spirit of lies—or to shrug off the lies and become an honest man worthy of respect both by one's children and contemporaries.

And then Solzhenitsyn provides a partial list of from that day onward he:

– Will not henceforth write, sign, or print in any way a single

---

[25] Solzhenitsyn, "Live Not By Lies" (1974).

phrase which in his opinion distorts the truth.
– Will utter such a phrase neither in private conversation not in the presence of many people, neither on his own behalf not at the prompting of someone else, either in the role of agitator, teacher, educator, not in a theatrical role.
– Will not depict, foster or broadcast a single idea which he can only see is false or a distortion of the truth whether it be in painting, sculpture, photography, technical science, or music.
– Will not cite out of context, either orally or written, a single quotation so as to please someone, to feather his own nest, to achieve success in his work, if he does not share completely the idea which is quoted, or if it does not accurately reflect the matter at issue.
– Will not allow himself to be compelled to attend demonstrations or meetings if they are contrary to his desire or will, will neither take into hand not raise into the air a poster or slogan which he does not completely accept.
– Will not raise his hand to vote for a proposal with which he does not sincerely sympathize, will vote neither openly nor secretly for a person whom he considers unworthy or of doubtful abilities.
– Will not allow himself to be dragged to a meeting where there can be expected a forced or distorted discussion of a question.
– Will immediately walk out of a meeting, session, lecture, performance or film showing if he hears a speaker tell lies, or purvey ideological nonsense or shameless propaganda.
– Will not subscribe to or buy a newspaper or magazine in which information is distorted and primary facts are concealed.

He acknowledges it is not a complete list, and that it must adapt to new circumstances. Today we live in a new epidemic of lies, and adapting these rules to the circumstances of our time is an urgent moral task.

Jeff Rich

The condescension of posterity
12 July 2020

Frank Furedi has proposed an intriguing idea. The spectre haunting radical identity politics, those Rainbow Guards of our raging Cultural Revolution, is a difficulty with borders: the boundaries between nations, genders, key characteristics of populations, the public and private spheres. These borders are being torn down, and replaced by a convenient chaos of fluidity and the new deity of Equality. All that is solid melts into fair.

Among the borders annihilated in this revolution of bad ideas is the ethereal crossing between the present and the past. Furedi sees the toppling of statues as a kind of conceptual confusion about the separation of the present and the past. The Red Guards of Antifa and Black Lives Matter topple statues in a virtual struggle that confuses symbols of the past with the realities of the present. In doing so they deny all particular, unique, given separateness to these figures of the past. The statues are contemptible caricatures of injustice that stand in place of a real past which others have tried to understand, even if it can never be perfectly known.

I am not sure Furedi quite grasps the mentality of the protesters and rioters. To me, the protesters have summoned phantasms of the past into a never-changing present where they will receive stern Maoist popular justice in all its vicious violence. All these fading figures in bronze, who in truth have been largely forgotten and neglected in mass education and popular memory, have been summonsed by new Committees of Public Safety to a trial like that of K: conducted without knowledge of their experience, without charge or process, without common decency or law. In the atrocious history told by the social justice warriors, the past is always guilty, the future is always innocent, and the present is a ceaseless struggle session. The Past is condemned as an Enemy of the People, guilty of the thought crime of pursuing different aims than the Party of the Present.

Furedi, however, responds to their arguments by asserting the need to respect the boundaries between past and present. He pleads for the benefits of strong fences between neighbours. Furedi restates the importance of constraints to the experience of freedom. He uses a concept of freedom that Patrick Deneen (*Why Liberalism Failed*) named the republican sense of liberty, understood as self-government within the boundaries of the law. From such a perspective, statue-toppling is the latest liberal illusion, based on the fallacy that we can free ourselves from the past and from constraints. As Deneen argues, such a concept of freedom is an illusion:

> The word "freedom" is embraced as the fundamental commitment of our age, but in vast swaths of life, freedom seems to recede – many citizens, for instance, believe they have little actual control over or voice in their government. Motivation by many voters in advanced democracies reflects not the confident belief that their voice is being heard, but the conviction that their vote is against a system that no longer recognizes the claim to self-rule.[26]

In my view, it is reasonable to take down and replace statues if it is done through civic dialogue and deliberation, not through violence and toppling. Otherwise we are simply giving in to unconstrained protesters who expel out-of-favour from the Big Brother House. So we have seen, for good reasons and bad, the crowd tear down the figures of Robert E Lee, then George Washington, Abraham Lincoln, Captain Cook, Christopher Columbus, even Miguel de Cervantes (himself enslaved for a time) and, most appallingly of all, Frederick Douglass. The pusillanimous leaders of the progressive liberal order admit there is no self-governing republic that can defend itself against this paroxysm of idiocy. Nancy Pelosi, the octogenarian grandee of the USA's Democratic Party, when asked how she would respond to this outbreak of iconoclasm, said revealingly, "I don't care that much about

---

[26] Patrick Deneen, *Why Liberalism Failed* (2018).

statues… People will do what they do".

Edmund Burke wrote in *Reflections on the Revolution in France* that society is a partnership. There is more than a social contract. It is still more than co-existence on a digital media platform. In *Reflections On The Revolution In France,* Burke wrote that this partnership is "not only between those who are living, but between those who are living, those who are dead, and those who are to be born".

To modern liberalism and its change-merchants, to modern radicalism and its identity-alchemists, this partnership must be revoked. In its place, the terror of Year Zero will spill the blood of the past and destroy the inheritance of culture. Patrick Deneen argues this attitude reflects the anxious burden of an unwitting inheritance of the past. Like Lady Macbeth liberals walk in the night and say out, out damned past to their bloodied hands. They cannot admit that their own minds, their very freedoms are formed by the culture of the past. Deneen writes:

> Culture and tradition are the result of accumulations of practice and experience that generations have willingly accrued and passed along as a gift to future generations. This inheritance is the result of a deeper freedom, the freedom of inter-generational interactions with the world and one another.

This inheritance passes as a gift between generations in what I call the infinite conversation. In the conditions of riotous protest, media-blown amnesia and liquid modernity, this infinite conversation is not possible. It is under attack, and so much political thought today is consumed with the question of how to live beyond this siege. Deneen proposes "building practices that sustain culture within communities, the fostering of household economics, and 'polis life', or forms of self-governance that arise from shared civic participation". I remain sceptical of localism, but do believe we can salvage simple disciplines and old traditions, that we may practise far from the Emperor's faraway throne.

One simple practice to sustain the infinite conversation is to change our attitude to the past. We ought to save the past from the terrifying *condescension of posterity*. To me, the ignorance of so many public commentators, politicians, journalists and twitterati is deeply saddening. Rather than see the past as some kind of .gif file to be manipulated into memes, we need to recall how the past really is very strange, enigmatic and enduring. When I was an undergraduate history student in the 1980's, I studied deeply E.P. Thompson, *The Making of the English Working Class*. It shaped my intellectual adventure – not the Marxism or New Leftism, but the moral claim of history so beautifully evoked in its preface. All the intellectuals of progressivism ought to read this passage, and consider whether their hatred of the past has led them into a new Old Corruption. Thompson criticised the leftist orthodoxy of his day, which he described as the Pilgrim's Progress interpretation of the progressive illumination of the working class to the correct ideas of the present. He criticised it for a flaw that we see in the arguments of Progressives today against the remnants of the Past.[27]

> My quarrel with the third ["Pilgrim's Progress" orthodoxy of leftist history] is that *it reads history in the light of subsequent preoccupations, and not as in fact it occurred* [my emphasis]. Only the successful in the sense of those whose aspirations anticipated subsequent evolution) are remembered. The blind alleys, the lost causes and the losers themselves are forgotten.

The Left's history has today become a Pilgrim's Progress of the Woke. It demands that most of the real people of history be both forgotten and obliterated, in the service of the preoccupations of the woke. But we have an alternative way of being with the past available to us. Thompson set it out in the most famous passage of his great work, which inspired how I try to understand and to recover the forgotten people of the past:

> I am seeking to rescue the poor stockinger, the Luddite cropper, the 'obsolete' hand-loom weaver, the utopian artisan, and even the deluded follower of Joanna Southcott [a prophetess of

---

[27] E.P. Thompson, *The Making Of The English Working Class* (1963), p. 12.

London radical artisans], from the enormous *condescension of posterity*. Their crafts and traditions may have been dying. Their hostility to the new industrialism may have been backward-looking. Their communitarian ideals may have been fantasies. Their insurrectionary conspiracies may have been foolhardy. But they lived through these times of acute social disturbance, and we did not. Their aspirations were valid in terms of their own experience; and if they were casualties of history, they remain, condemned in their own lives, as casualties.

Thompson's ideas are not mine, but his refusal to condescend to posterity inspired my own historical thought. Thompson believed, as a radical leftist, that these lost causes of the past may yet be the source of ideas and insights into "social evils we have yet to cure". He believed we (not any of us) are not at the end of social evolution, but there is a fitful progress driven forward by class. He certainly believed there was an ongoing class struggle in material life, political power and in culture. But he saw many sides and many small gifts from that struggle, even gifts made by apparent losers. One gift was the cultural inheritance of the poor stockinger, and from their seemingly outdated and hopeless ideas, Thompson believed, new grounds for hope and evolution rise. I do not share his confidence in social progress, and fear we are living in a time of demonstrable decay in many institutions. But I honour his belief that we owe duties to the inheritance of the past, which reveals its gifts in unanticipated ways, and from whose ashes we may hope the Phoenix of culture will be reborn.

From the Burning Archive

Anomie Today and Cultural Decay
13 August 2020

> The former gods are growing old or dying, and others have not been born.... A day will come when our societies once again will know hours of creative effervescence during which new ideals will again spring forth and new formulas emerge to guide humanity for a time. (Émile Durkheim)

Émile Durkheim (1858-1917), the French founder of sociology, studied deeply the fractures apparent in the modern society of late *fin-de-siècle* Europe. He saw the conflicts, the urban poverty, disorderly crime, the fragmentation, the division of labour, the demoralisation and the weakened bonds between society and the individual. He investigated suicide as the ultimate dissolution of the bond between society and the individual. Although his political beliefs were a kind of progressive rationalist liberalism, he discovered the power of the sacred. Despite his rationalism, he became intrigued by the rites of the sacred, and how enthusiasm for collective, social totems might be re-institutionalised in modern, individualist society.

He invented a concept to describe the waning regulation of the individual by collective, social moral regulation: *anomie*. *Anomie* described the absence of law in the sense of moral standards. Durkheim observed the social facts of *anomie* in the ways individuals were disconnected, exposed to anonymous and opaque market relationships, and how they drifted in lonely, futile lives without enthusiasm, lasting bonds or true purpose. The ultimate effect of *anomie* was suicide, which Durkheim studied in *Suicide* (1897), a work that in some ways founded sociology.

Durkheim did not despair about *anomie*, or at least not until it harrowed his family life. After the fragile society of *fin-de-siècle* Europe descended into the collective enthusiasms of the Great War (1914-18), the conflict destroyed Durkheim's son in 1915. The last two years of

Durkheim's life were then a hell of devastating grief. Until 1915, Durkheim argued in his sociology that modern societies generated adapted forms of moral regulation to counter *anomie* and and the risk of social breakdown. This new complex form of religious life was the cult of the individual, the inherited creed of the French Revolution – liberty, equality, fraternity. The cult of the individual celebrated the dignity of the individual, their rights, and their realisation through reason, free inquiry and disciplined work. These virtues were the social totems that the cult of the individual danced around, and that ensured that the holy spirit of society still inhabited the otherwise anomic individual.

For a while, Durkheim's optimistic vision of a remoralised society seemed to outlive the Great War. There were the achievements of the Cult of the Individual in the 20th century: the death of the aristocratic *La Grande Illusion* in the Great War, the explosion of mass communications and the consumer age from the 1920's, the victory in 1949 of the *Universal Declaration of Human Rights*, and the proliferation of individualism in politics, culture and economics for 50 to 70 years after the Second World War. Durkheim's new religion, his vision of a re-moralised society that could integrate extreme divisions of labour and intense social tensions, was realised. But as the Radio Age, near to Durkheim's death, cascaded into the Television Era, then into the Internet Age, and then into our own times of Religious War in antisocial media, this new form of religious life degenerated. Durkheim's Cult of the Individual was toppled in the riots of a new iconoclastic cult of identity politics. Once again, we wonder today if the individual drifts without law and order in a deranged society; and, even more profoundly, whether the deracinated individual is caught in a wild culture storm. If we follow the great anthropologist, Clifford Geertz, in thinking that cultures are an ensemble of ways, texts and performances to govern human behaviour, then the breakup of that ensemble will make us ungovernable. We see today proliferation of identities not rooted in any past, and cultural decay in all our important institutions. The contemporary individual lives without laws, unregulated, futile and without purpose. Surely, this is a new kind of cultural *anomie*?

Durkheim used another, more poetic term for *anomie*: *mal d'infini*, or the malady or illness of the infinite. Malady of the infinite may be the exact phrase to use for the cultural *anomie* we experience today. Tradition and bounded communities are dissolved. Each person faces a Sisyphean task to find themselves among the infinite array of cultural ensembles. We can never reach the end of our ever-expanding libraries. We can never preserve all the books of time from the flames engulfing our over-sized archive. With such proliferation of meaning, conversation collapses like the Tower of Babel – including the conversation between the past, present and future. Once upon a time the Muses guided us across time, space and strangeness, in disciplines we then knew as literature, history or art. But now we ride war-horses of cultural studies into the endless wars of identity. We suffer despair and find the malady of the infinite, rather than participate in the infinite conversation.

But we also long to hold something more. We reach out into the screaming emptiness of space, and declaim a poem in the cherished dream that someone may hear it, someone might read it, or that one solitary stranger may begin a new faith. As Durkheim wrote,

> A philosophy may well be elaborated in the silence of the interior imagination, but not so a faith. For before all else, a faith is warmth, life, enthusiasm, the exaltation of the whole mental life, the raising of the individual above himself.[28]

Durkheim teaches me that I cannot imprison myself in the magic fire of the interior imagination alone. To escape *mal d'infini*, I must find or even found faith. I must do more than merely stay sane. I must make this conversation endure in some school that can institutionalise, protect and preserve the ecstatic frenzy of shared mental life. I must find a way to some strong gods and stand in communion before them.

---

[28] Durkheim, *Elementary Forms Of Religious Life* (1912).

PART FOUR

THE INFINITE CONVERSATION

Mind of Winter
19 October 2015

Wallace Stevens is a poet for lovers of beauty among ruins. For people in the second half of life he is of unique importance because of the path he followed: youthful brio and brilliance, subdued as a diligent insurance executive, dimmed as a sometimes benighted husband, and then lit forever as a superbly deferred poet.

He first read his poetry aloud to an audience, with some awkwardness in 1938 at the age of 58. His "Man with the blue guitar" – things as they are are changed on the blue guitar – broke his chains. As Harold Bloom wrote, "the poet who had written *The Man with the Blue Guitar* had weathered his long crisis, and at fifty-eight was ready to begin again".

He is the model of not asking permission to make things of beauty from the world or critics or publishers or any circle of arts practitioners. His verse is ripened with complex subtleties of a mind of winter. Through his example, we know there never was a world for him except that he sang and in singing made. Sitting by the lamp he lit, we imagine our own interior paramour, and for good reason think the world imagined is the small good we can hold in our hands.

Jeff Rich

Staying Sane and the Infinite Conversation
15 November 2015

> He was a lonely ghost uttering a truth that nobody would ever hear. But so long as he uttered it, in some obscure way the continuity was not broken. It was not by making yourself heard but by staying sane that you carried on the human heritage. (Orwell, *1984*)

The lonely and arduous duty of the poet in destitute times is to obey this command: stay sane.

If you stay sane, you will defeat the monsters who torment you with their scorn for the finer arts of the mind.

If you stay sane, the writing will come slowly, and enigmatically crystallise into the forms that it demands.

If you stay sane, you will resist the temptations of fame, the distractions of media, and the follies of common thinking. Sanity is a reprieve from the world that presses against the resisting body of the poet, the authentic *dichter*, and importunes it with the latest sass and seduction.

If you stay sane, you will maintain the song lines of human heritage. When these songs appear to be destroyed in engineered fires; when they are smothered in the driving drums of a city in a rush; when war is declared again within the soul of civilisation, and the city of lights becomes the scene for new massacres; it is only the lonely tenacity of single sane souls that invests in the harmless runes of prophecy.

But from those chance meanings, spreading like disorder across time and space, will emerge the infinite conversation.

From the Burning Archive

Immortal Diamond
29 July 2016

Gerard Manley Hopkins was a poet I encountered on my parents' shelves as a child. A small 1960's Penguin paperback edition of his poems was one of the poetry books I met early in life. Unlike most of the poetry on the family shelves, which I remember reading with my father, this book belonged to my mother. Part of her spirit has always made Hopkins' poetry something I must understand.

As a child, I absorbed the sounds and the strange music, which I now know echoes Anglo-Saxon rhymes and alliteration within the line. I was astonished by seemingly invented words, and the idea that Hopkins was a nature poet. To think of Hopkins as a religious poet was then beyond my ken.

Hopkins sat unloved at the back of my mind for a few decades, and then in the midst of a deep depression last year I discovered a podcast about the terrible sonnets. For several days I wandered streets with "I wake and feel the fell of dark, not day" and "No worst there is none" singing in my head. And this was a transformational experience that took me beyond my depression towards flames of renewal.

Over the last few days, inspired by Bloom's exhortations to memorise poems, I have learned by heart the terrible sonnet, "No worst there is none." I also read, in a commentary on the sonnet, that Hopkins described the sin of *acedie,* that he even used its composition to exorcise this demon. I draw a different lesson from the poem. There, Hopkins taught me a name for the impassable obstacles of the melancholic mind-mountains.

Hopkins maintained an infinite conversation through his poems. In a later poem, "That Nature is a Heraclitean Fire and of the Comfort of the Resurrection" replies to his appeal to the uncomforting comforter of the terrible sonnet. The later, stronger Hopkins writes: "Enough! the Resurrection, /A heart's clarion! Away grief's gasping, joyless days, dejection". And a century later, in this antipodean darkness, this lame writer, who knows no religion, can still pass through flames to be reborn. So, I hope to join an infinite conversation; and so I find some stillness in the conclusion to Hopkins' redemptive poem:

> I am all at once what Christ is, since he was what I am, and
> This Jack, joke, poor potsherd, patch, matchwood, immortal diamond,
> Is immortal diamond.

My Lacunae in Bloom's *Western Canon*
26 July 2016

I admire Harold Bloom and his scorn for the New Schools of Resentment. I recognise my own motivations to read in his argument that "the self, in its quest to be free and solitary, ultimately reads with one aim only: to confront greatness.... Our common fate is age, sickness, death, oblivion. Our common hope, tenuous but persistent, is for some version of survival".[29]

So my list today is an honest, brief reckoning of who among the 26 authors in Bloom's *The Western Canon* I have confronted, my gaps and who I intend to read.

Shakespeare. Yes, a dozen or more of the plays and all of the sonnets. My favourite: *The Tempest*. More to read.

Dante. Only parts of the *Inferno*. Much more to read, especially as I have been long lost in *una selva oscura*.

Chaucer. The prologue, including reading aloud in middle English, and my recent reading of medieval history has intrigued me to read more.

Cervantes. No. I tried once with a new translation. Try again. Try

---
[29] *The Western Canon*, p 524.

better.

Montaigne. Yes. I used to model myself on his prefatory remarks about being long weary of the service of the court and retiring to his study.

Moliere. Yes, a long time ago.

Milton. I have an old leather-bound copy of his poems, and have read 'Lycidas' well. I still recall from my early 20's Howard Felperin's joy in this poem. But have not read 'Paradise Lost' - a sin, corrected since the first online edition of this text.

Dr Samuel Johnson. No. But I will have to read Bloom's case to overcome my aversion to ancient, port-soaked English gentlemen.

Goethe. No, except from some fragments and maxims. I confess guiltily, since I have had *Faust* on my shelves for decades.

Wordsworth. Yes

Austen. Yes, I read three or four of the novels in my 20's, but I have not rejoined the recent fashion.

Whitman. Yes, patchily, which may be all that is possible with such multitudes.

Dickinson. Yes, deeply and with profound fascination since she is one of the authors whom I most admire. She writes regardless of the publishing fates.

Dickens. Yes, but I have not read *Bleak House*, I think which is the one Bloom extols the most.

George Eliot. Yes, but again not the most canonical *Middlemarch*.

Tolstoy. Extensively, and from a young age. I read *Anna Karenina* in my eager teens. I returned to Tolstoy in recent years as the gloom fell upon the globe. It was 2010, amidst the political crisis in Australia and the darkening world of endless, failing wars, that I read *War and Peace* afresh in the Pevears and Volokhonsky translation.

Ibsen. Yes, again in my late teens and twenties.

Freud. Extensively. I once owned half a dozen of Freud's texts, but sold them for a pittance when the funds were low towards the end of my graduate student days. I regret selling off my Freud. Even though I disavow his therapy, I am thankful for his writings. He was a great essayist who inspired another in Adam Phillips.

Proust. Proudly, yes; and yes again in the more recent translation. I may read it again during this long break.

Joyce. Yes to *Dubliners, Portrait of the Artist as a Young Man,* and maybe a third to a half of *Ulysses.* I dip into *Finnegan's Wake,* now and again, which remains one of those projects for later liffey.

Woolf. Yes, with great waves of emotion as a young man.

Kafka. Necessarily yes. Though I, like Kafka, have yet to finish *The Castle.*

Borges. Splendidly yes.

Neruda. No.

Pessoa. Not when I first wrote this piece. But since then after a trip to Lisboa, I came to know his many personas and his books of disquiet.

Beckett. Yes, but mostly the plays. I have sampled the smaller fictions, like fizzles, and parts of the great trilogy - *Molloy, Malone Dies* and *The Unnameable* - but found them more exhausting than replenishing.

So the gaps are pleasingly few – Neruda, Goethe, Johnson, Cervantes. There are some who I need to read more deeply: Chaucer, Dante, Shakespeare, Milton, Dickens, Eliot, Joyce. And only one who I wish to avoid – poor old Dr Johnson.

Taking time with Szymborska

12 July 2016

I have been enjoying the pleasures of disconnecting, if only for a few months, from the real world – its rush and press, the deadlines and overloads, its grinding work and gasping wishes. I have taken the time to enjoy poetry again, both as a writer and a reader. The other night, with no obligations attached any more to the things I read, I took up the last collection of Wislawa Szymborska's poems, *Map: collected and last poems*.

I found Szymborska first when she won the Nobel Prize for Literature in 1996, and have long cherished the collection published on the heels of that fame, *View With A Grain of Sand*. She wrote with an unsentimental irony and a witty enjoyment of inverted perspectives. She asks, just how does a grain of sand view the world from its place on a window sill? She jolts us kindly into realising that is we who see the window as a view, not the grain.

Szymborska reflects often on the past. She apprehends the terrors of the world – after all she was a survivor of East European socialism – and sets them aside with a fetching lightness of touch. So in "The Letters of the Dead," she writes:

> We read the letters of the dead like helpless gods,
> but gods nonetheless, since we know the dates that follow.
> We know which debts will never be repaid
> Which widows will remarry with the corpse still warm
> Poor dead, blindfolded dead
> gullible, fallible, pathetically prudent.

And then at the end of this poem:

> Everything the dead has predicted has turned out completely different.
> Or a little bit different – which is to say, completely different.
> The most fervent of them gaze confidingly into our eyes:
> their calculations tell them that they'll find perfection there.

Szymborska, like a circle of her fellow East European writers (Milosz, Havel, or Zbigniew Herbert), represents a life of writing hidden below the whirligig of celebrity, consumption and false fame. She made her writing smile back to an often hostile world, and it is more courageous and authentic for its avoidance of defiance. In her early writing career, she adopted the values and propaganda of the socialist party. She broke with the party from the mid-1960's. Then later in her career, if that is really the right word, Szymborska contributed to *samizdat* publications as part of the dissident movement. Such writers, who turn away from commercially modified productivity and socially sanctioned words, present an alternative path for me at this blog. It too is nearly invisible and barely measures an audience. It abstains from becoming just another branded or affiliated product. Yet this blog belongs with a new *samizdat* movement, from which may bloom a true, distinct and original culture.

Szymborska's whole published opus is less than 350 poems. When asked why she did not publish more poems, she replied that she had a trash can at home. Her wit is exceptional. Her imagined worlds are undying and laced with artifice. Taking time with her has been *No End of Fun*, the title of her 1967 collection. Her poem from that collection, "The Joy of Writing" is the perfect ending.

> They forget that what's here isn't life.
> Other laws, black on white, obtain.
> The twinkling of an eye will take as long as I say,
> and will, if I wish, divide into tiny eternities,
> full of bullets stopped in mid-flight.

Akhmatova's Agony

22 August 2016

Late last week I rearranged my desk where I installed mementos of my single overseas trip, the long train journey from Beijing through Mongolia across Siberia and the Eurasian plains to Moscow and at the end to St Petersburg. There I encountered the history about which I had read so much, but now could touch.

I walked Raskolnikov's murder trail; stood in the cells of St Peter and Paul Fortress; followed Catherine the Great's collections in the Hermitage; stood at the sites of massacres and revolutions; and looked out onto the mist-laden Neva with Aleksander Nevsky at my back.

But the most moving visit was to Fountain House. In the late autumn afternoon, I honoured Anna Akhmatova Museum, enshrined in her old communal apartment. There you can look out at the gardens that were her refuge. You can stand in her modest shared kitchen. You can sit at the meagre table, where she would share the words of her 'Requiem' to a friend, who would commit them to memory, before the scraps of paper on which they were written were burnt in the ashtray. The poetry of Akhmatova then was a perilous rebellion in Stalin's Russia. For me five decades on, what happened here is a solemn reminder that writing is more than self-promotion, and ought to serve something, if hard to name, beyond the writer.

Her great poem, *Requiem*, is performed openly and beautifully today on the ether of the internet, with many superb readings, accompanied by music and images evoking the sufferings of the Russian people and the victims of the Gulag. But it was not until 1987 (16 years before my visit) that it was first fully published in Russia, more than thirty years after its initial composition.

The hour has come to remember the dead. Her fellow poet, Joseph Brodsky, whose desk now stands in the Museum apartment, wrote how Akhmatova's suppressed readers memorised her poems by heart "to temper their heart against the new era's onslaught of vulgarity." If my ability to remember poems by heart is weak, then at least I can repeat her words, and speak them into this new whirlwhind of vulgarity and decay that I am abandoned to. I practise the rite of poetry to absorb the infinite conversation through my mind, my tongue and my skin.

Doing so, as Brodsky says "betters one's chances of weathering the

drama of history".[30]
>
> Not only for myself do I pray
> But for those who stood in front and behind me,
> In the bitter cold, on a hot July day
> Under the red wall that stared blindly.

Parables of Shame

19 August 2016

Franz Kafka was a poet of shame and guilt, writes Saul Friedländer in his biography of the eternal enigma. Friedländer reveals Kafka's sexual fantasies, his spurned homo-erotic thoughts, his disgust at his sexuality and animal drives. Through Friedländer I learn that Max Brod lightly censored his editions of Kafka's writings to remove these stains. But this Kafka does not fascinate me.

In my 20's I was mesmerised by a different Kafka. It was the Kafka who was wretched in life, and whose fitful, frustrating search to pursue the immutable in writing converted me to a dangerous religion. I absorbed from Kafka's life the belief that writing could not be reconciled with a life of contentment; that contentment was a sign of corruption that would take me adrift from the winds of my inner life; and that writing would demand the sacrifice of all loving relationships, just as Kafka himself spurned Felice Bauer.

It is 20 years or more since I read much Kafka, but his torments can still mesmerise me. In Friedländer's biography, I find Kafka's diary entry on 6 August 1914, when the great war swelled in the world's

---

[30] Akhmatova, *Poems*, 'Introduction by Joseph Brodsky', (Norton, 1983), p xix.

belly:

> What will be my fate as a writer is very simple. Any talent for portraying my dreamlike inner life has thrust all other matters into the background; my life has dwindled dreadfully, and will not cease to dwindle. Nothing else will ever satisfy me. But the strength I can muster for that portrayal is not to be counted upon.[31]

So, Kafka sings the song of shame I know too well: I am not good enough, my inner life is not good enough, my inner life cannot survive contact with the human world. Contact with the angelic orders, evoked in Rilke's *Duino Elegies*, will destroy my earthly self. So, Kafka goes on:

> Thus I waver, continually fly to the summit of the mountain, but then fall back in a moment. Others waver too, but in lower regions, with greater strength; if they are in danger of falling, they are caught up by the kinsman who walks beside them for that very purpose. But I waver on the heights; it is not death, alas, but the eternal torments of dying.

I too have told my own story through this image of the mountaineer. He scaled the mind's mountains alone, without a kinsman, and beyond his strength. He stood there in the snow drifts, beyond help, lost, disoriented, but needed to go on. Committed to scale the heights, he had one path home: death on the mountain.

But I must free myself from this image and this torment, and, like Rilke's Orpheus, find my way back to infinite praise. For Kafka, his nights were spent writing through insomnia, shame and self-hatred. He was maladapted to a world which prompted so much disgust and shame. He could only make his "descent to the dark powers".[32] But I believe I can leave the underworld, and celebrate the spring that comes after from my losses. I have found in later life a form of writing that Kafka professed not to know.

Still, there are in Kafka these haunting parables of the doomed

---

[31] Quoted in Saul Friendländer, *Franz Kafka: Poet of Guilt and Shame* (2013) p. 130.

[32] Letter to Brod, July 1922.

quests of life, which Friedländer glosses as the search for an unattainable goal, on which "the possibility of entering (or returning to) some land imagined as free and promised is blocked by insuperable obstacles". Despite the doom, we must go on. This is the immutable call to the writer to scale the heights of terror, to test the world's powers of destruction, and to trust that your words can withstand them. In 1917, Kafka wrote in one of his aphorisms,

> Man cannot live without a permanent trust in something indestructible in himself, though both the indestructible element and the trust may remain permanently hidden from him.

Despite the futility, despite the inevitable failure and self-destruction, Kafka made images like the silk-worms in Sebald's *The Rings of Saturn*. He stole from the immutable fires. He made a life as artistry into undeniable affirmation, just as Beckett, Kafka's Irish heir, would later say. Keep going. Going on. Call that going. Call that on. In "The Burrow," an animal makes a seemingly secure, perfect fortress, but knows, at any moment, its defences may be shattered. The burrowing animal, like Sebald's weaving silk worms, says of its labours:

> All this involves very laborious calculation, and the sheer pleasure of the mind in its own keenness is often the sole reason why one keeps it up.

The most perfect parable of the shamed writer is 'Before the Law'.[33] There a man comes upon a powerful doorkeeper who stands at the gate of The Law. For years he had sought admission through the gate, but did not have the words, the character or the questions to speak his way past the obstinate, inscrutable gatekeeper. Finally, in his last hours, in darkness, with his last spark of vitality, he gathers all his knowledge, all that he has learned from his many failures, and weakly puts one last question to the gatekeeper: "'Everyone strives to reach the Law', says the man, 'so how does it happen that for all these many years no one but myself has ever begged for admittance?'"

---

[33] From Franz Kafka *The Collected Short Stories of Franz Kafka* (Penguin, 1988), p 4.

The gate keeper sees the man has reached his end. He has finally realised the question he must ask, the question his shame and his obsessive goals had prevented him from seeing until his death. Then, triumphantly the gatekeeper roars in his ears: "No one else could ever be admitted here, since this gate was made only for you. I am now going to shut it".

Fragments of Fragments
August-September 2016

A blog is a fragmentary artwork. The aesthetic philosophy of the blog – a dissonant phrase of paradox – is at odds with the virtues of the masterpiece. You do not find here completion, mastery, comprehensiveness, or any perfectly realised vision. Some blogs do present their niche as an encyclopedia of their author's thought-world. But the evanescent writing that I enjoy reminds us to be

> Here among the disappearing, in the realm of the transient,
> Be a ringing glass that shatters as it rings.
> (Rilke, *Sonnets to Orpheus*)

Before the internet, much of the best writing survived and was made in fragments. This afternoon, for example, I picked up a book of aphorisms, only turned into one whole piece after Kafka's death and in only partial fulfillment of his design. In this collection of fragments, this remarkable parable on tradition survived

> Leopards break into the temple and drink the sacrificial vessels dry; this is repeated over and over again; finally it can be calculated in advance and becomes part of the ceremony.

Jeff Rich

(Franz Kafka, *The Collected Aphorims*, 20)

I was introduced to this parable by Howard Felperin in the only year at university when I studied literary studies. And Felperin had been taught by Harold Bloom who placed Kafka in the *Western Canon* because of his fragments. It was not the whole works, not the Kafkaesque essence, that Bloom saw as canonical. The canon was mined only from the good parts of the incomplete novels, the aphorisms or parables, the stories, some not finished, and parts of his diaries and letters. Bloom wrote:

> one must range widely in his writings, because no particular genre that he attempted holds his essence. He is a great aphorist but not a pure storyteller, except in fragments and in the very short stories we call parables.[34]

Kafka's writings only survived because Max Brod, his friend and executor, defied Kafka's instructions to burn all his writing. Brod made other small breaches of faith to edit and smooth Kafka's shards into a coherent whole. But like the entropic energy of a collapsing star, the fragments fragmented again.

I celebrate and commemorate writers like Kafka who made their art in fragments or who only survive in fragments. Among them, fragments perhaps of all writers, are Sappho, Maurice Blanchot, Émile Cioran, Walter Benjamin, and Heraclitus. When we read, no fragment stands in the same river twice

This morning, while reading Harold Bloom on Ralph Waldo Emerson, I found another sage's voice shattered into fragments. In *Anatomy of Influence* Bloom commented that Emerson thought in isolated sentences. The best of Emerson is found in fragments that shimmer in those sentences within the wild growth of his paragraphs and the loose forms of his essays.

Here I found a model for myself. My writing and my thought prefer the fragmentary, where I see glints of prophecies of a long transformation of the self. The long haul novel or well structured book,

---

[34] Harold Bloom, *The Western Canon* (1994), p. 448.

comfortable in its genre, is not for me. The path of the masterpiece is blocked, but the way, the trail of curiosity, intuition and curation of the fragmentary, is open to me.

From Bloom, I learned of Emerson's *Journals*. Here Emerson was most himself. They are vast miscellanies of a self-reliant spirit in search of wisdom. They show the drama of a mind conflicted about its cultural heritage. The *Journals* are full of snippets of quotation and commentary on the literary heritage, like a polymath's field notes. Despite his practice of the fragment, Emerson dreamed of a transcendent remaking of the poet. Bloom calls this dream, Orphism. This philosophy urged the self-reliant thinker not to destroy the written past, but to leave behind its ruins. So Emerson wrote: "When we have new perception, we will gladly disburden the memory of its hoarded treasures as old rubbish".

As I read fragments of the *Journals*, available in a complete edition online, I imagine Emerson as a precursor of the blogger, with his weekly lectures, his frequent sermons, and the vast random curiosity of his *Journals*. He is a precursor of my own dream of writing in fragments. In the *Journals* Emerson transcribed this anticipation of the burning archive from Goethe:

> Literature is a fragment of fragments: the least of what happened and was spoken, has been written; and of the things that have been written, very few have been preserved.
> (Goethe, *Maxims and Reflections*, 404)

Goethe spoke in lapidary phrases what I have struggled to express in these fragments. In maxim 80, Goethe wrote: "History writing is a way of getting rid of the past". And in the first maxim of this collection, he wrote "There is nothing worth thinking but it has been thought before; we must only try to think it again".

So, I find in these fragments an infinite conversation carried on from Goethe to Emerson to Bloom to myself. Was Goethe's maxim the beginning of the sentence that Bloom describes as the most Emersonian of all? "In every work of genius we recognize our own rejected thoughts; they come back to us with a certain alienated majesty." Fragments, conversation and rejected thoughts affirm the curious path I have taken.

Repeat Great Words. Repeat Them Stubbornly.
7 August 2016

Tonight I have been memorising, learning, and getting by heart Zbigniew Herbert, *The Envoy of Mr. Cogito*.

Herbert is one of the East European writers I seek to emulate, who spoke in dissidence from the comforts of power. I believe that Western societies or parliamentary democracies suffer a kind of cultural impoverishment through, as Havel wrote in *The Power of the Powerless*, the "automatism of technological civilization and the industrial-consumer society". These dissident poets were beacons of a kind of 'existential revolution' (Havel's term) that still challenges us, despite all our freedoms and all our wealth. It is an existential revolution because, as Havel wrote, it takes place in the heart and the voices of the powerless. The revolution occurs in daily existence in the sense of ways of being. Simple ways turn the tide: speaking your mind in an office meeting, refusing to adopt brands and slogans, avoiding the habits of endless consumption.

Herbert's poem is an anthem of moral courage, but marks the boundaries of defiance. I used to display it on my pin-board above my cubicle desk in the office. For a year or more, after I had a breakdown or breakthrough, it displayed dissent itself. But no-one ever asked me about it. This anthem is also the poet within the poet laying out the code that rules his voice. Towards the end, the envoy of Mr Cogito is urged to return to "humanity's old incantations". These songs give both courage with apotropaic words. They also define the noble and likely futile task of the poet who must repeat words "like those who crossed the desert and perished in the sand".

All men must die. True. But in the small time we live, we must give testimony with no expectation of reward beyond the company of cold skulls.

The Golden Fleece of Nothingness
12 August 2016

Out of curiosity and a certain doggedness, I chose this afternoon to confess my uncertainty about an allusion in the first lines of a cherished poem by Zbigniew Herbert, *The Envoy of Mr Cogito*, which I once learned by heart. Herbert begins this defiant testimony of the poet:

> Go where the others went before to the dark boundary
> for the golden fleece of nothingness your last reward.

I knew this fleece was a classical allusion; but precisely what, I did not. So I opened my *Complete Dictionary of Symbols*, which described the Golden Fleece, as "the famous symbol of the near impossible goal". This very Jungian reference guide explained that the golden fleece incorporated two solar images – the winged ram (whose fleece it was) and gold (ore of the sun). And I learned, as I so faintly recalled, that the fleece is part of the story of Jason and the Argonauts.

The Golden Fleece had been stolen by King Aetes of Colchis, (a territory proximate to Georgia today), by seizing it, and then taking flight on the back of this magical flying sheep. After his theft, Aetes grew obsessive about his stolen precious. He came to believe through a prophecy that if he ever lost the fleece he would lose his fortune. So, Aetes had the ram shorn, and the fleece hung in a sacred grove guarded by a sleepless dragon, which could conjure skeleton guardians by plunging its fangs into the ground. Jason was tasked to recover the Fleece, and by charming the dragon to sleep he accomplishes this heroic quest.

But the story itself interested me less, than how this admission of unknowing led me through the ever-opening doors of the interpretation of literature. Curiosity liberates you to discover more than one truth out of anything you read. So I found on Wikipedia – always a comically authoritative source – a list of 18 possible symbolic meanings of the Golden Fleece: royal power, alchemy, the spring power, the technology of the East, the wealth of Colchis, and on it goes. Yet, this quest is its own reward, and that reward is nothingness in Herbert's poem. So in writing, in the quests that we all pursue through life, the golden fleece is the magical door that takes us to the impossible quest, in which we may never succeed, but that enriches us for trying.

Finnegans Awwwake agoin
4 August 2016

Out of a whim, I opened again, as if for the first time, that great scary book of twentieth-century literature, that dream book of all language and all literature, James Joyce, *Finnegan's Wake*. For the first time in my life, I got past the second page. I dutifully bought a second-hand paperback edition in my twenties, knowing it was the uncontrollable and infinite jest of Joyce's late life, but despite all my pretensions I could not persist with its polysensical language. This time though, I read through the first twenty pages and made some kind of peace with this war on words.

I entered the maze, despite all the warding off spells of those first pages and experienced my first encounter with: bababadalgharaghtakamminarronnkonnbronntonnerronntuonnthunnt rovarrhounawnskawntoohoohoordenenthurnuk! (the thunderclap marking the fall). The thread I carried to enter the maze was the story that Joyce conceived his work like *The Book of Kells,* as a masterpiece of miniature elaboration. The compounded words, the echoes and shouts of 85 languages, the joyous variation of names and myths and quotation, the puns, the penetration of ancient ideas with modern demotic potty language ('penisolate wars') and the ideas of the modern fall ('jung and eerily freudened'), the puns that make you laugh before you understand, and the proliferation of meaning were all intricate illuminations that made this artwork uniquely identifiable and yet universal in its celebration of the glory of language and literature.

Finnegans Wake would seem, at a glance, the most esoteric of works, the ultimate symbol of a book that might consume the life of a modern scholar. It would take a lifetime to read this work, and still it would not be possible to know what it was all about. That failure to master the work indeed, or in plain waords, said Beckett, was exactly what it was and remains all about. Yet critics still think it was a mere cruel joke – the ultimate fodder for a Joyce industry of academics, who dedicate their lives, with other people's money, to making one sense of this magnisense. The book cannot be explained, you would think, it can only be admired or explored. The common reader, such as I, would run away rather than enter this inexplicable maze, if they knew its reputation for consuming the lives of the few rare graduate literature students who dared enter. The common reader would run away from the danger, and ask to store this artefact away in the closed, dark and dusty parts of our burning cultural museums.

But, no. The book that can defeat any single reader is reborn by the network of readers of the world wide web. So we read that the *Wake* was the book the web was invented for. A thousand lives of scholarship – or should we just say readership? – can live forever on a single web page. So I discovered, after reading my twenty pages, that the whole marvelous thing can be read online (http://finwake.com), where you can consult over 90,000 glosses, and notes and explanations (fweet.com) and hints for this gargantuan and Rabelaisian cryptic crossword. There I learned that solely in the first word on the first page ('riverrun') – there is a running motif of a reverend's letter, a running river (the Liffey, or, the beautiful to say, Anna Livia Plurabelle), an allusion to Samuel Taylor Coleridge's *Kubla Khan* ('In Xanadu… Where Alph, the sacred river, ran'), a hint of Italian *(riverranno,* meaning they will come again), and two ambiguous hints of French dreams *(rêverons*: we dream) and reunions *(reverrons*: we will see again, or we will meet again).

This joyous celebration by the everyone of the internet of literature's greatest wonder is open for all to see and to build on. The *Finnegans Wake Extensible Elucidation Treasury* allows all to comment, and so add meanings that others have not seen, like a never ending twitter feed (fweet.com). The waywords and meansigns project sets the Wake to music. A visual artist began but could not continue the project of meticulously illustrating each image of the work, so circling back on *The Book of Kells* and making this modern gospel into an illuminated manuscript again, named *Wake in Progress*, itself an allusion to Joyce's working title of the book, 'work in progress'. And so do we not see here the *commodius vicus* of a true cyclical view of history and culture? Do we see how paradoxically the great invention of modern mathematics and science has allowed a return to "religious, truthful, and faithful" pursuit of Giambattista Vico's "poetic wisdom" (*Stanford Encyclopedia of Philosophy*, on the web) as practised by the illuminators of *The Book of Kells*, by Joyce, and by the everyone elucidators of the wake? And this is happening beyond the walls of the academy, returning poetic wisdom to a deep, if rare, popular culture.

So can we say then that, even if the archives are burning, the great flowing riverruns of culture give back the eternal life of words to those who live and wake outside the ashen towers?

The Book of my Soul
28 October 2016

Why do we write poetry? In a world of inexhaustible archives, where we are overwhelmed with voices, why would we ply our own into the unending and infinite conversation? Why do this when although we have control over the words we write, we have no control over their reception in the world or the fruits of the work?

> Alas! What boots it with incessant care
> To tend the homely slighted shepherd's trade,
> And strictly meditate the thankless Muse?
> (Milton, *Lycidas*)

My last post on conceptual poetry prompted me to think on this, since there is a way in which the proponents of the cutting edge have abandoned the thankless muse and turned their poetry into a species of barren, mechanical marketing. They abolish the anxiety of authentic authorship by turning everything into a cheap showman's trick.

My post also prompted thoughtful responses from one of my readers, Daniel Paul Marshall, who says, quite beautifully, that "my entire reason to write poetry is due to Wallace Stevens saying it isn't everyday the world forms into a poem". Daniel pointed me towards the *Inflectionist Review* (www.inflectionism.com), which articulates a sense of poetry as belonging to a long, deep tradition of infinite conversation between readers and writers, who in turn are readers, rather than a ceaseless war of the new against the old, of radicalism against tradition. The *Inflectionist Review* described their poetry movement as part of this unending tradition of conversation:

> The literary tradition is as ancient as our capacity for verbal communication. Through ages, most of the core human concerns have remained the same, although our ability to analyze and discuss them has evolved. Poetry has remained essentially the same in that it elicits our reaction by appealing to those concerns indirectly.

They look to poetry, or literature, for the exchanges between people that cause a "positive spark, an epiphany, a sense of growth". Poetry connects to psyche or soul, and that is why Wallace Stevens spoke of the nobility in poetry. The poet's special privilege and responsibility is an ecstatic freedom of the mind. The literary *avant-garde* abandons and abuses this privilege. Now, I am not one to raise an aesthetic war banner and plant it in the ground, but I do see my poetry, my prose and this blog, if we take that as an artform, as part of a longer, humbler and more secret tradition than the loud brash declarations of self-promoters and the *avant-garde*.

When I write, I apprentice myself to Milton's homely slighted shepherd's trade, and to the spirit worlds of all the unknown shamans of the world, who sang their chants, struck their drums, and soared to unknowable journeys into the night. Instead of a statement of an aesthetic philosophy, my mind turned to a poem I wrote some years back, and included in my first self-published e-book, *After the Pills*, and which I later included in *Gathering Flowers of the Mind*. It was one of the first poems I wrote after I began to take medication for my mental health. It marked and broke open the ground where I began a productive, enjoyable and free writing life. I end the poem with this stanza.

> In the mandalas, strange mazes, of this book
> I encircle, tame, and then hold fast
> The sound of the blowing wind.

The poem refers to the music of Arvo Pärt, the Estonian composer, who fled Soviet repression, and produced some of the most beautiful music of the twentieth century, springing from the traditions of church music. If this kind of writing practice makes me a traditionalist or even a conservative, who will never be fashionable, so be it. I do not seek fame or fashion from what I do with my voices, and I draw inspiration from others who write the book of their living souls.

Thomas Bernhard's Soliloquies
11 October 2016

Looking around my study this morning for a prompt for a post, still with the idea in the back of my head of experimenting with list posts, I pulled out Thomas Bernhard, *The Loser* from the shelves.

Selecting a page at random, I came upon this passage:[35]

> Our starting point is always that we don't know anything about anything and don't even have a clue about it, he said, I thought. Immediately after setting to work on something we choke on the huge amount of information that's available in all fields, that's the truth, he said, I thought. And although we know that, we continue to set to work on our so-called human-science problems, to attempt the impossible: *to create a human-science product, a product of the intellect. That's madness!* he said, I thought. Fundamentally we are capable of everything, equally fundamentally we fail at everything, he said, I thought.

That pattern of overlapping layers of speech acts and cognition – 'he said, I thought' – is characteristic of Bernhard. In these traps of language dramatised the madness of the intellect in strange, fugal rants of despair.

---

[35] Thomas Bernhard, *The Loser* (1983, tr 1991), p 66.

Jeff Rich

This kind of narrative – from inside the head of an obsessed intellectual – is the one that I often default to, or it might be better to say it is the one that I am currently practising in the 'work in progress'. The overlapping layers of speech acts and cognition (I do not know the term for this figure of speech, sorry) create dialogue from the lonely, obsessed monologues that are Bernhard's novels.

As I am practising it in the 'work in progress', this kind of soliloquy is not even a stream of consciousness, so much as an essay of consciousness, in which I take up and reflect upon my own mental events from different perspectives. And it allows a kind of interpenetration of the theme of an essay with the biography and self-presentation of the narrator. So my prose work does not seek to reproduce the typical scenes, dialogue and narrative arc of fiction. It follows my internal monologue about a set of related stories – about a breakdown, Ivan the Terrible, my encounters with the powerful, stories of violence and power from history, a train journey from Beijing to Moscow, and many reflections, fantasies and observations triggered by recalling all these narratives. If it works, it interests the reader or the writer through the associations and discoveries made when interleaving these stories, which, as the writing unfolds, reveal many symbolic kinships between these several layers of the story.

Writing this down here reflects a new found confidence that this prose work will be completed. I had tried different forms before to tell the story of Ivan the Terrible. But, having read Bernhard and Sebald, and having been entranced by this style of voice, I found writing a conventional prose historical fiction ultimately uninteresting. So I am giving birth to this odd monstrosity that perhaps only I will ever love.

Let me say my thanks, however, in this list post to those authors and their works that have influenced me in this project. I do not say I will match these authors' artistic achievement. I only say that I am working through my own response to their influence by writing this book. These books from my shelves have influenced how I am writing this 'work in progress'.

1. Thomas Bernhard, *The Loser* – which is an account from

Wertheimer of his struggle with not matching Glenn Gould's artistic virtuosity, leading ultimately to his self-destruction.

2. Thomas Bernhard, *Correction* – which is a kind of account of a murder or a suicide through constant correction of differing perspectives.

3. Thomas Bernhard, *Lime Works* – which is another portrait of a strangely obsessed intellectual, which has the epigraph: "But instead of thinking about my book and how to write it, as I go pacing the floor, I fall to counting my footsteps until I feel about to go mad."

4. Thomas Bernhard, *Wittgenstein's Nephew* – which is perhaps his most accessible work, and is a deeply moving story of his friend Paul Wittgenstein, the philosopher's nephew, who suffered from mental illness and the treatment that society gives to we, the mad.

5. W.G. Sebald, *Rings of Saturn* – Sebald has acknowledged Bernhard's influence, and for me this is Sebald's most mesmerising work that interleaves essays on Thomas Browne, Roger Casement, Joseph Conrad, silk worms and much besides, all with a dark bass note obsessing about the traces of destruction and ruin that can be found everywhere you look. This book is very much the model for my 'work-in-progress'.

6. W. G. Sebald, *Austerlitz* – a purer narrative than *Rings of Saturn*, more fictional, less essayistic, but still with the echoes of refracted thought.

7. W. G. Sebald, *Vertigo* – a divided work, less cohesive than *Rings of Saturn*, and with more accounts of the author's own difficulties, and his experiences of vertigo when traveling to his homelands.

8. Marcel Proust, *In Search of Lost Time* – Of course, Proust wrote before both Bernhard and Sebald, but his great book, which is the tale of the symbolic redemption of his life through art, is also a model for my 'work in progress', in which I must symbolically destroy power in order to serve art.

On Reading Ambitions

Jeff Rich

17 January 2017

> It should be known that the above-mentioned *hidalgo*, during the periods when he was idle – which was most of the year – devoted himself to reading romances of chivalry with such eagerness and pleasure that he almost completely neglected the hunt, and even the administration of his estate. His curiosity and folly got to such an extreme that he sold many acres of farmland to buy romances of chivalry to read, and he took home every one of them he could find. (Miguel de Cervantes[36])

Today I strolled through the city during my lunchtime break, and wandered down to the best bookshop in the CBD, or central activity district as it has been recently renamed, with a determined plan to return only after I had acquired one classic work of literature that I had not yet read or had too long neglected.

I did first browse through books of current affairs, since I felt I should familiarise myself at least with the terms and titles of current debate in my lowly role as an under-castellan of a minor and sleepy provincial government in the Southern Pacific. From those racks I collected a recent essay proposing Australia quarrel a little more with our great ally and imperial friend, the United States of America. Surely this course is sensible, at least in a world made less secure each day by the chest-beating of the US national intelligence community and its grand old men and women.

Then I turned to deeper interests in the long rack that held classics of plays and poetry. I paused a while over the *Saga of Volsung* and the *Elder Edda*, and passed over reams of Austen and Dickens and the comfortable favourites. Then I thumbed through a new edition of Yeats' selected poems. In 'Why should not old men be mad,' I read how the poet gave all the good reasons curmudgeons like me might grumble when:

> Some think it a matter of course that chance

---

[36] *The Ingenious Hidalgo Don Quixote de la Mancha* (1605) [tr. Lathrop, 2014], p 19.

> Should starve good men and bad advance,
> …
> Observant old men know it well;
> And when they know what old books tell
> And that no better can be had,
> Know why an old man should be mad.

Yeats told indeed how there was no single story of an unbroken happy mind. It was perhaps the affirmation to know what old books tell, and the noble madness of old aged truth, those monuments of unageing intellect, that led me like a bloodhound on the scent of its hare to that grandest of tales of old men and the folly of their books.

So I walked home with a 2014 translation of Cervantes, *Don Quixote*, or to give the full name from the early frontispiece, reproduced in translation for this edition by Alma Classics, *The ingenious hidalgo Don Quixote de la Mancha*.

Cervantes' great comedy is one of those books that you can believe that you know but have not read, and especially so for someone like me, who is inclined to tilt at false dragons, clothed as windmills, and more inclined to know people in books than in real life. Yet I have not read *Don Quixote*.

But now I intend to read its 700 pages, full of comedy, classical and early modern literary references, which I will rely on notes to understand, and flavoured by the humane understanding of a writer whose story I have begun to be intrigued by. It is on a first pass a much funnier book than many that I have ploughed determinedly on with, such as Proust, Vikram Seth, *A Suitable Boy*, and *War and Peace*. With Tolstoy, I must confess, I did skim over the long essay on his pet theories of history near the end. On the other hand, there are many long books that have defeated my overly ambitious plans to ingest whatever wisdom and creative spark they still hold: a six volume history of private life, that stands embarrassed on my selves, the Bible, Musil, *Man without Qualities*, and of course, *Don Quixote*.

It makes me wonder about ambitions in reading. Today's literature is so vast. It is an ocean beyond ambition's compass. There is too much to read, even when you do not explore the shores expanded exponentially with all the internet samizdats to which I contribute and celebrate. Do we live in a time when the sheer enormity of all the written words leads us to surrender the classics, the great challenging works, the necessary elements of a humanist education, and instead to skim social media feeds for the remaining years of silence?

Then again, ambitions in reading surely serve some good ends. They set a course across that vast uncrossable ocean that is the literature of everything that could be read, and allow this poor reader to tack close to at least some known shores. If I say I were to read Cervantes, and still I failed, then at least I would have tried, and, even if taken in fragments, the attempt would have made me stronger. What I fail to read, still makes me stronger?

So I will go to bed tonight with my heavy old Spanish master, held in my weak old wrist, and thank ambition for letting me know, if only for moments, the imagination of the dead. There, will I know that in our madness is our truest dignity?

Sebald's Sentences

17 April 2017

"Max" W. G. Sebald wrote some of the most mesmerising and *sui generis* texts of 20th century literature. His *Rings of Saturn* is a collection of essays on silk, travel, depression, genocide and the elaborate prose master, Thomas Browne – a Borgesian list sewn together with deep meditation. This great work transformed my sense of possibility with writing, and my own meditations on power, madness, journeys, and the awesome, fearsome sovereign, Ivan the Terrible. This enigmatic writer, like his master, composed exceptional sentences.

I have spent the afternoon, as if in retreat from a world that does not welcome me, lying in bed and reading, much as I did as a teenage boy, when I fled a family that tormented me into the world that I conjured from the novels of Trollope, Dostoyevsky and Tolstoy, a world which came to wrap my senses in muslin cloth and made me into a walking apparition of a no longer living sensibility; and the book that I have read, itself composed in a modern ghostly form of nineteenth century style, is *Austerlitz* by the great German emigrant writer, Winfried G. "Max" Sebald.

Sebald enjoys a renown that comes in part from the unclassifiable genre of writing that he practised; he combined personal memoir, fiction, travelogue and history into a cabinet of human curiosities, lined with a dark soft cloth of sadness: yet underneath all the strangeness of his forms, there is the ornate, stately, otherworldly beauty of his sentences.

The story is told of some writer who once was asked by a budding practitioner of the art what might sustain them on a journey to fame. "Do you like sentences?" the writer replied. That after all is the stuff of each day of writers in every context – making sentences. So, to dwell on Sebald's sentences seems the best way to honour his memory, and to hope to emulate his art, which found a way to speak of human destruction outside the boundaries of our own time and through a style schooled in the writing of German naturalist description of the nineteenth century.

Throughout *Austerlitz*, there fall these delicate strings, which also provide some kind of clue to the seemingly directionless perambulations of his melancholy mind. So from the early sentences of *Austerlitz*, Sebald writes, as if inscribing the fractal pattern of his intention deeply in the enigmatic curls and twists of his maze:

> From the first I was astonished by the way Austerlitz put his ideas together as he talked, forming perfectly balanced sentences out of whatever occurred to him, so to speak, and the way in which, in his mind, the passing on of his knowledge seemed to

become a gradual approach to a kind of historical metaphysic, bringing remembered events back to life.[37]

There is too this graceful concatenation of, on the one hand, the precisely descriptive details of the outer world, of memories, of photographs, of the minor details of fortifications, and the forgotten stories of ambition behind the construction of the Central Railway Station of Antwerp; and, on the other hand, an ethereal uncertainty about our minds' ability to grasp the experiences that beset them and to stop the torrent of emotions with which we perceive the world. Sebald's enigmatic prose is born from this coupling of a strangely meticulous prose with the constant evocation that much of our lives are spent in mirages of our own conception. The very first sentence of *Austerlitz* contains this quality of a dream; a dream made through the miscegenation of gentlemanly scholarship with the perplexity of a mind that knows its own madness.

> In the second half of the 1960's I travelled repeatedly from England to Belgium, partly for study, partly for other reasons that were never entirely clear to me, staying sometimes for just one or two days, sometimes for several weeks.

The phrase, 'partly for other reasons that were never entirely clear to me', disrupts the reasoned preoccupations of the apparent narrative, and opens the reader to the disordered world of Sebald's deeper meditations, which come to him with many qualifications, always with a question of whether he has been deceived. Many states of mind 'seem to be' in this prose. They visit the narrator uninvited, unexplained, and lead from the seemingly solid into the always uncertain mists of our own minds.

This theme is conveyed in a passage in which Sebald looking upon a caged nocturnal animal in the Antwerp Zoo. He finds in the image of a captive raccoon in the Nocturama of Antwerp, a projection of the longing we have, those of us who sit and polish our words like the raccoon, to reach beyond the darkness that we see all around us.

---

[37] Sebald, *Austerlitz* (2001), p 14.

The only animal which has remained lingering in my memory is the raccoon. I watched it for a long time as it sat beside a little stream with a serious expression on its face, washing the same piece of apple over and over again, as if it hoped that all this washing, which went far beyond any reasonable thoroughness, would help it escape the unreal world in which it had arrived, so to speak, through no fault of its own. Otherwise, all I remember of the denizens of the Nocturama is that several of them had striking large eyes, and the fixed, inquiring gaze found in certain painters and philosophers who seek to penetrate the darkness which surrounds us purely by means of looking and thinking.[38]

Thoughts on the Unnameable
2 April 2017

It was some time in my teens or early 20's that I listened, with fitful attention on a Sunday afternoon, to a literary arts documentary that was maybe about Joyce, or maybe about Dublin, but certainly presented a fragment of a reading by a fine British actor of Samuel Beckett's prose works. "Keep going, going on" – I remember the lilting slow Irish voice that seemed to linger on all the irony of each and every word – "call that going, call that on".

It has stayed with me all of these years, as a watchword of a kind of ironic literary mindfulness. But the work from which it was detached thirty or more years ago, back when you could still occasionally watch quality literary arts documentaries on television, that prose work has long eluded me. Until this morning, with the

---

[38] Sebald, *Austerlitz* pp 2-3.

ubiquitous solutions of Google, that anti-mystery machine, I discovered that these phrases came from the opening sentence of *The Unnameable*, which has long sat on my shelves unread, forgotten, an isolated fictional narrator, lost to time and culture.

> Where now? Who now? When now? Unquestioning. I, say I. Unbelieving. Questions. Hypotheses, call them that. Keep going, going on. Call that going, call that on.

As I read on this morning, I wondered why this great dramatic monologue had not captured my attention before. He conjured my own compulsion to speak, to go worstward ho, and to write. In all the fragments, in all the destitution of these times, still there is this compulsion to speak, to write, to leave the words we share in our breath, and cast them to the winds that will destroy us. Is this not the same dilemma I have wrestled with? Nothing to say except the questions and hypotheses—let us call them that—of the weak and fading Malone of my own imagination. Nothing but skeletons only, caricatures, and some ghosts in an uncontrolled machine. Still I must say something: "At the same time I am obliged to speak. I shall never be silent. Never."

It is surely a cruel joke that Beckett, that stylist of epic failure, that artist of impoverishment, who exceeded even Kafka's hunger artist in staging fizzles and events of no, that this Beckett should have become the source of motivational images on the internet. His 'Fail better' lines have been inscribed on an ascending stair, photographed and shared for all the world on social media. They have even found their way into speeches by sportsmen, who summon the most unlikely ghost of Malone to spur on their Olympic striving.

And who would be a bad sport and dispute the value of that? If I can drift my life towards the spirit I heard that long forgotten Sunday afternoon, in the steady renaming of each of our failures as some kind of going, as some kind of on, then why cannot others take his words, and accent 'better', not 'fail'. We writers, after all, do not control our words; we do not control how they are forgotten, ignored and misread.

Failure and futility have their sorrows, but also their comforts.

They are the ends we all meet in the end. They are the ultimate defiance of the rulers of the world. They evade and defeat all those who believe in systems, in logical prose, in the rationality of our errant minds. As Beckett wrote, "The thing to avoid, I don't know why, is the spirit of system".

The Infinite Conversation and Survival
27 June 2017

I have written before in *The Burning Archive* of the very abstract metaphor for writing and reading, those eternal companions, that I have prised from the title of Maurice Blanchot's work, *The Infinite Conversation*.

I have written in 'On Wastebooks and Epigrams' of how writing secures our rare, precious fragments of understanding against likely destruction, and bequeaths them in frail forms to those who wish to take part in the infinite conversation.

And I have also written, in more cryptic, plangent terms of how writing is my chosen method of going sane and staying sane. To chant the songlines of human heritage, regardless of audience and social esteem, is my path. As I wrote in 2015, surprising myself with this record of my thoughts preserved from the flames:

> It is only the lonely tenacity of single sane souls that invests in the harmless runes of prophecy. But from those chance meanings, spread like disorder across time and space, will emerge the infinite conversation.

The guiding metaphor of the infinite conversation emerged from a dialogue with my psychotherapist. She posed the question: what values are important to you when you write? For me fame is not the spur, nor wealth, nor even impossible immortality. But a kind of survival through braiding my gentle voice with the never-ending threads of literature.

I do not have ready access to Blanchot's text to deepen my imagination of the meaning of a mere title to his work. The best I could do was to find the text (and lose the reference) of a brief tribute by Jean-Luc Nancy on the occasion of Blanchot's still living centenary.

> This existence is not life as immediate affection and self-perpetuation, nor is it its death. The 'dying' ['mourir'] of which Blanchot speaks — which is in no way to be confused with the cessation of life, and which is, quite on the contrary, the living, or 'living-on', or 'sur-viving' invoked by Derrida when he was at his closest to Blanchot — forms the movement of the ceaseless approach to absenting as true sense, destroying in it all trace of nihilism. Such is the movement that, being written, can 'give to nothing, in its form of nothing, the form of something.

It is this form of survival that I cherish in writing. In the borderlands of the mind, I listen for the survival of ghostly incantations and keener sounds, As I wander these ranges alone, I pay loving attention to these voices in my head. This survival promises renewal from isolation, dreams to mend the injuries of the day. It makes from our evanescent words fragments of beauty that may wander the earth forever.

When I have fears

29 October 2017

I have over the last year or so frequently relaxed in a meditative trance while listening to soft-spoken readings of poetry. The softly but precisely enunciated words, set against moody electronic music, penetrate to unknown chambers of the mind. Who this poet trance reader is, I do not know, but I appreciate her readings, stripped of any theatrical reading of the kind that famous actors sometimes make.

The readings I listen to most are those of Keats, Dickinson, Gerard Manley-Hopkins, and a reading from Rilke's letters of advice to a young poet. But my favourite is the reading by the Poet Trance YouTube channel of the poems of Keats.

I did not know the poem, "When I have fears", before I discovered it, read in this way. I had been searching for quality readings of poems, as a way to aid memorisation and to fill the well with things of beauty. Instead of showing me the way to famous actors rendering well known poems with their robust personalities, the world wide web pointed me to this anonymous lyricist of trance, who showed modestly how beauty is truth, truth beauty, and that is all ye know on earth, and all ye need to know.

The poem itself echoes in my mind. What writer of a certain sensibility has not feared they may never live to trace the shadows of the visions that come without fanfare, without announcement, yet fatefully deciding the inner life?

These fears are not resolved in the poem; and instead they are endured. The poet patiently waits out these fears, with their origins in the mysterious illusions of fame and love. He stands alone on the shore of the wide world, thinks, and waits for his fears to subside and for his dreamt illusions – the high-piled books of literary fame, the faery power of unreflecting love – to sink beneath the lapping waves. He is left alone to write, and to make things of beauty from this world, with no expectation of admiration, applause or recognition. These fears hold a cruel paradox – they are fears of not having things that cannot be. Beautiful, evocative, satisfying, alluring illusions. But these illusions also crush words of truth under the heavy weight of impossibility – huge cloudy symbols of a high romance.

In the face of death, in the face of oblivion, in the face of insignificance before the grandeur of the wide world, in the face of losing love, the poem realises all those things are true. They may be feared, but they cannot be averted. So, when I have fears, I endure them. I stand on the shore of the wide world, and I sing my song.

Keats chose this inscription for his tombstone: "Here lies one whose name was writ in water". I imagine this inscription for mine own: Here lies one whose name was writ on burning paper.

Conrad's Darkness

5 November 2017

> I have never been able to find in any man's book or any man's talk anything ... to stand up for a moment against my deep-seated sense of fatality governing this man-inhabited world. (Joseph Conrad, Correspondence with Bertrand Russell, 1922)

A new biography of Joseph Conrad has come out. *The Dawn Watch: Joseph Conrad in a Global World* is written by Maya Jasanoff, an American historian, who has set out to make sense of this dark pessimist who saw the troubles of the first globalised century.

Her book has prompted a rash of reviews, not the least of which is by John Gray, the mordant critic of censorious liberalism and all beliefs in progress. It is from John Gray's review, "Homo Duplex," that I have taken the epigram of this post.[39] It is an epigram I could subscribe to.

I first encountered Conrad in reading a little grey, worn cloth-bound student's guide to English literature, which had been handed down to me from my grandmother's student days in the 1920s and 1930s. This textbook presented Conrad as a plain stylist, in contrast to the complex eloquence of Thomas Browne, and a novelist of the high

---

[39] John Gray, 'Homo Duplex', *Literary Review*, 459, Nov 2017.

seas. I went on from this coy introduction to read much of Conrad – *Lord Jim*, *The Secret Agent*, *Nostromo*, and, of course, *The Heart of Darkness*. He evoked like few other writers the gloom and glower of the world, and the futility of all our grandiose enterprises.

The passages that have had the most impact on my intellectual life are the portraits of his narrator, Marlow. This wandering storyteller was separated from his society by both experience and vision. His tales are those of a dark prophet spurned in his own country. They are tales of the barbarism in all civilisations.

At the start of *The Heart of Darkness*, Conrad described the floating steamer on the Thames, on which Marlow tells his tale of the horror, the horror of the Belgian Congo. Conrad evoked the great historical voyages of English navigation and English piracy – "the Golden Hind returning with her round flanks full of treasure" – and exclaimed:

> What greatness had not floated on the ebb of that river into the mystery of an unknown earth!... The dreams of men, the seed of commonwealths, the germs of empires.

Then he turned to the sun setting on the great metropole of London – "the monstrous town was still marked ominously on the sky, a brooding gloom in sunshine, a lurid glare under the stars." Then Conrad made Marlow speak. London also "has been one of the dark places of the earth".

The crew did not respond to Marlow. They accepted his dark words in silence, as expressing the enigma he was. He did not tell tales like the other sailors. He did not look for simplicity or easy satisfactions in life. He did not share their awkwardness with secret knowledge. Marlow was not a typical sailor sharing tall tales so

> to him the meaning of an episode was not inside like a kernel but outside, enveloping the tale that brought it out only as a glow brings out a haze, in the likeness of one of these misty halos that sometimes are made visible by the spectral illumination of moonshine.

This story laid down a way of being I would emulate in my own life, in my own writing. Marlow spoke of the mysteries and the strangeness we only see in darkness. He spoke as one sailor among others who yet pursued another course. He spoke as a man who made his way through the world, and yet was forever marked off by the cultures he connected to in his mind. His stories made him into a stranger in every world he passed through. Of Marlow, Conrad wrote: "he had the pose of a Buddha preaching in European clothes and without a lotus-flower". He made enlightenment of darkness.

It would seem, therefore, the most natural thing in the world that Conrad made an appearance in the strangely beautiful tales by W. G. Sebald, *The Rings of Saturn*, which changed forever my sense of what it means to write. Sebald's meditation on melancholy turned to Conrad "whose protracted bouts of despair were henceforth [after his trip to the Belgian Congo] to alternate with his writing". Conrad appeared in *Rings of Saturn* as both a witness to the human destructiveness that haunts the narrator and as a prelude to the tragic story of Roger Casement's fatal opposition to the horrors of King Leopold's monstrosity. Casement's compassion and courage led to his brutal execution and the extirpation of his name.

Sebald, Conrad, Marlow, and if this does not seem an imposture, myself: our thoughts are connected by a deep pessimism, from which writing is the only escape. Action in the world is too marked by fatality; but writing allows us to say the things that our silent readers will ignore and accept, just as Marlow's companions on the Thames did.

It is this dark magic too that John Gray summons in his undefinable political philosophy marked by scepticism towards all illusions of progress. If I maintain the tradition of Marlow, speaking my strange stories on a floating steamer as the sun sets on our monstrous world, then John Gray maintains the traditions of Conrad's dark tales of the failure of imperial power. As Gray writes in his review of Jasanoff's biography of Conrad:

> If Conrad sounds cynical to readers today, it is because he voices truths that are now deemed unmentionable. He did not believe in what Russell, in a 1937 essay, called the 'superior virtue of the

oppressed'. All human institutions, including newly independent states, were steeped in crime; barbarism and civilisation would always be intertwined, with old evils continually reappearing in new guises. It is a vision as disruptive to the censorious liberalism that holds the reins today as it was to imperial fantasies of progress a hundred years ago.

Sailing to Byzantium
4 January 2017

Since I am on holidays, and not consumed with duties and obligations, I have returned to an old habit of virtue, committing poetry to memory. Today's poem is Yeats, *Sailing to Byzantium*.

The choice of this poem itself was prompted by reading Richard Fidler's *Ghost Empire*, which is an uncluttered, vivid telling of the main story lines of the Byzantine Empire. Fidler reconnects threads of Byzantium to our own culture in surprising ways – the story of little Red Riding Hood, the use of the fork in Europe, the adaptation of chess, the theft of sericulture from China. This mysterious still neglected story haunts our imagination, without us really knowing how or why. As Fidler writes:

> Once you know the story of this lost empire, you feel the ghost of Byzantium pressing against you at the crumbling land walls.... The story of how Constantinople flourished into greatness and expired in terrible violence is one of the strangest and most moving stories I know.[40]

---

[40] Richard Fidler, *Ghost Empire* (2016), p. 9.

And it is a story that very much belongs in the *Burning Archive*, devoted to remembering the ruined cultures and disappearing stories of the world, and the yearning of this tattered cloak upon a stick to enter into the infinite conversation. Fidler titles his final chapter, "The Artifice of Eternity," in a tribute to Yeats' poem. And towards the end of this chapter, *Sailing to Byzantium* itself appears, crowning a discussion of Constantinople's place as the "immortal city of imagination." Fidler quotes Yeats own reflections on the poem from a BBC lecture:

> When Irishmen were illuminating the *Book of Kells*, and making the jewelled croziers in the National Museum, Byzantium was the centre of European civilization and the source of its spiritual philosophy.

Fidler omits, however, the final clause of the sentence, which unlocks the poem. Yeats said "so I symbolise the search for the spiritual life by a journey to that city". I wish I had a symbol of a holy city to which I could sail, fleeing from the fires in the archive and the depredations of merchants and treasonous clerks. Through loving attention, perhaps I can create one. In the meantime, I can sing and commemorate the beauty of Yeats' language.

Regaining Time

12 March 2018

The other evening, I pulled from the shelf the sixth and last volume of Marcel Proust's *In Search of Lost Time,* or to use the Scott-Moncrieff translation, still evocative across the Anglophone countries with their Shakespearean heritage, *Remembrance of Things Past.* This volume, *Finding Time Again*, in the awkward 2002 translation of Ian Patterson, or *Time Regained*, still so in my mind from Scott Moncrieff's 1920s translation, is the culmination and summation of Proust's long circumambulation through the illusions of society, friendship, love, introversion, aestheticism and misguided ways through literature. It is in *Time Regained* that Proust makes his ultimate discovery within his own experience of how to find redemption. Redemption lies not in faith nor science nor reality. Redemption is achieved through literature, and how it reactivates memory to synthesise fleeting subjective perceptions with the persistent sensual world.

> Real life, life finally uncovered and clarified, the only life in consequence lived to the full, is literature. Life in this sense dwells within all ordinary people as much as in the artists. But they do not see it because they are not trying to shed light on it… Thanks to art, instead of seeing only a single world, our own, we see it multiplied, and have at our disposal as many worlds as there are original artists, all more different one from another than those which resolve in infinity and which, centuries after the fire from which their rays emanated has gone out, whether it was called Rembrandt or Vermeer, still send us their special light.[41]

Proust encounters involuntary memories that transport the narrator beyond the constraints of past and present. The narrator stumbles on the cobblestones as he leaves his coach, and he regains the sensation and perception, enclosed within a memory, of his past and ever-changing self, searching the streets of Venice for the experience of John Ruskin's ideas of beauty. It is the turning point that allows Proust or the narrator of *In Search of Lost Time* to put aside his doubts about his literary ability, his many diversions, his weak will grounded in the indulgence of his mother, and settle down to write. These are the moments when time is regained. These are the moments when life becomes one with literature.

---

[41] Proust, *Finding Time Again*, trans. Ian Patterson (1927; tr 2002), p. 204.

But Proust's theory does not turn life into an art object. Rather, life inundates literature. The experience of recalling a loving aunt in your childhood through the scent of a madeleine cake dipped in lime blossom tea does not belong to writers or artists alone. These processes of perception and symbolisation, which Proust meticulously recreates throughout *In Search of Lost Time,* are available to all people. They are ways of seeing. They are moral challenges – to see life aright, finally uncovered and clarified. We all experience these moments, even if we do not all dedicate our lives to document in those strange tapestries of experience, symbol and mind that we call great literature. But each of us compose in our minds the books of our souls, and this book "whose characters are forged within us, rather than sketched by us, is the only book we have".[42]

Involuntary memory, indeed, may have prompted me to pull *Time Regained* from the shelf at this time. The death of my mother has prompted reflection on memory, old age, death and the disappearance of treasured worlds. These are the themes in the great coda to *In Search of Lost Time* that Proust composed in *Time Regained*. I recalled, as I read the book again, the sunny, spacious room in a Victorian terrace, with a rush mat floor and a view onto nothing but another terrace's wall, in which, in my early twenties, I fervently read all of Proust in search of an aesthetic philosophy of life, just as Proust had read Ruskin. I travelled like a post-Romantic adventurer through Proust's strange and unfamiliar scenes of social comedy – the life of the French aristocracy in *La Belle Époque,* the flowers and landscapes of Europe, the Romanesque churches and the travel to Venice, the Dreyfus Affair and the demoralisation of French society during World War I. They created a beautiful pageantry for me.

But the heart of the drama was the long delayed realisation of the vocation of the writer. When and how would Proust's narrator finally sit down, or lie down in the bed of his cork-lined room, to write his book?

---

[42] Proust, *Time Regained*, p 188.

For years I have felt, like Proust's narrator, that:

> I now had proof that I was no longer good for anything, that literature could no longer bring me any joy, whether through my own fault, because I was not talented enough, or through the fault of literature, if it was indeed less pregnant with reality than I had thought.[43]

Then Proust and his narrator entered fatefully the library of the aristocratic family, the Guermantes, and conceived the great artwork he would live and die for. There Proust's narrator had taken from the shelf Georges Sand's *Francois Le Champi*, which his mother had read to him long into the night to soothe his anxiety. From that memory he recovered the magic of story-telling. So, when I pulled *Finding Time Again* from my own humble shelf, I stumbled on my own involuntary memories within deep house of culture.

Axel's Castle, a mirror, and an encyclopedia
2 April 2018

When I was about fifteen, I found Edmund Wilson's *Axel's Castle* in a library. It was my introduction to literary modernism and its progenitors, such as the French symbolists. Over time I would read most of the authors to whom Wilson was my accidental guide: Yeats, Joyce, Proust, Valéry, Eliot, Stein, and the French symbolist author who wrote the play, *Axel's Castle*. In time, I would find other guides to the great modernist canon. But the symbol of *Axel's Castle* remained as a ghostly survivor of my initiation into high modernist culture.

---

[43] *Finding Time Again*, p. 174.

There was nothing in the outward circumstances of my teenage life that would have led me to value the pursuit of writing as a form of symbolist transcendence of mundane reality. My parents were primarily interested in science, but with an occasional indulgence of Rilke and Hopkins. I spent much of my childhood reading *Wisden*, and playing cricket, in the forlorn dream of overcoming my physical limitations to become a professional cricketer. My maths teacher at school, impressed with my talent with trigonometry, algebra and arithmetic, urged me to become an actuary. I had no literary friends – few friends really – except perhaps two girls, whose literary tastes involved a love of Leonard Cohen songs, which I could not share, and who I have not seen again since high school.

But, while the pain of my family breakdown compounded, driven by my mother's madness and my father's greed and grandiosity, I grasped for symbols of inner experience beyond the real. So, *Axel's Castle* became my symbol of a higher inner life. Yet it was, and has long been, an oppressive illusion. I could never live like the disdainful aristocrats of the soul imagined in Comte de Villiers de l'Isle-Adam's lonely, isolated tower: "Living? our servants will do that for us." Nor could I ever bring together around me the salon of the spurned genius, Mallarmé, who puffed smokescreens between himself and reality, and engaged in the most radical experimentations with the limits of poetry, its incarnation in the letter and its instantiation by chance. Nerval's ecstatic transportation into madness frightened me, since for years I would help my mother find her way to treatment amid her hypomanic fantasies. The dream of *Axel's Castle* enriched me through its night journey of torments, but paralysed me in fear of its dénouement: the suicide pact and the renunciation of life.

Axel's lonely, Gothic, occult tower took me down a path of self-destruction; but ultimately the path opened into a clearing, where I learned to write in my own way. Now that I have shaken off its curse, I can walk with my pen into the great forest again.

But as I write these words of reflection, prompted by this persistent memory, a strange nagging doubt questions me. I begin to doubt whether I ever read *Axel's Castle* at all. Certainly, I have not read the original text by Comte de Villiers de l'Isle-Adam, *Axel*, from which the archetype that has ruled my literary life was born. But now, I think to myself as I clarify these memories, that I only ever learned of Edmund Wilson's book through a footnote reference in a compendium volume of studies on modernism, edited by Malcolm Bradbury. Maybe it was this book of commentary on commentary that I acquired at the age of fifteen from the school library. Maybe it was only from this distant mask that I was captivated by the symbolism of *Axel's Castle*. Could it be that all I had imagined in that title truly only came from my preexisting imagination, and I have long imprisoned myself in one of my own illusions?

I have stumbled into my own version of Borges' story, "Tlön, Uqbar, Orbis Tertius". In that labyrinthine story, Borges' narrator tells the history of Tlön which he discovered, through the "conjunction of a mirror and an encyclopaedia", in a singularly rare edition of the *Encyclopaedia of Tlön*. The narrator devoted much of his scholarly life to studying the history of this country, glimpsed in a single moment in the rarest of books. But then he reveals in his narrative that no-one else can find this edition of a book on which he has constructed his imaginative life:

> already a fictitious past occupies in our memories the place of another, a past of which we know nothing with certainty – not even that it is false.... A scattered dynasty of solitary men has changed the face of the world. Their task continues. If our forecasts are not in error, a hundred years from now someone will discover the hundred volumes of the Second Encyclopaedia of Tlön.[44]

Was my reading of Axel's castle an illusion, or was it the anticipation of knowledge that will change the face of the world?

---

[44] Jose Luis Borges, *Labyrinths* (1964), pp. 41-42.

Jeff Rich

Cantos from a Cage
15 April 2018

> What thou lovest well remains,
> the rest is dross
> What thou lov'st well shall not be reft from thee
> What thou lov'st well is thy true heritage
> Whose world, or mine or theirs
> or is it of none?
> First came the seen, then thus the palpable
> Elysium, though it were in the halls of hell,
> What thou lovest well is thy true heritage
> What thou lov'st well shall not be reft from thee.

(From Ezra Pound, *Canto LXXXI*)

If modernism was a kind of Renaissance of this last century, as the critic Peter Craven intimated, then Ezra Pound is surely one of the greatest and most troubling figures of these dying generations, this botched civilisation. His poetry reaches across cultures and centuries like a prophet in a tower. He is the great progenitor, whose heritage is stained by both his politics and his madness.

Overshadowing his poetic achievements and the magnificent difficult music of the *Cantos* are his failures as a man of judgment. Broadcaster for Mussolini. Convicted traitor. He was spared from an American hanging by a much questioned sentence of insanity. But what else than madness was Pound's experience as a prisoner of war when, caged outside Pisa, in the arid ruins of Europe, he sang the broken magnificent threnodies, the defiant laments of *Canto LXXXI*: 'what thou lovest well shall not be reft from thee'. There is a surviving recording from the 1960's of the aged Pound himself reading from this most enduring Pisan canto. Pound's voice gives an extraordinary timbre to his lines, a shaking echo of suffering, as if the scars of his captivity, his betrayals and his torments modulated his voice.

There remains a great controversy over Pound's stay in St Elizabeth's lunatic asylum, after his trial for treason ended with a plea of insanity. But his madness became a political trial. Was he mad? Was he bad? Did his poetry spring from a mind of poison or of greatness? It is strange that Pound should not be a symbol of the language of madness in Foucault's histories as well as the contemporaneous Artaud at Rodez. Was the salon Pound kept a corrupt indulgence for affluent writers? Were the poets who gathered around him, who forgave him his misjudgments, naive fools, willing traitors, or unwitting collaborators with the atrocities of antisemitism?

What do I learn from Pound? Neither acclaim nor ostracism can extinguish the voice. Neither tradition nor its breaking can constrain the voice. Neither madness nor politics can define the voice. Out of the cages of our lives, we sing our greatest cantos.

> But the beauty is not the madness
> Tho' my errors and wrecks lie about me.
> And I am not a demigod,
> I cannot make it cohere.
> If love be not in the house there is nothing.

(Ezra Pound from *Canto CXVI*)

Oakeshott and the Infinite Conversation
17 January 2019

Michael Oakeshott, the conservative philosopher, has appeared once or twice before in the *Burning Archive*, mostly in association with my discussions of governing. I discussed how Paul Kelly took ideas from Oakeshott – specifically that "citizenship is a spiritual experience" – to diagnose the morass that is our contemporary political conversation. Oakeshott was, perhaps most famously, the inventor of the term, *conservative disposition*, which I increasingly recognise in myself. As he wrote in "On being conservative":

> My theme is not a creed or a doctrine, but a disposition. To be conservative is to be disposed to think and behave in certain manners; it is to prefer certain kinds of conduct and certain conditions of human circumstances to others; it is to be disposed to make certain kinds of choices.

This approach was consistent with his broader philosophy that distinguished between different modes of thought, so that the world of science, art and practical judgment contained different ways of being. Oakeshott went on to characterise conservative dispositions and choices so:

> To be conservative, then, is to prefer the familiar to the unknown, to prefer the tried to the untried, fact to mystery, the actual to the possible, the limited to the unbounded, the near to the distant, the sufficient to the superabundant, the convenient to the perfect, present laughter to utopian bliss.

Then, Oakeshott continued:

> Familiar relationships and loyalties will be preferred to the allure of more profitable attachments; to acquire and to enlarge will be less important than to keep, to cultivate and to enjoy; the grief of loss will be more acute than the excitement of novelty or promise. It is to be equal to one's own fortune, to live at the level of one's own means, to be content with the want of greater perfection which belongs alike to oneself and one's circumstances.

To prefer the actual to the possible is an unpopular disposition in our world today, ravaged by the mercenaries of change who bring all familiar institutions to their knees to worship some form of "this must be". How often have I longed for some present, familiar laughter to dissolve the utopian bliss of the stern, ruthless parrots of change?

It is hard to imagine a pair of writers more different than Oakeshott and Maurice Blanchot. Oakeshott wrote a book on wagering on horse races. Blanchot ghost-wrote manifestos for the disastrous radical movements of the 1960's, as some kind of expiation for doing the same for the French authoritarian and antisemitic right in the 1930's and early 1940's. But today I discovered an uncanny connection between them – the infinite conversation.

Conversation was a dominant metaphor for both Blanchot and Oakeshott. Both writers valued conversation as a way of being that was open to the interlocutor, that followed open-ended paths of inquiry. Conversation held no fixed positions. All participants had the freedom to redirect this flow of words, to respond to this cascade of prompts with good manners, courtesy and mutual affection. If only we could bring that spirit to today's political and cultural conversations.

Blanchot entitled one of his books, *The Infinite Conversation*, and despite his reclusive manner of life celebrated in his obscure prose friendships found in writing and reading. And Oakeshott, I discovered today, wrote the best description of the infinite conversation, and why it is such a precious and rare thing that we should seek to conserve against the flames.

> As civilized human beings, we are the inheritors, neither of an inquiry about ourselves and the world, nor of an accumulating body of information, but of a conversation, begun in the primeval forests and extended and made more articulate in the course of centuries. It is a conversation which goes on both in public and within each of ourselves.

Jeff Rich

Encountering Fernando Pessoa in Lisbon
23 May 2021

Travel – I am finding – is for me an exploration of the cultural, the imaginary, the infinite conversation as much as it is sightseeing in the material world. So my travel to Lisbon has been an encounter with a new writer, who I may add to my collection of the fragmentary, unsuccessful and unpublished: Fernando Pessoa.

Lisboa has a museum dedicated to Pessoa, that projects into space a digitized version of the great trunk of his enigmatic writings that was discovered after his death. I was unable to visit the museum in the two days in which I walked, like Pessoa the cobblestone streets and the blue and white, tiled pavements of the old city, but the trip here has led me to read about his writings, his life and to begin to read the strange book, *The Book of Disquiet*.

I find in this text that is not a book, this prose of heteronyms and avatars, the courage to continue my own literary practice.

> In these random impressions, and with no desire to be other than random, I indifferently narrate my factless autobiography, my lifeless history. These are my Confessions, and if in them I say nothing, it's because I have nothing to say.

Reconnecting with Franz Kafka in Prague
18 June 2019

In the struggle between yourself and the world, second the world. (Kafka, *The Collected Aphorisms*)

A highlight of my recent trip to Europe was the three days I spent in Prague, renowned for its beauty, and home, at least in some ways, to three writers important to me: Vaclav Havel, Rainer Maria Rilke and Franz Kafka.

I learned a little about each of these three very different authors in my days in Prague, and it was perhaps most of all Franz Kafka who stood out in the trip. On my first full day in Prague, after visiting the Castle in the morning, where I stood outside the small house in the Golden Lane where Kafka lived for a time with his sister, I went to the Franz Kafka Museum. There I remembered the reasons Kafka was important to me, and began to dwell in his uniquely realised terrors again.

The Kafka Museum displays artifacts, texts and imaginative projections from Kafka's life and writing in an innovative and moving way. It recreates the mood of the short story, "The Burrow," by taking the visitor down a narrow staircase into an underground hall, surrounded with disturbing music and sounds, and into a long gallery of filing cabinets labeled with the characters of Kafka's texts. It is deeply affecting.

I also remembered the affinities I had with Kafka: his self-loathing at times; his hatred of his father; his profound doubts about his writing, and yet the urgent, spiritual necessity of his writing to his existence – so deeply imagined in "The Hunger Artist"; and the troubled necessity of his work in the bureaucracy.

> The strange, mysterious, perhaps dangerous, perhaps saving comfort that there is in writing: it is a leap out of murderers' row; it is a seeing of what is really taking place. This occurs by a higher type of observation, a higher, not a keener type, and the higher it is and the less within reach of the "row," the more independent it becomes, the more obedient to its own laws of notion, the more incalculable, the more joyful, the more ascendant its course.[45]

Yet I also saw how and why I drifted away from my earlier

---

[45] Kafka, *Diaries*, as displayed at Kafka Museum, Prague.

obsessive reading of Kafka's diaries and letters. My temperament has never truly been that of the hunger artist, and I have not suffered Kafka's terrible, disabling fear of simple human intimacy and family life. Among the most affecting displays in the exhibition was the case that showed the women in Kafka's lives whom he failed and betrayed from within the prison of his literary torments.

During the trip I acquired a recent translation of Kafka's *The Castle*, and began another effort to finish reading this unfinished work, in a translation stripped of some of its early English translators' rhetoric of spiritual search. I know his parables and short stories better than his novels, and perhaps that is how it should be. Kafka is another artist of the fragmentary. Coincidentally, when in Stockholm a week or two later, I saw a performance of Kafka's *The Trial* at the Swedish Royal Opera House. It was as if the world of Kafka was breaking on my shores, and retelling me this strange parable of self-destruction through literature that suggests self-realisation is a religious myth.

Bloom's last lilac: the death of Harold Bloom
19 October 2019

The American literary critic, or rather lover of literature, Harold Bloom is dead at 89. There are the usual range of bad obituaries, collected over at *aldaily.com*, prepared by scornful journalists ('staff writers') on the make or by embittered post-modern pedants envious of his gifts of memory, language and understanding. But these fashionable madmen cannot mar the grief I feel at Bloom's fading into the infinite conversation. The enduring charity of his reading will not be undermined by the Schools of Resentment that peck at his grave.

I first encountered Bloom in the early 1980's, confusingly mingled with the critical fashions he would disarm, such as Paul de Man and Jacques Derrida and other names who have passed from my memory now. Howard Felperin, who taught me at the University of Melbourne to appreciate Milton's *Lycidas*, spoke of Bloom as his true home master in his long Southern exile from American academic ambition. Peter Craven, when editor of *Scripsi*, long lost (since 1994 I read, though I still imagine its ghost stalks this ersatz city of literature), may have even brought him out to Melbourne. I recall or I imagine hearing Bloom speak with his gentle erudition to Craven, on the radio show Craven then hosted on 3RRR, back before the schools of resentment took over the culture. I may have even seen him speak at a guest lecture somewhere in Melbourne, but I mistrust my fogged over memories. Certainly, there is an interview with Bloom that appeared in *Scripsi* that was conducted by the then young literary scholar, part of Peter Craven's circle, Imre Salusinszky, who would later give up much of his life to be a political adviser to a failed Premier. Ultimately, I made my way from Bloom's appearances in the chat shows of literary culture to his substantial books, and I recall reading *The Anxiety of Influence*, alone and anxious, in the university libraries of Melbourne and Canberra.

But it was not that strangely birthed book of misreading – Bloom's own account of its place in his life appears in the much later, *An Anatomy of Influence* – but his later, deeper readings of longing and tradition that influenced me most. Bloom's *The Western Canon* sits on my desk as I write this shambles of grief. I open it at random in the first chapter, *An elegy for the canon*, and read the sentence: "Where did the idea of conceiving a literary work that the world would not willingly let die come from?".[46] This idea grips me – that our task, when surrounded by the flames of the burning archive, is to do what we can not to let the books burn, not to let the culture die, not to let what thou lovest well to be reft from thee.

---

[46] *The Western Canon*, p 19.

Jeff Rich

In an interview from 1991[47], Bloom said:

> I don't believe in myths of decline or myths of progress, even as regards the literary scene. The world does not get to be a better or a worse place; it just gets more senescent. The world gets older, without getting either better or worse and so does literature. But I do think that the drab current phenomenon that passes for literary studies in the university will finally provide its own corrective. That is to say, sooner or later, students and teachers are going to get terribly bored with all the technocratic social work going on now. There will be a return to aesthetic values and desires, or these people will simply do something else with their time.

I can only hope that there may be some stirrings amid our ruins for such a return to aesthetic values. It took courage for Bloom to defy the technocratic creed that had invaded the culture. It took faith to defend the infinite conversation with tenacity. For that long defence of his tower against the schools of resentment, I will always be grateful. There hope bloomed. One obituary in the *Paris Review* said that, by teaching us, Bloom made the inter-weaved world, opened by literature, "richer, more alive, redeemed".

I never responded as warmly to Walt Whitman, as did Bloom. He called Whitman the "American Homer", and found the echoes of "When Lilacs Last in the Dooryard Bloom'd" in other modern members of the canon, such as Eliot and his Waste Land. But in honor of Bloom's protection of the burning archive, read the verses from that act of mourning for Lincoln and for more.

---

[47] I have lost my notes on the source of these remarks, or perhaps like the Encyclopedia of Tlön, they were an illusion.

Fragments from the Burning Archive—Anna Akhmatova
29 December 2020

In my study is a box of old index cards with fragmentary thoughts, notes on narratives and characters, and quotations taken from my reading. The box is labelled, "Notes to Digitise," and perhaps the transcription of all my youthful scrawl will one day be a retirement project. But for now it is a stimulus to dig deep down into the Burning Archive and recover some old treasures.

Take this card, for example, on which I have transcribed Anna Akhmatova's "Inscription on a book" – or so google names it, though my own referencing derived from Orlando Figes' *Natasha's Dance: a cultural history of Russia* (2002) that points to a poem "Leningrad, 1959" from Akhmatova's *Complete Poems*.

> From beneath such ruins I speak,
> From beneath such an avalanche I cry
> As if under the vault of a fetid cellar
> I were burning in quick lime.
> I will pretend to be soundless this winter
> And I will slam the eternal doors forever,
> And even so, they will recognize my voice,
> And even so they will believe in it once more

This "expression of lonely suppressed prophecy", as I noted on my card sometime in the early or mid 2000's, evokes the trope of Cassandra, scorned yet prophetic. Others have described Akhmatova as "Russia's Cassandra," who became an "icon of suffering and authenticity in Russian literature," and I return repeatedly to this story in my song of myself. Twice, in 2003 and 2019, I have visited the Akhmatova Museum in Fountain House in St Petersburg, and a card with her portraits sits on my desk, inspiring me to emulate her. She was one of the great survivors; and inspires me to survive too; and so to keep writing poetry until the end of a long life; to make poetry a long run of insight, and not a Romantic burst of self-immolation; and to find in suffering the words that speak for a city under siege. So I might yet write an unforgettable Requiem, that like Akhmatova's, that created a "resurrection song... a literal incarnation of the spiritual values that allowed the people of that city to endure the Soviet night and meet again in Petersburg".[48]

Fragments from the Burning Archive — Mikhail Bakhtin

30 December 2020

I plunged again into my white box of old handwritten index cards today, and pulled from the archive, laid down in my twenties and thirties, a fragment from Mikhail Bakhtin (1895-1975), the Russian literary critic and philosopher. The text comes from a late work of Bakhtin, *Speech Genres*, although I took the text from Clark and Holquist's biography[49] which, unlike most of Bakhtin's own texts, I then had access to through the libraries of the University of Melbourne and Australian National University. The card reads:

> There is neither a first word nor a last word. The contexts of dialogue are without limit. They extend into the deepest part and the most distant future. Even meanings born in dialogues of the remotest past will never be finally grasped once and for all, for they will always be renewed in later dialogue. At any present moment of the dialogue there are great masses of forgotten

---

[48] Orlando Figes, *Natasha's Dance: A Cultural History of Russia (2002)*, pp. 520-521.

[49] Katerina Clark and Michael Holquist, *Mikhail Bakhtin* (1984).

meanings, but these will be recalled again at a given moment in the dialogue's later course when it be given new life. For nothing is absolutely dead: every meaning will someday have its homecoming festival. (Mikhail Bakhtin, *Speech Genres*)

Bakhtin was a fascinating figure to me when I was a student, as I struggled to find a form of historical writing that preserved the enigmas of literature, resisted the drudgery of rational academia, and yet did not become the indulgence of fiction. I was intrigued by his idea of the *polyphonic* voices in Dostoyevsky's novels and the *carnivalesque* in Rabelais. I never studied his ideas systematically – perhaps the very idea of such an approach to Bakhtin is *grotesque* – but his ideas were a provocation, and an invitation to see the world dramatically, as a storm of events and perspectives, and not only from the tyrannical single perspective of the *cogito*.

In an interview near his death in 1975[50], Bakhtin said:

> In order to understand, it is immensely important for the person who understands to be located outside the object of his or her creative understanding—in time, in space, in culture. For one cannot even really see one's own exterior and comprehend it as a whole, and no mirrors or photographs can help; our real exterior can be seen and understood only by other people, because they are located outside us in space, and because they are others.

This is a challenging thought for a recluse, and yet also true. It is why I believe, to step away from literature for a moment, that governing requires talking to strangers – for only then will the glimpses of a new reality appear in the theatre of public discussion. Yet I wonder also if looking back after thirty years on these cards is a way to get a perspective on the real exterior, and to see these traces of my life with new insight. If nothing else, I noticed two odd coincidences between this fragment of Bakhtin and my later writing.

First, Bakhtin was sent into internal exile in 1929, due to his errant mind in the Stalinist purges, and, while my punishment is not nearly

---

[50] *Mikhail Bakhtin: The Duvakin Interviews, 1973*, eds. Gratchev and Marinova, (2019).

as severe, yet still I have long felt myself to be a dissident in our decaying regime, and only recently wrote, in my year in review post, of the freedom of internal exile. Perhaps, this dim awareness led to my affinity with Bakhtin.

Second, reading this card from my box archive after all these years surprised me because there, lurking in that quotation transcribed thirty years ago, was the idea of the infinite conversation. For Bakhtin, literature, or less grandly, writing makes for a dialogue that is infinite. The meanings of this extendible dialogue can never be fully grasped, and its flames can always be renewed by a succeeding reader or writer breathing out into its embers. I absorbed that lesson from my fellow internal exile, my fellow scorned intellectual, and I found in that lesson an enduring hope – "nothing is absolutely dead: every meaning will someday have its homecoming festival".

My last words on 2020: Thomas Browne, *Urn Burial*
31 December 2020

Oblivion. Death. The rites we practise to farewell the dead. What better themes to end this year, 2020?

This afternoon I have begun a reading plan for 2020 that incorporates listening to audio books, and in one afternoon I have completed, while talking a lunchtime walk and doing the pre-dinner dishes, the magnificent sentences of Thomas Browne's *Hydrotaphia* or *Urn Burial*.

This essay or short book, published in 1658, is a meditation on the customs of burial that farewell the dead. Browne was prompted in that year to pick up his doctor's pen by the digging up of 40 to 50 Roman burial urns in a field of old Walsingham. He meditated on burial practices across cultures, and even animals, such as "bees; which civil society carrieth out their dead, and hath exequies, if not interrments". What would Browne have made of the strange sterile practices of farewelling the dead, behind glass and protective personal equipment, during this 2020 pandemic of the fear of death?

To Browne death extinguished dreams of immortality – even amidst the intertextual ether of the infinite conversation – and not even a recovered burial urn could resurrect perpetuity. Disease made Browne contemplate oblivion, not survival: "the iniquity of oblivion blindly scattereth her poppy, and deals with the memory of men without distinction to merit of perpetuity". Oblivion ripped tears in the fabric of history, culture and ancestral remembrance. Browne wrote:

> Who knows whether the best of men be known? or whether there be not more remarkable persons forgot, then any that stand remembered in the known account of time? Without the favour of the everlasting Register the first man had been as unknown as the last, and Methuselahs long life had been his only Chronicle. Oblivion is not to be hired: The greater part must be content to be as though they had not been, to be found in the register of God, not in the record of man.

So ends the year. May we put the remains of 2020 in a burial urn, and consign it to oblivion.

This grey spirit seeking a sinking star
5 January 2021

This morning I felt a sinking regret and clutched with fear at the prospects of making something of my life. But despite these fears, I also knew a kind of courage forged in the adventures of the mind and the journeys of the spirit that have been my lot. I saw a few short years ahead for me before retirement, and wondered what might be the prospect of ever freeing myself from my office as a lowly under-castellan in a minor provincial government, and making a living instead as an author.

I had turned last night to AuthorTube and BookTube for guidance, but saw more appeals to enterprise and marketing than to the search for knowledge, wisdom and survival in the infinite conversation. These were not my goals, however practical they may be. If I do pursue an author platform – and I intend to commence in February a podcast and Youtube Channel of the Burning Archive, together with later in the year a sub-stack newsletter – it will not be for social media fame, but to find some heartfelt fellowship in tradition with a band of true seekers of the sinking star I search for in the infinite conversation.

To check the sparring of despair that I felt this morning, I turned for my daily poetry reading to Alfred Tennyson's "Ulysses". Truly I felt this morning, outcast and downcast, like Ulysses, an idle king,

> Match'd with an aged wife, I mete and dole
> Unequal laws unto a savage race,
> That hoard, and sleep, and feed, and know not me.

But more so than the moulted carapace of governing that lies at my feet, I connected to the adventurer of the spirit, weakened by age and misfortune, that Tennyson saw in Ulysses. It was this grey spirit that I turned to this morning for the courage to continue.

> This grey spirit yearning in desire
> To follow knowledge like a sinking star
> Beyond the utmost bounds of human thought.

I also saw in Ulysses's contrast with his son, Telemachus – "centred in the sphere/ Of common duties, decent not to fail/ In offices of tenderness" – the wrestle between domestic settling and mindful striving in my own heart.

But it is the magnificent final stanza where I sought the deepest courage to continue, and to believe "to sail beyond the sunset, and the baths/ Of all the western stars, until I die." Even though I am frail, unknown and alone, here I found the courage I needed this morning:

> We are not now that strength which in old days
> Moved earth and heaven, that which we are, we are;
> One equal temper of heroic hearts,
> Made weak by time and fate, but strong in will
> To strive, to seek, to find, and not to yield.

Harold Bloom wrote, in a commentary on this poem, from which I read this morning, that these lines echo "the defiant Satan of Milton's *Paradise Lost*, I-II". But to me the closing lines are not a defiance of God, but a defiance of extinction. They clap the hands of an old man, and sing into this tattered cloak on a stick. They call me to choose the way of life that is mine, even acknowledging how I differ from those I love (domestic Telemachus) and the image of the world with which the world has shackled me ("I am become a name"). The poem is not the poisoned illusion of a soul that defies God, but the lay of a grey spirit who knows both his growing weakness and his true way of being.

> Yet all experience is an arch wherethro'
> Gleams that untravell'd world whose margin fades
> For ever and forever when I move.
> How dull it is to pause, to make an end,
> To rust unburnish'd, not to shine in use!

This grey spirit strives to find some glimpse of immortality, to search for the sinking star that falls beyond the horizon, and to yield his treasures only to the infinite conversation.

Jeff Rich

Ezra Pound, the unavowable fury of thy true heritage in fragments
24 February 2021

The story of Ezra Pound's mind cannot be told in plain and simple affirmations. Three twisted trees grow from this mind in all accounts: poetry, unavowable politics, and madness. They stand tangled and tragic in a strange, haunted copse that very few today will see as an holy trinity. The iconoclasts of today's fanatical cancel churches do not need to come to burn this copse down – Pound was canceled decades ago, if in the more tolerant ways of the last years of the dying generations of literary scholarship. But still, no-one can stand at this decaying copse today without exorcising the ghosts of Pound's fascist politics (if we accept that term for now), his antisemitic furies, and his contempt for demotic culture.

> 'All things are a flowing,'
> Sage Hercleitus says;
> But a tawdry cheapness
> Shall outlast our days.
> (Pound, "Hugh Selwyn Mauberley")

Every critic or reader must ask, sometimes with shuffling feet and wringing hands, sometimes with deep remorse and wretchedness these difficult questions. Can we admire Pound's poetry without shame for his politics? Can we excuse Pound's treason as the price of his madness? Can we celebrate Pound's genius without the stain of his disordered and unwanted ideas? Can we form one true, beautiful song from the great rambling fragments and documents of the *Cantos*?

It is almost as if Pound embodies the spirit of Antonin Artaud, in his archetypal madness, and the thought of Theodor Adorno that "writing poetry after Auschwitz is barbaric". Yet Pound did write such poetry in the *Cantos*; is it a record of barbarism or civilization or like all art, is it both? Daniel Swift works through the wake of Pound's trial for treason and his madness, its reverberation in a circle of post-war American poets from the Ezraversity of St. Elizabeth's Hospital in his *Bughouse: the poetry, politics and madness of Ezra Pound* (2017). At times he moves us to look beyond the exorcised ghosts and find a way to come to terms with this great troubador. But his treatment never quite reaches to the greatest heights of tragic biography. As Peter Craven has written:

> The trouble is that *The Bughouse* is constantly outgrowing its own status as a work of interpretation without quite turning into the thing it might be – a biography which is also a work of intrinsic literary quality. What we tend to get is a kind of travelogue and personal journey into the environs of Pound's incarceration.[51]

Over the last month I have tried a new practice of focusing in depth on a single writer over a month, and Ezra Pound has been my writer of the month. I have long taken casual glimpses at Pound as if in a literary dream, as in my post "Cantos from a Cage," and yet it has only been over this last month that I have made my way through many of the *Cantos* and Pound's other better known longer poems.

In reading Pound's *Cantos* I have found a shattered memory book of a loved heritage after a storm of destruction. The great fascination of the *Pisan Cantos*, in particular, is how they hold the story of his art, his beauty, his grandeur, his pettiness, his madness and his unawowable, yet not betrayed, politics. Ira Nadel writes, "The *Pisan Cantos* is Pound's memory book decoding and recoding his past in a kind of quest for internal harmony in the face of destruction".[52]

The ordeal of detention in a metal cage on the plains outside Pisa, in the shadow of an imagined *Taishan*, makes Pound's story that of an artist who has endured great suffering for indeed furious hatred. Coetzee admired how Pound endured "exile, obscure labour and obloquy for his art," and I, in my more self-dramatising moments,

---

[51] Peter Craven, "Old Master, Old Monster: *The Bughouse* by Daniel Swift," Sydney Review of Books (2017)

[52] Ira Nadel, *Ezra Pound: a literary life* (2004).

identify with the same struggle as an outcast and a wanderer, who is out of temper with his times. And can we forgive Pound his political misjudgments – in these times when the degradation of the American republic is even clearer; when the collapse of our culture more imminent; and ostracism for errant words is the new black? After all, which poet of any political stripe ever really exercised sound judgment in matters of state?

But it is the fragmentary and documentary nature of the *Cantos* that makes it both an extraordinary testimony, and a strange and difficult text to read. It is a strange mix of visionary poetry, diary, reminiscences, texts of world literature, and texts of daily life. Pound breathes beauty into all these fragments like the divine furies, or perhaps merely like the wind that will be how we all leave this life.

In a vivid, loving and regretful recollection of his meetings with Pound now preserved on Youtube, the American poet Donald Hall recalled meeting Pound in the late 1950's. Pound greeted him with a declamation: "Mr Hall, you find me in fragments.' So Pound echoed the great nineteenth century essayist of America, Ralph Waldo Emerson – who Pound did inherit after all – who said, somewhere I have not recorded, "I am a fragment and this is a fragment of me."

In his latter years, after his return to Italy, Pound deliberately fell into a deep perhaps prophetic and willed silence. Perhaps he had lost the electricity that he had as a young man espoused as the true hallmark of great art. Perhaps he protected himself from further exposure of unsoundness of mind. Perhaps he created, ever the impresario, a supreme fiction of the poet as a prophet in exile from language itself. Yet still in the late *Cantos*, Pound would wander among dross and rants, then seemingly stagger out towards shafts of beautiful light. Here, to conclude this post, is the last will and testament of Ezra Pound from the last completed *Canto* of them all, *Canto CXVI*:

> But the beauty is not the madness
> Tho' my errors and wrecks lie about me.
> And I am not a demigod,

> I cannot make it cohere.
> If love be not in the house there is nothing
>
> Ezra Pound, *Canto CXVI*

Thank you, *il miglior fabbro*. And good night, sweet ladies, good night.

A revelation from Rumi

28 February 2021/ 29 December 2018

This morning I read some poems from Hafez (c 1315-1390) that celebrated love and wine and striving of a mysticism. Notwithstanding the art, the sentiments left me cold, and so I recovered from an earlier post this different sentiment of Rumi that speaks more to my sense of the spirit of the times: "Sometimes the cold and dark of a cave/ Give the opening we most want".

Sitting in a shopping centre cafe, I am reading *A Year with Rumi*. I am waiting for a back massage, sipping a coffee and listening to Sam Harris and Johann Hari speaking about addiction, depression and the loss of connection and control in our society. I woke this morning with the thought that I wanted to deepen the response of the Victorian Royal Commission into mental health from a service design frolic for health bureaucrats to engagement with the place of mental health/illness in culture. I read from my book the poem, 'Backpain' by Jalāl ad-Dīn Muhammad Rūmī (1207-1273), written 800 years ago.

> Walk with grief like a good friend.
> Listen to what he says.
> Sometimes the cold and dark of a cave
> Give the opening we most want.

Jeff Rich

The Poet W as Comedian
18 April 2021

I have discovered over the last six weeks that Wallace Stevens is, after all the strife and seclusion of this last sixteen months, surely the best antidote to our troubled times. Why is that? Wallace Stevens is a poet of comedy, and comedy relieves the distress of tragic history. Comedy reconciles the restless, Romantic imagination with the present and the real. When the world falls apart, one must cultivate one's garden, but also tell some comic stories over dinner. It is comedy, not alone but inseparable, that moves the infinite conversation on.

That is what I have discovered in making Wallace Stevens my writer in depth over the last month and a bit. While over many years I had seen Stevens as a serious conceptual poet, maker of supreme fictions, full of the maker's rage to order words of the tragic-gestured sea, I have now discovered that Stevens took more delight in the glassy lights, which dance and bobble on the fishing boats at anchor offshore, and so arrange abundant days into a deepening, enchanting night.

> Ramon Fernández, tell me, if you know,
> Why, when the singing ended and we turned
> Toward the town, tell why the glassy lights
> The lights in the fishing boats at anchor there,
> As the night descended, tilting in the air,
> Mastered the night and portioned out the sea,
> Fixing emblazoned zones and fiery poles,
> Arranging, deepening, enchanting night.
>
> Wallace Stevens, "The Idea of Order at Key West"

Comedy can never reign supreme. Yet, for all of us subjected to those who seek domination, comedy frees us to escape from our cages, and to dance in the truth. Comedy lightens up Cassandra when there is no hope. Comedy mocks authoritarianism. Comedy finds the object of delight amid months of despair – a blooming flower, the ripples on a crafted lake, a rich plum upon a table. Comedy schools the riotous mind, discontent with both present and past, that yearns only for a future that never arrives. In "The Comedian as the Letter C," Wallace Stevens narrates the comic odyssey of his persona. Crispin is a poet who tries to find his place and time on a journey from the East to West coast of America (via Yucutan, as the sea route then went). Crispin strove to be a Modernist rebellious poet – to make it new, to invent a terrible new beauty, to shock the contented masses to live among his monsters. But he lost his angry energy on his American odyssey where he found the sun and and touched the earth.

> Crispin dwelt in the land and dwelling there
> Slid from his continent by slow recess
> To things within his actual eye, alert
> To the difficulty of rebellious thought
> When the sky is blue. The blue infected will.
>
> Wallace Stevens, "The Comedian as the Letter C"

This Ulysses found he loved Penelope more than smiting the sounding furrows to seek a newer world. Crispin discovered in the comic denouement of the beautiful world the true harvest of his imagination – the unquenchable plum.

> … It seemed haphazard denouement.
> He first, as realist, admitted that
> Whoever hunts a matinal continent
> May, after all, stop short before a plum
> And be content and still be realist.
> The words of things entangle and confuse.
> The plum survives its poems….

This passage from *The Comedian as the Letter C* comes in the fifth section of the poem and is entitled "A nice shady home." After all adventures, who does not wish to return to a nice, shady home? So, Stevens showed us the way to navigate through modernism, romanticism, realism and yet stranger doctrines to the comfort, comedy and comity of a quiet, normal and noble suburban life.

The wisest art, the most blessed stories, the deepest poems are comedies. The comedians tell us the emperor has no clothes. The fools coax Lear back from the brink. They make treaty with our all-too-human weaknesses, and let us marry our faults with forgiveness. It is comedy, gently holding the hand of tragedy in truth, that we ought turn to in our time of troubles today. In the world of pandemic and uncontrolled technocracy, we all may learn to stop short before a plum, and find there content with the real.

Part Five

Histories of our Times

Jeff Rich

Millennial Predictions—the return of totalitarianism

14 October 2015

The second speculative prediction in Fernández-Armesto, *Millenium* was that rival totalitarian regimes would return. This prediction was bravely conservative or pessimistic, when drafted. He wrote it a few short years after Fukuyama's rush of Hegelianism to the head in *The End of History*. Unlike the American neo-conservative Fukuyama, the European conservative Fernández-Armesto saw the worldwide installation of liberal democracy as a false dawn. His prediction rested on the assumption that people liked endless change rather less than technophiles, innovators and reformers might believe. Fernández-Armesto also judged liberal democrats to be too pusillanimous to defend political and cultural authority against nihilist or fascist or religious or radical challenges. The nub of his argument was:

> In increasingly complex societies struggling to cope with rising expectations, gigantic collective projects, baffling demographic imbalance and terrifying external threats, order and social control will come to be more highly valued than freedom.[53]

He saw new totalitarian movements on the rise in the populist right, law and order appeals, a new fundamentalist Christian movement, a faith in Marxism, only inured by failure, and Islamic fundamentalism, if with the qualification that it seemed on the wane as he wrote. We have since seen totalitarian ideas return, but, with the exception of Islamic fundamentalism, not quite with the longing for order that he anticipated. Authority as a whole is fragmented in the new society of the spectacle, and even its death cults rarely seek to assume total power, but compete for cultist passion on the fringes. Western liberal societies have warded off law and order totalitarianism

---

[53] *Millennium*, p 700.

because security is now central to defeating both the greatest cultural threat of all – Islamic fundamentalism – and the emerging geopolitical threats of post-communist democratic authoritarianism – China and Russia.

Western liberalism has been hounded less by its moral queasiness, as Fernández-Armesto feared, and more by its unleashed shadow, market totalitarianism. In a long elite-driven civil war of market against society, the new class of "there is no alternative" market ideologues has terrified society. Freedom has degraded to no more than the freedom to sell to the market, and human dignity has been enfeebled by fear of the loss of wealth. In this way, Vaclav Havel saw clearly into the spiritual disease in Western societies when he pointed to the same existential dilemma of living a lie in both communist and capitalist societies.

So I mark this prediction of Fernández-Armesto as wrong, since it misses the mark on both phenomenon and causes.

Millennial Predictions—big states will fragment
9 November 2015

Fernández-Armesto makes unusual observations as an historian, framed in remarkable prose and piquant with exceptional learning. His third millennial prediction is that big states will continue to fragment. He shares his intuitions that people give loyalty to the global only partially, and that they prefer local identity. He writes, "In a world where the bell tolls for all, people prefer to listen for only part of the peal".[54] Over the long course of deep history, fickle human

---
[54] *Millennium*, p. 704.

attachment pumps strong tides – the inflow of expanding identity and contracting diversity and the outflow relaxing diversity.

In this account, the formation in the relatively recent past of larger state or even global entities represents the end of a surging wave of Big Identity. In time, however, the forces of divergence, provincialism, and preference for the idiosyncratic over the universal will undermine Great States. Fernández-Armesto writes, "whenever a big state is nestled, smaller-scale identities and political aspirations incubate under its shell until eventually they poke their beaks through the cracks and take flight". So he foresees the breakup of European nations, and those megaliths that seem immune to disunion, China and the United States of America. We imagine one of these Great States to be too young, and the other to be too old, to disintegrate, but Fernández-Armesto's most provocative prophecy is that both may splinter. And the emerging great powers of the Global South, India and South Africa may also crack as states, even while they grow in status. In Fernández-Armesto's view, India may become the home for "more rounds of ethnic cleansing," and South Africa may be doomed with a flawed constitution that cannot contain divergent cultures.

Twenty years after, Fernández-Armesto's prediction, I cannot say whether he will be right or wrong in the long term. These states still cohere, and yet troubles brew. The United States appears on the brink of social and political collapse, but still continues to limp on. But with each Presidential election round, the probability of a catastrophic democratic failure rises. Here is a society that will have no single ethnic group in the majority within years or decades; and yet this electorate taunts the world by encouraging Donald Trump's candidature, including his promise to expel millions of Mexicans. China, on the other hand, fights its inner demons of corruption and dissent, and suppresses the identities of its citizens within a newly great China – Xi Jinping's New Chinese Dream. This authoritarian wave is on the rise, and may be the prelude to the Twilight of the Superpowers that Fernández-Armesto imagined.

But Fernández-Armesto has his own attachment and loyalty to

quaint, local and idiosyncratic cultures. His preference leads him to be too optimistic that these local identities can survive and reform into political states. His preference for the odd exception blinds him to the death of culture, even eccentric local cultures, in the society of endless spectacle. We may see a darker vision of the Twilight of the Cultural Gods. The authority to govern states may breakdown and all cultures may fragment and decay, but alternative identities at a smaller scale may not grow to recreate nation or civil society or canon. The state is breaking down, but is not partitioning into multiple viable unions. It may remain a husk of institutional identity for many years, unless a countervailing current can walk from the ruins. Collapse, not fragmentation, may be our fate. From collapse, dark riders may come.

The Armenian Genocide

1 November 2015

In the latter part of the nineteenth century, the Ottoman Empire began to crumble. The elites of the European empires pitied this 'Sick Man of Europe,' and this disdain caused resentment in the Turkish elite, on whom the Europeans still depended for their brittle control. When Ottoman authority collapsed, Turkish elites could see the cost of weakness in the subjection of the Chinese imperial dynasty to European commercial empires. To avoid the same fate, modernising elites in Turkey (Türkiye) sought to strengthen their state by turning on one former Ottoman client, the Armenians.

From the 1890's, Turks massacred and deported Armenians. These massacres and deportations were accelerated by World War One, the collapse of Ottoman authority, and the rise of the 'Young Turks'. This group of the Muslim elite feared the loss of their state as well as the empire. So they forged a modern, nationalist, Turkish successor state through ethnic cleansing: the genocide of the Armenians and massacres of other minorities, such as the Pontic Greeks. These peoples suffered forced marches into the Syrian desert, labour camps, mass killings, starvation, forced conversions, mass deportations, mistreatment of refugees as they fled, renaming villages, and the conversion of churches to mosques.

At the end of World War One the young Turks fell from power, and for a short time a liberal group ruled. They sponsored trials and investigations of these crimes. Indeed, the historian, Arnold Toynbee, led a historical commission that documented crimes against humanity. Woodrow Wilson led a conference at Sèvres, in a side meeting to Versailles, that negotiated diplomatic solutions to create self-determined nations within the boundaries of the fallen Eurasian empires. This conference defined the boundaries of an Armenian state to be excised from the new Turkish Republic. But a revolt against the liberals defeated this plan because it appeared to serve Anglo-American, not Turkish interests. This revolt brought to power, Mustafa Kemal, better known as Atatürk. Ever since, the Turkish state has acted to extinguish Armenian identity, culture and memory. Of course, it denies these actions are crimes. It presents the national myth of Atatürk as the founder of the nation, who opposed the imperialists by purging Turkey of Armenians and Christian culture. In these accounts, Atatürk was a warrior of honour who purified Turkey against the Armenian collaborators with imperialism.

But there is a shameful under-current to this nationalist myth. Atatürk's nationalist ethnic cleansing in the early twentieth century provided a model for Hitler and the German, Nazi Holocaust. There is, as you would expect, controversy and some uncertainty in the surviving documents that support this claim. But the evidence points to Germans directly participating in the Armenian massacres and forced marches, and to the Nazis learning from and applying the Turkish methods to their own genocide. Hitler even sought to model his own cult of leadership on the style Atatürk himself used, and that gained such adulation.

It is regrettable that today in Australia each Anzac Day Atatürk is honoured because of some words he spoke in flattery to our young nation in the 1920's. There he paid tribute to the 'johnnies' he fought against. We ought to do better. We ought to read this likely fabricated statement as a warrior code tribute, insinuated against British imperialism. We ought especially to know these things, and say these things, since Anzac Day is tomorrow, and today, April 24, is the day chosen to commemorate the Armenian genocide.

Lest we forget.

Thoughts on Coasts
8 February 2016

We think about history in categories. They are the imprints of tradition, how generations have told the wide story of the past: rise and fall of civilisations; the phases of nomadism, agriculture and industry; the gradual mapping of a world defined by the lands of continents, not the boundaries of ungovernable oceans. We forget the many migrations that peopled the world, and tell a simpler story of categorised civilisations that radiated out from the Fertile Crescent and rice paddies of East Asia. Our categories deceive us into believing all the decisive innovations of Civilisation stem from this continental core – farms, factories, and a certain idea of freedom. We push back into the long forgotten past social categories of our own over-described world, and ignore the more diffuse experience of another world.

The history of coasts show the insidious effect of this story of civilisational archetypes. Coasts may have been our first home, our salvation from inland drought, and our beacon lights of discovery. The first bands of humans left inland Africa and found the abundance, the variety, and the cultural encounters with others on the coast. They peopled the world by following its long chain to other lands. It was here trade bloomed. It was here our earliest forebears combined their talents to fish and to farm, to hunt and to gather, to war and to trade, to speak and to succumb to the greatest force we can touch, the ocean swell.

My own nation is a land of coastal dwellers. Its inner heart is red but dead. Most of the peoples of the world now follow our example, with close to three-quarters of them settling in cities and towns near the coast. We are all beachcombers now.

Inspirations from Roberto Calasso

28 March 2016

I aspire to write history not like a dry professor, but more like the shimmering mysteries of the past conjured by writers like W. G. Sebald or the sometimes ponderous, but often astonishing, Roberto Calasso.

"There is no essential reason for history to be distinguished from literature", he writes in the most enigmatic history of modernity, *The Ruin of Kasch*. This thought is more invitation, than conclusion. With the following thought, Calasso springs his surprise. Historical research is the gradual reconstruction of an artificial memory, made in the process of opening archival boxes of the unexpected. If the historian clings to his prior ideas, he leaves the past imprisoned in the present's preconceptions. "History finds itself," Calasso declares, "when it decides to let the sources alone – and understands that these sources can be *anything at all*, can be whatever there is".

So he discards a thousand dull lectures about the holy trinity of race and class and gender, a thousand dull homilies about critical readings and interpretations of interpretations, and a thousand dull sermons on the text as an act of power. What Calasso finds instead in the surprising gift box of the archive is the mysterious questions of the true historian. How do I reanimate the voices, the bodies and the minds of the dead? How can they walk amongst us again?

The Enigmas of Ivan the Terrible
10 April 2016

Ivan the Terrible tests the limits of historical understanding. All that we know of him, we only seem to know of him. All the stories we tell of him, we can only separate from legend with difficulty. His experience of the world, to the extent that we can reach that interpretation beneath other interpretations, was a reality that we accept only with a troubled mind: borderline madness; a belief in an idea of sovereignty, consecrated by a Byzantine political tradition that has disappeared from the world; an intimate familiarity with violence and trauma, and the dissociation of memory, image and culture. Here are seven enigmas of Ivan *Groznyi*, fourth of his name, Tsar of Holy Mother Russia.

First, how did he die? The English commercial agent, Jerome Horsey, left the only account. Horsey placed Bogdan Belsky and Boris Godunov, the two principal counsellors and rivals in the court, in the Tsar's private room, where Ivan spoke of death, and called for cures by gemstones and magic. He called for apothecaries and summoned his confessor. Then, Horsey wrote, "In the mean he was strangled and stark dead." Was Ivan murdered, and if so by whom and why?

Second, was he mad, and, if so, how? It is difficult to explain the events of his life without believing there was some kind of derangement in his mind. His fits and turns of violence were so savage. His revenge against loyal diaks and priests were so spectacularly cruel. His ceremonies of debauchery and violence were so ritualistic. Yet these events also displayed something more controlled than a deranged mind. He ruthlessly and violently imposed his will on the world. Could it be that Ivan IV suffered what we would today call borderline personality disorder?

Third, what purpose was served by the creation of the *oprichniki*? The *oprichniki* was the separate state within a state of terrorising guards, loyal solely to their sovereign. Older Marxist histories described this brutal state experiment as a class attack on the feudal boyars. Though animated by Ivan's enigmatic violence, the *oprichniki* was similar in ways with the formation of stronger centralised military states by sovereigns across Europe. But it was also influenced by the raiding and ruling traditions of the Horde. Was Ivan's creation of a personal estate and band of warriors, loyal to no-one but their Khan or their Caesar, Ivan's own imaginative extrapolation of the Mongol and Byzantine traditions of governing he inherited?

Fourth, what were the reasons for his feigned abdications? Before the creation of the *oprichniki* he feigned abdication, taking himself on a pilgrimage. Was this only a masquerade, which worked strategically to force quarrelsome boyars to choose loyalty to their ruler? Or did Ivan have a psychological discomfort with power and sovereignty – especially since his concept of sovereignty brooked no opposition to his will? What are we to make of the later episode when he gave the crown to a Tatar prince, and with dramatic revenge took it away, so creating through his personal humiliation of this prince a theatrical symbol of his absolute power? Was this a calculated ruse or a desperate psychodrama?

Fifth, what was the nature of his religious belief, especially his belief that he was a dread angel? Deep religiosity pervaded his life. He prayed in day-long sessions. He took a monastic name on his deathbed. For periods of his early rule, he was faithful to the Priest Sylvester and the Metropolitan Filip. He wrote strange poems that expressed his belief that he was an incarnation of a Dread Angel. Yet magic, debauchery, rites and sacrificial violence haunted him. He may have held chiliastic beliefs: that he was, in fact, living in hell on earth; that his time was the end of days; that his violent tempers expressed the judgment of the damned by God. How do such strange and powerful currents of good and evil inhabit the same mind?

Sixth, are the stories of his traumatic childhood produced by later dissociation and reconstruction? In the letters to Prince Kurbsky he described his treatment by the boyars after both his mother and his nurse were taken from him and killed. The rage and traumatic memories of these letters ring true. But could they be screen memories? Were they justifications of a sulking anger, an indulged bloodlust? Were they indeed later fabulations by a cruel tyrant who pulled wings off flies as a child?

Seventh, is his famous correspondence with Prince Kurbsky a later forgery? Is indeed anything that we say we know of him reliably true? Is there any real primary source from which we might extrapolate the truth of this legend? Edward Keenan, who died only in the last year or so, made this argument, and it may be true. But if it is, then how are we to speak of this character, whose life is too real, too implausible to be mere invention, forgery or fiction? Surely whereof this life of which we must speak, we must not be silent.

Jeff Rich

Inga Clendinnen, Dancing with Strangers
11 May 2016

If I were to teach a course on the history of Australians in the global nineteenth century, I would begin with a reading of Inga Clendinnen's most remarkable book, *Dancing with Strangers*. I would invite my students or my fellow scholars to turn their attention to a close reading of the episode of the 'Spearing of the Governor', Arthur Phillip. Clendinnen's anthropological reconstruction of this misunderstood stumbling dance of strangers shows how history is divided profoundly by culture. Culture is, as she understands it, "the context of our existential being: a dynamic system of shared meanings through which we communicate with our own".

Clendinnen's treatment of the strange dance of culture through history is exemplary. She carefully communicates those near-lost shared meanings through the sources. She searches for clues to mental states in action, with scrupulous intelligence that avoids empty 'isms' and abstractions. Her limpid prose provides the exquisite music for the dance. Above all, she has listened to the attentive but imperfect witnesses of the past. She has allowed their voices to speak of small matters that hold great moments, and so let significant episodes murmur to us again. Towards the end of her book, she writes:

> History is not about the imposition of belated moral judgements. It is... based on the honest analysis of the vast, uneven, consultable record of human experience. To understand history, we have to get inside episodes, which means setting ourselves to understand our subjects' changing motivations and moods in their changing contexts, and to tracing the devious routes by which knowledge was acquired, understood and acted upon. Only then can we hope to understand ourselves and our species better, and so manage our affairs more intelligently. If we are to arrive at a durable tolerance (and it is urgent that we should), we

have only history to guide us.[55]

I can imagine few more curious, compassionate and steady guides to the *danse macabre* of history than Inga Clendinnen.

Madness and History
10 July 2016

I am reading Andrew Scull, *Madness in Civilization*.[56] The title is a wink to the English translation of Foucault's *Folie et Déraison*, that is *Madness & Civilization: a History of Insanity in the Age of Reason*. The wink is not kind. Scull's book is in some ways the culmination of his life's work to rectify the errors of Foucault. At its core; *Madness in Civilization* disputes Foucault's poetic argument that madness is the shadow of reason, or a transgression that must be ostracised. Scull places madness firmly within the boundaries of civilization. But at times Scull puts his argument gracelessly. He makes offhand snipes at the philosopher's scholarly errors, and holds off with scholastic charms the strange beauty of Foucault's poetry enclosed in history.

Take, for example, Scull's brief discussion of the theme of the ship of fools, as depicted in Hieronymus Bosch (c1450-1516), *Das Narrenschiff*. Scull notes the image of the Ship of Fools was created as a literary trope, as in the 1494 text by Sebastien Brant, illustrated by Durer. These artists created, Scull writes, "allegorical images which captured the sense of the mad as liminal figures, haunting the imagination, lurking half-seen on the very margins of civilized

---

[55] Inga Clendinnen, *Dancing with Strangers: Europeans and Australians at First Contact* (2005).
[56] *Madness in Civilization: a cultural history of insanity from the Bible to Freud, from the Madhouse to Modern Medicine* (2015).

existence." So striking were these compositions and images, Scull acidly writes, "that, six centuries later, they would tempt the famous French philosopher and historian Michel Foucault (1926-84) into embracing the wholly mistaken notion that these powerful paintings were representations of something real, instead of merely an artistic conceit".[57]

That closing sneer at Foucault's "artistic conceit" betrays the weakness of Scull's book. It struggles to convey the experience of madness. It does not map the imaginative world of insanity from both sides of the borderlands of reason. It is heavy with real context, and reprises a stale, American-Western history of one 'civilization' in which the mad dwelt, but is light on deep appreciation of its claimed topic – the culture of insanity. Its early chapters, and I am just part way through, tell us much background about empires and historical developments that follow a tediously Eurocentric or Atlanticist course. But the stories surprisingly do little to elaborate the images, stories and voices of insanity. If Scull had been prepared to question why a mere 'artistic conceit" exercised such a hold on the imagination, as evidenced by the selection of topic by so many artists and storytellers, then he might have written a book with more poetic power, a book more like Foucault's *Madness & Civilization*. Instead, he seeks to tame the images of madness, to school the wild fertility of its symbolism with the dull discipline of pedantry, and domesticate madness securely within civilization, no longer a threat, but a "fundamental puzzle, a reproach to reason, inescapably part and parcel of civilization itself."[58]

In contrast to Scull's desultory dismissal of the imaginative resonance of the Ship of Fools, Foucault teased out the image and the social practice of the expulsion of the mad. He balanced, if sometimes in too grandiose prose, the mundane realities of disordered minds with the magical flight of their symbols. At the outset of his discussion of the Ship of Fools, despite Scull's uncharitable sneer, Foucault noted

---

[57] Scull, *Madness in Civilization* pp. 114-5.
[58] Scull, *Madness in Civilization* p. 411.

that this trope was a literary composition, possibly derived from the Argonaut cycle, and part of the mythic themes, revived and rejuvenated in the Renaissance. He claimed that these images, however, had a real existence, even though his text was blurry about whether this reality was in the form of an actual boat, as in two cited examples, or in the form of real, practical and symbolic expulsion. The expulsion drove the mad from the cities. Foucault wrote:

> Madmen then led an easy wandering existence. The towns drove them outside their limits; they were allowed to wander in the open countryside, when not entrusted to a group of merchants and pilgrims.[59]

What mattered to Foucault was not proof that the mad were transported on an actual ship, but that "the expulsion of madmen had become one of a number of ritual exiles".[60] For a cultural history of insanity, the symbolism of an image is as important as the realities of its more humdrum real world enactment. And Foucault dwelled on how madness moved between image and reality, and how the Ship of Fools became a primary symbol that registered how people imagined madness in history. So Foucault wrote this passage, inwhich even now 35 years after first reading its strange poetry, I recognise its importance for my own exiles in the borderlands of reason:

> Navigation delivers man to the uncertainty of fate; on water, each of us in the hands of his own destiny; every embarkation is, potentially, the last. It is for the other world that the madman sets sail in his fools' boat; it is from the other world that he comes when he disembarks.

Foucault imagines the madman in a position on the edge of society, who is both outcast and prisoner. He is forced to take passage from the city, but then imprisoned in the floating city gates. He is imprisoned in the threshold, that crucial symbol for Foucault.

> A highly symbolic position, which will doubtless remain his until our own day, if we are willing to admit that what was

---

[59] Scull, *Madness in Civilization*, p. 8.
[60] Foucault, *Madness and Civilization*, p. 10.

formerly a visible fortress of order has now become the castle of our conscience.[61]

This passage makes history into poetry. Its marked words denote a private symbolism for the writer. It evokes a modern dilemma of imprisonment in our rational minds. It reminds me of Weber's reference to the iron cage of rationality and vocation. It evokes the manifestation of madness in history in a way that is beyond the powers of Scull's more pedestrian prose.

To write of madness in history is a special responsibility: to prowl these borderlands and to come back and speak truthfully of the fears, the beauty, and the simple mundane practicalities of what you find and how you experience it. It is not a challenge that can be readily undertaken within narrow academic conventions, and it is not a challenge that Scull ultimately rises to. Scull domesticates madness with scholarly precision to a trite chronology of Atlantic civilization; Foucault reanimates the history of madness poetically, with all the necessary errors of imaginative speech.

Third Rome

13 March 2016

First, there was the Latin empire, polyglot and legal, with its legions centred on Rome. Then there was the Eastern Empire, religious and magnificent, radiating out from the seeming impregnable perfection of Constantinople, then sucking itself back in when defending itself against Goths, Slavs, Persians and Arabs. Then, at last, there was the third Rome – Holy Mother Russia.

---

[61] Foucault, *Madness and Civilization*, p. 11.

Holy Mother Russia was formed by many strands of Byzantine orthodoxy, Slavic peasants, Viking warriors, Tatar raiders and more ethnicities of Eurasia. But after the fall of Constantinople in 1453, the Patriarch and Grand Duke of Muscovy lived out one strand of this story, the rise and fall of this Third Rome. The Byzantine collapse gave them their mission to be the new centre of Christendom. For the next 160 years – four generations – its rise would lead to some of the most exquisite expressions of beauty and holiness, and the most terrifying acts of sovereignty and the madness of power.

Those twisting stories came together exquisitely in St Basil's Cathedral, formally known as the Cathedral of the Intercession of the Most Holy Theotokos on the Moat. Built by imported Italian Renaissance architects for Ivan the Terrible, the awesome Tsar blinded its designers so they could never make anything as beautiful again. This cathedral, named for the blessed intercession of the virgin, and meant to commemorate Ivan's victory over the Muslim Tatars of Kazan would, however, come to be known for the holy fool, *yurodovi*, who wandered barefoot here and across the beautiful red square, *krasnaya ploschard*. One time on this square Basil scolded this Tsar for living immodestly before God. Yet still here Ivan committed atrocities, executing his former loyal *diaks* with personal cruelty.

Ivan was the crest of the wave of the great Third Rome, and his savagery undid his dynasty. In the Kremlin he murdered his capable son in a fit of rage provoked by his daughter-in-law's unseemly dress. His remaining son was pious but an idiot, and real power passed, after Ivan's poisoned death, to the brother of this Feodor's wife, Boris Godunov. Amidst the stories of murdered children, fleeing courtiers, plagues, famines and the end of Christian days, the Riurokivich dynasty was extinguished. Godunov became Tsar, and despite some glories was soon challenged by the pretender, False Dmitri. This Dmitri ultimately made his way to rule in Moscow if briefly.

The time of troubles proceeded in confusion, and Poland and the Swedes invaded. The country almost collapsed in its civil war. The Third and last Rome fell. Amid its ruins and violence, two patriotic

Russians fought back and saved Russia from extinction. The invaders and Catholics were repelled, and in their place the Romanov dynasty was crowned. So the Third Rome passed from the world, and the Russian empire began.

Ivan's Singer

31 August 2016

No-one knows for sure how Ivan the Terrible died. The Tsar of all Russia, Grand Prince of Vladimir and Moscow and all the rest, died in 1584, but just how he died, we do not really know. The uncertainty, together with the availability of scientific methods, led to the exhumation of his bones from his grave within the Cathedral of the Kremlin that houses all the bones of the fallen Tsars, except, of course, the last Romanov.

There is an account of his death from the unreliable commercial adventurer, Jerome Horsey, but it is an eyewitness account, which is an uncommon thing in the history of the death of kings.[62] Ivan the Terrible suffered from multiple ailments and was a believer in all kinds of magic and religion, and so, according to Horsey, he called in his last hours for precious stones to be brought to his private chamber. He placed coral and turquoise stones on his body and declared to his private court: "I am poisoned with disease; you see they show their virtue by the change of their pure colour into pall; declares my death".

Ivan then spent the last hours of his final day with the comforts of his doctor and his alchemist. Ivan had denied these comforts to

---

[62] Jerome Horsey, 'Travels' (1598) in Bond, *Russia at the Close of the Sixteenth Century* (Hakluyt Society, 1856).

thousands upon thousands who he listed in his *sinodiki* (prayers for the dead, listing the many names of his victims) which Ivan sent to monasteries in the deranged grief that followed his murder of his son and heir. He took a bath and there "made merry with pleasant songs as he useth to do". Ivan had always loved the singers of his court, the *skomorokhi*, who sang ballads and ribaldry and performed clowns. They had roots in peasant and even pagan culture, and were suspected by the Russian church of fomenting heresy and disrespect for priestly authority.

Indeed, such was Ivan's love for the *skomorokhi* that as part of perhaps his most infamous act – the sack of Novgorod and the massacre of its citizens – he captured all the loved and artful *skomorokhi* of Novgorod, and after using them to shame the insubordinate Archbishop of this city, still too proud of its religious and republican traditions, carted them off to Moscow. Russell Zguta identified at least one of these *skomorokhi* who would later serve Ivan for over 20 years, indeed most likely till the day of his death.[63]

Was it one of these captive artists of this perfect monster of power who helped Ivan approach his death, stained with sin, but merry with song? I like to imagine that one of these *skomorokhi* became the cruel man's most loyal singer, and so found in captivity, like much art does, a comfortable life. But such a lowly singer does not appear in the next scene of Jerome Horsey's account of the Tsar's final moments.

Returning to his bedchamber fresh from his bath and in new linen, the Tsar called for a chess board. Beside the bed stood the two rivals for the Tsar's favour. Boris Godunov would later become Tsar, uniquely so since he was not part of any dynastic family. Bogdan Belsky was the sly and surly drinking partner of the Tsar. Would they have been the Tsar's chess opponent? It seems odd indeed. But perhaps it was the singer, who like Roy in *Bladerunner*, used a game of chess to confront his maker?

Then Ivan suddenly fainted and fell back, and now the confusion and omissions of details in Horsey accounts demand the imagination.

---

[63] Russell Zguta, *Russian Minstrels: a history of the skomorokhi* (1978).

Ivan called for the apothecary, and the more usual remedies, the doctor and the confessor. Horsey depicts a strange scene of rivals in power, who stood apart from a minstrel clown in their suddenly vulnerable terror. And then, Horsey wrote, most enigmatically of all, "In the mean he was strangled and stark dead".

The great biographer of Ivan the Terrible, Isabel de Madariaga wondered, was Ivan murdered?[64] It was not poison. A 20th century autopsy found no markedly irregular traces of poison in his body. But there were other means to kill and many motives for murder. The Tsar had been in disarray with grief and madness and sorcery. His war plans were ruined. His own dynasty had been brought to the edge of extinction by his rage-filled impulse to kill his own son.

Madariaga formed the cautious view the Horsey's strangling was a spasm or suffocation of a heart attack. But I see another possibility. There in that room, the captive artist finally struck out at the domination of power and terror. It was too late, of course; far too late for all the dead souls whose fate the singer did not celebrate. It was too convenient. But does not patronage always support art so? The artists imagine they seduce power, when power controls their every step. So I imagine, in the black spots of history's recall, that the moment the Tsar fell back, and panic filled the room, his friendly chess opponent, his loyal *skomorokhi*, saw his power wane, reached across the board, and strangled the Tsar to death. Belsky and Godunov looked on and did not intervene. In the hours after Ivan's death, the two rivals conspired together to take the sad and broken life of Ivan's Singer. Maybe? And to think, we can only begin to know this drama because the clumsy Horsey let slip one stray word – 'strangled'.

---

[64] Isabel de Madaraiaga, *Ivan the Terrible* (2005), pp. 351-2.

Civilizations and natures
9 August 2016

From time to time, I am tempted to be a prophet of doom, and like Cassandra abandon myself to "the awful pains of prophecy... maddening as they fall" (*Agamemnon*); but something in my temperament holds me back to a more tempered and sane view. History is neither progress nor complete decay. In some times, the archives do burn; but manuscripts are saved from the fire, and cultural life finds a way to go on. There are always losses, which I mourn, but there are so many splendours to celebrate and so many gardens to cultivate.

My favourite wise companion in maintaining a sane and generous view of our global history is Felipe Fernández-Armesto. He wrote in *Civilizations* that in both people and in civilizations:

> vices and virtues mingle, in the greatest saints, and in the most politically-correct common rooms. For every good intention, there is a frail deed: each provides the standard by which the other is measured. Civilizations, compared with other types of society, certainly have no monopoly of virtue. But a true pluralist has to relish the diversity they add to life.[65]

His *Civilizations* experimented with writing a new universal history of plural civilizations as versatile adaptations of the environment. Civilizations is remarkable for its wit, its literary allusiveness, and its compelling experiment: to write all history as historical ecology. In Fernández-Armesto's account, civilizations have no common characteristics, but share a process: the effort to transform the natural environment. Humans, unusually, if not uniquely, among animals, have populated all parts of the earth, all types of environment and climates. Our history is inseparable from these many natures – and here too Felipe Fernández-Armesto insisted food is central to the

---

[65] Felipe Fernández-Armesto, *Civilizations* (2000), p. 30.

human story, as our most daily and intimate encounter with nature. And, "wherever humans can survive, civilization can happen".[66]

The list: 17 cradles of civilizations

So, in *Civilizations*, Fernández-Armesto told the story of how civilizations have adapted, transformed, and remade 17 natural environments. Only a few of these belong to the classic story of the cradles of civilization, and he found in these environments many lesser-known treasures worth preserving from destructive fire. My fragmentary notes of this splendid list of 17 cradles of civilizations follows, with Fernández-Armesto's evocative chapter titles. The list is a brief illustration of how the past can be explored and its strangeness recovered with this enigmatic balloonist.

The Waste Land (Desert, Tundra, Ice)

1. *Ice Worlds and Tundra (The Helm of Ice)*. The Sami of Arctic Scandinavia created a civilization from the great herds of reindeer. The reindeer supplied most of the needs of life, and indeed their name, *jil'ep*, in the Nenet language means life. These ways of life were recorded in Olaus Magnus' *Description of the Northern People (1555)*, the "unacknowledged work of genius" of a Christian bishop who, in voluntary exile from protestant Sweden, travelled to the North to convert pagan souls but still stooped to understand the twenty forms of snow described by the Sami.

2. *Deserts of Sand (The Death of Earth)*. There is the tantalising mystery of the Garamantes in ancient times in the Fezzan in the Libyan interior, and speculation that the modern day nomads of the Sahara, the Tuareg are their successors. The Tuareg use an alphabet which is very similar to an ancient Libyan writing system, and is used magically, transmitted by women, and to cast spells on household objects, but not to record the ballads and stories of war spoken by the men. Tuareg is an Arabic term meaning abandoned by God; they call themselves *Imohag* or free men. They continue to practise their martial

---

[66] Felipe Fernández-Armesto, *Civilizations* (2000), p. 27.

code, fighting for Qadaffi and in Mali.

Leaves of Grass (Grasslands)
3. *Prairie and Savannah (The Sweeping of the Wind)*. Where we learn of old Mali, near the upper reaches of the Niger, and headwaters of the Gambia and Senegal Rivers, a great trading state controlling the passage of gold, and access to the great market and scholarly city of Timbuktu. It was here in 1352 Ibn Battuta described the majesty of Mansa Musa's court.

4. *Eurasian Steppe (The Highway of Civilizations)*. In 1034 the scholar-administrator and poet, Ou-Yang Hsiu, advocated standards of merit, and, in response received the reward that was at hand for the powerful who ran patronage networks in the bureaucracy. He was exiled to Yi-Ling at the mouth of the Yangtze gorges, where he observed the remoulding of Szechwan. He sought a conservative revolution by instilling the "perfection of ancient times" through reforms to the examination system, and he and his like advocated the true, humane diplomat's policy – "If indeed Heaven... causes the rogues to accept our humaneness and they ... extinguish the beacons on the frontiers, that will be a great fortune to our ancestral altars".[67]

Under the Rain (Tropical Lowlands and Post-Glacial Forests)
5. *Post-Glacial and Temperate Woodlands (The Wild Woods)*. On the Northern shores of the Great Lakes, the Iroquois built distinctive social spaces, such as the longhouse. The Iroquois built these longhouses out of elm, and not for practical, but for aesthetic reasons. Fernández-Armesto gives this example of the efflorescence of the cultural drive.

6. *Tropical Lowlands (Hearts of Darkness)*. In the jungle or rainforest of the Peten region of Guatemala was the great Mayan city of Tikal, in which despite the profuse growth there was monumental building from about 400 BC, and inscribed names and memorials of kings from AD 292.

---

[67] Fernández-Armesto, *Civilizations*, p. 120.

Jeff Rich

The Shining Fields of Mud (alluvial soils in drying climates)
7. *The Near East [if you live in Europe] (The Lone and Level Sands).* Where Fernández-Armesto takes us to the "the garden of the Lord" that used to exist at the ancient city of Jericho, back eleven millennia ago when it looked over an alluvial plain, and not a salted sulfurous desert.

8. *China and India (Of Shoes and Rice).* Where we meet the gentleman archaeologist, Charles Masson, stumbling on the ruins of the Harrapan civilization in 1826, and fooling himself that he had rediscovered one of the lost cities of Alexander the Greek.

The Mirrors of Sky (Highlands)
9. *Highlands of the New World (The Gardens of the Clouds).* Before the Incas, at a vast height, fed by maize and potatoes, lay Tiahuanaco and Chavin de Huantar, a place of pilgrimage thousands of years old.

10. *Highlands of the Old World (The Climb to Paradise).* We encounter the isolation and the martial culture of the New Guinea Highlands, itself an independently evolved place of agriculture. Here, in the 1980's, a Kerowagi elder told an anthropologist interviewer: "We thought no one existed apart from ourselves and our enemies."

The Water Margins (Seas)
11. *Small Islands (The Allotments of the Gods).* The wonder of Polynesian navigation is told, including the remarkable map produced by the navigator and holy man, Tupaia, who sailed with Captain Cook.

12. *Seaboards (The View from the Shore).* Here we learn of the mystery of the sea peoples who raided Ancient Egypt, the Vikings and Phoenicians, and navigators of the Atlantic Rim, including the old Celts who edged out to the outer British Isles.

13. *Maritime Asia (Chasing the Monsoon).* We rediscover Palembang on Srivijaya, which prospered on Chinese trade for sandalwood and frankincense. Surely proof that wealth has always been built on "experiences", and the material economy has always been saturated with symbolic significance.

14. Greek and Roman Seaboards (The Tradition of Ulysses). Since too much has been written on the origins of so-called Western Civilization in the classical world, I note only Fernández-Armesto's judgment on its strangeness:

> In spite of the unique contribution made by the ancient Greeks to the rest of the world, we should beware of idealizing them, as so many historians have done in the past. What was most enduring in their heritage was, in its day, the most eccentric: Socrates was condemned to suicide; Aristotle was driven from Athens and died in exile.[68]

So true; we create legends from shadows.

Breaking the Waves (Oceans)

15. Oceanic Civilizations (Almost the Last Environment). Fernández-Armesto retells Ibn Battuta's travels across the Muslim Lake of the Indian Ocean, and points to the regularity of the monsoonal wind-system as the basis, if such a metaphor is possible for a wind system, of the seafaring traditions of the Indian Ocean. His awareness of the direct effects of varied wind systems on the history of exploration and global exchange is also the basis of one of his many aphorisms: that in the history of the world there should be less hot air, and more wind.

16. Making of Atlantic Civilizations (Refloating Atlantis). Where with deep scholarship of exploration and navigation, he points to the many attempts to launch sea-borne empires in the fifteenth century. What distinguished the Western European seaboard's creation of the Atlantic civilization was, despite all the founding myths of Western civilization, the accident of being in the right place, so having access to favourable winds and currents.

17. Atlantic Supremacy and Global Outlook (Atlantic and After). In this last chapter, he contemplates the limits and limitations of the Western Civilization floated on this Atlantic environment. So, he zeroes in on the "bewilderingly paradoxical" twentieth century, with superb flowering of culture, creativity and freedom, matched by the most

---
[68] Fernández-Armesto, *Civilizations*, p. 425.

terrifying destructiveness. "It promised so much and betrayed so many" wrote Fernández-Armesto. But the twentieth century ended in mysterious, disappointing questions. "Why did civilization yield? Why, in other words, did progress fail?"[69]

It is an awkward question to end on, and the basis for what may be a true conservative argument, that our values can never be firmly based in progressive beliefs, since progress is an illusion. They all misrepresent a more chaotic experience of change, full of loss and gain. And this means that faced with the many difficulties that our societies and cultures encounter we need to avoid the willing delusion that we are moving with the spirit of the times. Instead, we may turn to our homes and gardens, our flawed traditions and treasured archives, and take care of them. So, in the concluding paragraph of *Civilizations*, Fernández-Armesto echoes the themes of this blog:

> After all the disillusionments with which the history of civilizations is studded – the triumphs of savagery, the bloodlettings of barbarism, the reversals of progress, the reconquests by nature, our failure to improve – there is no remedy except to go on trying, and keeping civilized traditions alive. Even on the beach and in the shingle, *il faut cultiver notre jardin*.[70]

The Tiger's Eye Closes for the Last Time
13 September 2016

The great Australian historian and writer, Inga Clendinnen has died. Clendinnen wrote cultural histories in the tradition of Clifford

---

[69] Fernández-Armesto, *Civilizations*, p. 543.
[70] Fernández-Armesto, *Civilizations*, p. 566.

Geertz, including an astonishing study recreating the mental world of the Aztecs. She then contracted a devastating disease that forced her early retirement from the academy, and after a period of recuperation, a blessed rebirth as a free-ranging writer and essayist. Her publisher, Michael Heyward, has written a moving obituary over at *The Australian*, in which Heyward quotes Clendinnen saying that her turn to writing in response to her life-threatening illness "liberated me from the routines which would have delivered me, unchallenged and unchanged, to discreet death".

Her books are exemplars for me. Her writing is so lucid and so insightful about human psychology and culture. She respects formal genres, but writes beyond them, with a graceful grief for the loss of formal well-written academic scholarship. They take good parts of history, memoir, essay, anthropology, and serve the reader on a quest to imagine all the possibilities of being human.

As a tribute to this great thinker and writer, who I wish I could emulate, let me quote from her essay on her understanding of historical writing:

> The most assured historians reveal their moral vision in everything they do: through tone, the sequencing of topics, the interspersion of comment, the selection of particular moments for deeper inquiry. That is why my most engrossing aesthetic/intellectual pleasure from words on the page, excepting only poetry, comes from watching a master historian at work. It is a preposterously ambitious enterprise, trying to make whole people, whole situations, whole other ways of being out of the dusty fragments left after real lives end, but that is what the best historians set out to do.[71]

I have written elsewhere about Clendinnen's masterful account of the first encounters between the first Australians and the Europeans who arrived on one small part of their shore in 1788 – *Dancing with Strangers*. I have yet to read her great book on the Aztecs, which preceded her illness, but often think about the themes of *Reading the*

---

[71] Clendinnen, *The History Question* (2006), p 55-56.

Holocaust, which she wrote as a non-specialist after her illness. This work is especially important to my own reflections on the Royal Commission into Institutional Responses to Child Sexual Abuse. Close to the end of that work she writes, in response to the conflicting emotions stirred by a photograph of an act of violence from the Holocaust:

> An awakened, outraged sensibility demands systematic inquiry… it is not enough to loathe the perpetrator and to pity the victim, because in that scene they are bound together. We must try to understand them both.[72]

So she goes on to say "only disciplined, critical remembering will resist the erasure of fact and circumstance effected by time, by ideology, and by the natural human impulse to forget". And then with a graceful turn, so characteristic of Clendinnen, she turns to the words of Wislawa Szymborska, frankly admitting she had only recently discovered her with her Nobel Prize award, and with her poem, 'Could have,' ends her great essay on the holocaust, with the observation that Szymborska "says much of what I have been trying to say over these many pages in as many words".[73]

So, let me end this elegy of sorts by urging the reader to read Szymborska's poem. Her kindred spirit has guided me and perhaps also this great tiger of the mind, Inga Clendinnen, whose eye has finally closed against the world.

---

[72] *Reading the Holocaust*, p. 206.
[73] *Reading the Holocaust*, p. 207.

Red Nostalgia
22 October 2017

During the week I attended a lecture at my old university on the meaning of the Russian Revolution today, 100 years on from Red October. The lecturer, Mark Edele, gave an entertaining and insightful talk to perhaps 600 guests, some alumni, some students, some dignitaries associated with the large philanthropic donation that had enabled the creation of the professorship, of which this was the ceremonial inaugural lecture.

The event was not without some pain or embarrassment for me since I had a year or more ago applied for a job as one of the new lectureships in History at the University of Melbourne, created by this gift from the Hansen Trust, and meant to be dedicated to improving the teaching and public engagement of history. Here was the professor appointed in that batch, alongside a number of lecturers whose experience in the world outside the academy was not exceptional. Here was the living example of the path I did not take, and that still mourn, but which despite my brief hopes in the winter of 2016, I will not ever be able to return to.

While there was mingling offered with drinks and nibbles before the event, I took myself to one side and wrote down some reflections on my day, which had seen rejection for one job, and an interview, despite expecting rejection, for another. It made me recall the note I had written to the former head of the History Department, as I sought to return there over a year ago. I had titled the email, 'advice for a prodigal son'. But though I received the advice, wandering son I remained. I scanned the mingling faces, and saw no-one whom I could recall, except one faded Peter Pan, with unruly hair and modest clothes, who I remembered as a tutor from my university days, who now had become professor.

The lecture itself provided a stimulating account of the many processes of revolution, civil war and breakdown of authority that constituted the events of the Russian Revolution. I learned of the new scholarly account of the revolution as an event that spanned the years 1916 to 1923 and all regions of the vast Russian empire, not only the familiar events of Red Petrograd.

Indeed, before this lecture I had not realised the significance of the containment by the Soviet Union of the imperial breakdown, with revolts across Central Asia, the Caucasus and European Russia, provoked by the breakdown of central authority in 1917. Lenin had sought to contain the revolts through a structure of federated soviet republics, based on frustrated national identities. I had read indifferently of the discussion of the nationalities question, but had not realised its significance. Indeed, it was a principal dispute between the old Bolsheviks, Lenin and Stalin. Lenin's view prevailed. He sealed the imperial breakdown in amber, despite Stalin's objections. In doing so, Edele pointed out, he left what Vladimir Putin described as a "time-bomb" in the constitution of the Soviet Union. The time bomb duly exploded after 1989.

Edele spoke about the conflicting views of historians of Red October as a coup or a popular revolt. In his summary view, it was a coup with the backing of the power of the radicalised crowds on the streets. Edele seemed less critical of the Bolsheviks as cynical manipulators of this radicalised crowd, compared to the account of paid demonstrators, funded by German money, orchestrated through the German agent, Lenin, that appears in McMeekin's recent account of the Russian Revolution, which I read a short time ago.

The "radicalised" crowd is a trope of revolutionary history, and part of a kind of Red Nostalgia. I recall reading, in my undergraduate years, George Rudé's celebration of the revolutionary crowd in the French Revolution, and his portrayal of this crowd as a serious actor in an historical drama. The radicalised crowd is a contrast to the violent mob. A long tradition of thought, which began at least one source of the history of emotions, sought to find an explanation in group psychology and emotional response to the phenomenon of violence in the radicalised crowd. In response to this tradition, Rudé tried to find the reason, indeed the emerging class consciousness, of this radicalised crowd in their material conditions. Not fury, but bread prices explained the crowd in this Marxist view. Simon Schama's *Citizens* inoculated me forever against this view.

Despite the new fashion of Marxism in some intellectual circles, Edele's only concession to this view was to speak of the radicalised crowd. This simple word, radicalised, is, despite all attempts at academic civility, a trigger for red nostalgia. It contains within it whirlpools of emotion, strange psychologies, and much responsibility for violence. Today, we try to explain to ourselves how relatively prosperous settled people can radicalise as terrorists. There is no simple explanation, and no single process that leads from grievance to fighting in foreign wars and seeking martyrdom in Islam. It was likely no simpler in Petrograd in 1917.

The sentiment of radicalism is immune to scholarly inquiry. It lingers on, and surely some level of red nostalgia played a part in the large audience attracted to this lecture. Edele was polite towards this nostalgia, only gently chiding the sentimental Marxism that has hidden the violence and the chaos of Red October for so many years.

But one unrepentant revolutionary spoke out in question time after the lecture. With only a brief time for questions, one ragged, aged Trotskyist, whose face seemed familiar from decades ago handing out the dreadful rags of propaganda put out by the Socialist Workers Party and similar organs, stood up and made a comment. He was disappointed in the lecture. Edele had not conveyed the grandeur of the Russian Revolution – surely the greatest of them all, better than the French or the Glorious English Revolution. And why should we care if the Constituent Assembly was abolished? It was a corrupted institution. And did not Alexandra Kollontai bring feminism to the world as part of the Revolution? Why did not Edele speak more of the great and true historians of the Russian Revolution – Isaac Deutscher, Stephen Smith and E.H. Carr?

Professor Edele politely demurred. Those books are now very old.

It is true that even factions were banned under the Communist Party – how could that represent a true democracy? I was left to question: where do our political passions come from, and in what kind of thought process are they grounded? Surely, it is not in the material facts of history. But there, alas, the time for questions was exhausted, and so the evening ended in a bitter red sunset.

Forgetting Foucault
26 November 2017

Over recent weeks I have chanced upon a few biographical articles on Michel Foucault. One was an account of Foucault's use of LSD in Death Valley on a road trip with some fellow academics in the 1970's. Another was speculation that in the late 1970's Foucault was too close to neoliberal ideas that would attack the French welfare state. They have led me in turn to revisit some of the discussion of the biographies and hagiographies of Saint Foucault, including his fevered embrace of sadomasochistic practices in the 1970's and 1980's San Francisco.

For a long time Foucault was an icon for me, driven by the mesmeric appeal of some of his thought and his personal struggle to think and to write. I read everything he ever wrote, and most of his interviews. Whether I understood them, I am not so sure. I have a copy of *The Order of Things*, which I bought as part of a prize for first year history at the University of Melbourne and so is signed by historian, Geoffrey Blainey (only four years younger than Foucault himself), and the writer who donated the prize, Judah Waten (who died the year after Foucault). It sits on my shelf now unread for twenty or more years, and is treasured more for those signatures than for Foucault's melodramatic evocation of the effacement of humanity in sands of time. But in my twenties I collected Foucault's thoughts obsessively, as if through the incorporation of these texts I would transform my status from benighted outsider into a public intellectual of standing. I tracked down his very early work on dreams and the practice of Ludwig Binswanger. I remember now more of Binswanger's descriptions of ways of being-in-the-world, than I recall the details of Foucault's radical co-option of those ideas. It was symptomatic of my strange quest that, in the end, I found Foucault's subject matter more interesting than his ideas.

I even translated one text of Foucault's that I could not find in an English translation, Foucault's essay on Blanchot's thought of the outside. I pursued the authors he was fascinated by, such as the strange, enigmatic but ultimately tediously absurdist procedural writer and spoiled rich kid, Raymond Roussel. The works that most deeply moved me were his tales of madness – in life, in writing, in suffering. It was not political Foucault that I found fascinating, although I tried to systematise all I knew of his erratic and unhinged statements on politics into some form of critique of 'governmentality'. I even conceived my PhD thesis as a kind of Foucauldian history of work and unions: I was tracing the ways in which a certain truth, a certain identity, was framed around the more fluid and undifferentiated lives of these workers. But while this idea fascinated me, it did not really help me write the work. It was his method and his style, the ravings of a self-proclaimed outcast, that both mesmerised me and paralysed me.

I wanted to borrow Foucault's identity, his postures, his self-dramatisations, but found myself in a completely alien situation, and ultimately Foucault's ideas and choices left me cold. He was a histrionic advocate of violence who wore a black velour suit. But what violence did he practise and against whom? He championed the rights of spoiled, privileged men to practise sadistic cruelty on north African boys. He imagined himself into a dramatic cultural revolution, and supported people's justice. Yet he petitioned the French Government to abolish the age of consent and liberate paedophile men to practise their child sexual abuse on unprotected children. He loved death too much, and knew too little of life. His own judgment that taking LSD in Death Valley was the most important experience of his life, to my current mind, condemns him.

The most important thing I learned from my fascination with Foucault was how to forget Foucault. He was a Nietzsche without the suffering – the conscious self-presentation of priestly radicalism mesmerised me and millions more. Miller's biography of Foucault presents itself as "one man's lifelong struggle to honor Nietzsche's gnomic injunction, 'to become what one is'". And perhaps this is what fired my imagination, even if I mistook Foucault's fame and fashion for authenticity and value. Now I think a truer model of the transvaluation of all values was the lonely wandering of Friedrich himself. As Roger Kimball writes:

> But whatever one thinks of Nietzsche's philosophy and influence, it is difficult not to admire his courage and single-minded commitment to the philosophical life. Wracked by ill-health—migraines, vertigo, severe digestive complaints—Nietzsche had to quit his teaching position at the University of Basel when he was in his mid-thirties. From then on he led an isolated, impoverished, celibate life, subsisting in various cheap *pensioni* in Italy and Switzerland. He had but few friends. His work was almost totally ignored: *Beyond Good and Evil*, one of his most important books, sold a total of 114 copies in a year. Yet he quietly persevered.[74]

The contrast with Foucault, the wayward scion of privilege, could not be stronger. Kimball uses Nietzsche's words against Foucault himself, saying,

> He epitomized to perfection a certain type of decadent Romantic, a type that Nietzsche warned against when he spoke of "those who suffer from the impoverishment of life and seek rest, stillness, calm seas, redemption from themselves through art and knowledge, or intoxication, convulsions, anaesthesia,

---

[74] Kimball, Roger. "The Perversions of M. Foucault by Roger Kimball." *The New Criterion* 11, no. 7 (March 1993).

and madness." Foucault's insatiable craving for new, ever more thrilling "experiences" was a sign of weakness, not daring.

By my 30's, despite all the obsession, I had left behind this icon of cruelty. By choosing life in all its mundane beauty, and not the radical intoxication of a melodramatic death, I learned to forget Foucault.

Return of a King
16 January 2018

I have finished reading William Dalrymple's mesmerising and tragical history of the first Anglo-Afghan War (1839-42).[75] It tells the story of the British invasion of Afghanistan, or, as it was known by its local rulers then, Khurusan.

The king who returns in this story is Shah Shuja of the Sadozai dynasty, who would hold court in the Bala Hissar fort and royal palace of Kabul. In 1800 the Sadozai dynasty had been ousted by its main rival, the Barakzais. The Barakzais clan would be led ultimately by the formidable Dost Mohammed Khan (1779-1863). Shah Shuja lived in exile in Ludhiana in the Punjab, and suffered many humiliations and defeats in his efforts to reclaim the throne, not least yielding the Koh-i-Noor diamond to Maharajah Ranjit Singh, the Lion of Punjab, one of the most effective military rulers who resisted the British. The British made a strategic decision to ally with Shah Shuja. They supported him with a pension, and kept his tattered court intact for thirty years before deciding in the 1830's to reinstall the Shah as ruler of Khurusan.

The British motive to return this King was geo-strategic rivalry with Russia, and the secure control of Britain's Indian Empire. Fears

---

[75] William Dalrymple, *Return of a King: the battle for Afghanistan* (2013)

were spread in doctored intelligence reports that the Russians planned to take control of Afghanistan, ally with Persia, and squeeze Britain's imperial heart from the north. These fears were unfounded, but give Dalrymple's book some of its most intriguing and tragic characters – the three key local intelligence officers of Britain and Russia, Alexander Burnes (a relative of poet, Robert Burns), his Afghan colleague Mohan Lal Kashmiri, and the Russian/Pole, Ivan Vitkevitch or Jan Prosper Wietkiwicz. These three spies were the central players in the opening gambit of the Great Game of espionage and geo-strategic rivalry in Central Asia between Russia and Britain. All their lives ended tragically, perhaps none more so than Wietkiwicz. He had been exiled and sentenced to death at the age of 14 for opposing Russian rule of his native Poland. His death sentence was commuted and he made a life as an extraordinary military officer, linguist and early intelligence officer in the Russian army, which he had resented as an adolescent. He outwitted the British, and achieved Russia's initial objectives of securing an alliance with the Barakzai clain, but then was withdrawn when Russia made a diplomatic pivot. He died suspiciously in St Petersburg in an apparent suicide on the eve of being honoured by his Tsar. Some historians, including Dalrymple, credit a plausible hypothesis that he was assassinated by British agents.

These men's lives were consumed and destroyed by rulers and decision-makers full of delusions and misjudgments. The mystery at the heart of the book is the incompetence of power. Why did the least able generals, diplomats and rulers control the command boxes, while the able ones were shunned, ignored, overlooked and slighted? The greatest tragedy that flowed from that incompetence was the invasion of Afghanistan, ordered by the remote and inattentive governor, Lord Auckland, executed with ferocious stupidity by Major-General William Elphinstone, and overseen politically by the pompously self-certain, deluded Sir William Hay McNaghten.

The invasion began with a disastrous unprotected march through the Bolan Pass, where the British army, principally made up of Indian sepoys and camp followers, was attacked by snipers from the high cliffs, and lost most of its supplies. Still, they made it through and were surprised by the withdrawal from Kabul of the Afghan rulers. The British took it over and engaged in outrageous looting and destruction of some of the commercial centres of Kabul. They reinstalled Shah Shuja as a puppet ruler, and settled in for a year or more of British proxy rule. That rule was characterised by arrogant errors and contempt for the local population, and even for the nominal sovereign, Shah Shuja himself. McNaghten was the real ruler of Afghanistan, and he inspired an Islamic uprising against mistreatment and foreign infidel rule.

Dost Mohammed had withdrawn strategically to gather his strength. By 1841 he marched his armies and coordinated a network of urban insurrection. The British were trapped in Kabul, and overrun by this urban insurrection. Alexander Burnes – a figure of hate in Afghanistan for his espionage and his private harem of Afghan women – was murdered. Dost Mohammed outsmarted the vain British rulers. He offered them safe passage out of Kabul. In reality, he continued to harry and to attack the retreating army, shepherding it into ambush after ambush, while claiming these attacks were made by uncontrollable rival tribes. Almost the whole retreating army and its camp followers died or were captured and sold into slavery in the most terrible scenes. Starving, frostbitten husks lined the mountain passes to Peshawar. Ultimately, a single man – the British surgeon who survived misadventures through luck, more than heroism – rode alone and exhausted into the last British stronghold of Jalalabad. This is the scene depicted in the melodramatic painting by Elizabeth Butler, *Remnants of an Army* (1879).

Shah Shuja had earlier been attacked on his march out of Kabul by a band of vengeful Afghani warlords who he had alienated and offended. His palanquin was found and attacked. The last Shah of the Durrani empire, the last Timurid ruler of Khurasan, was shot and left to rot in the barren sands outside Kabul. The British had done much to ruin Afghanistan. It would no longer be a commercial cross-roads of Central Asia. Still, Dost Mohammed ruled successfully for another twenty years, increasing the revenues and security of his country. He would become a national hero, but, for a ruined nation, an imperial "war for no wise purpose" had wrecked so many lives.

In another of Dalrymple's histories of Mughal India, he writes:

> Public, political and national tragedies, after all, consist of a multitude of private, domestic and individual tragedies. It is through the human stories of the successes, struggles, grief, anguish and despair of these individuals that we can best bridge the great chasm of time and understanding separating us from the remarkably different world of mid-nineteenth century India.[76]

The *Return of a King* is a masterpiece in bridging that chasm through the interweaving of exceptional individual stories with profound public tragedies, and the presentation together of uncanny contemporary parallels with all the strangeness of a lost but recoverable world.

Cultural Collapse, Delhi 1857

4 February 2018

This whole city has become a desert. (Ghalib, 1861)

William Dalrymple's *The Last Mughal: the Fall of a Dynasty, Delhi 1857* is a great tragedy, and its fallen hero is the culture of the Mughal court.

Under Emperor Bahadur Shah Zafar II (1775-1862), the Mughal court and Delhi society experienced a cultural renaissance of sorts. Zafar, the last Mughal, presided over a liberal regime that practised

---
[76] *The Last Mughal: the Fall of a Dynasty, Delhi, 1857* (2006) p. 13.

toleration between Hindu and Muslim, the equal parts of Delhi society, and Zafar himself regularly visited Sufi shrines, and was even known as a Sufi *pir*. He practised forms of Sufi mysticism and eschewed a growing Wahhabi fundamentalism that began to spread from Medina to Delhi through the nineteenth century. He also himself wrote poetry, and sponsored *mushairas* (poetic symposiums) as among the most important and celebrated cultural events of Delhi.

Dalrymple quotes from a fictionalised account of one of the mushairas – *Delhi ki akhri shama, The Last Musha'irah of Delhi* by Farhattullah Baig. It told how the poets of Delhi would seek to outdo each other with the wit, cleverness and beauty of their ghazals and other forms. In a brightly lit room the poets and audience sat, ate sweets and smoked from their huqqas, until the Shah's herald entered the room to read the ghazal from which they would improvise their variations.

At Zafar's court there were two great poets who competed for renown and the favour of the Shah: Ghalib (Mirza Asadullah Khan), and Zauq (Sheikh Muhammad Ibrahim Zauq). The two poets were a contrast in lives and style. Ghalib was more formalistic, and more prone to drink, gambling and love affairs. Zauq used simpler diction and forms, and perhaps for this reason appealed more to his Sufi master, Zafar. Zauq was appointed the chief poet of the Mughal court at a young age, and was the poetry master to the Last Mughal. But Ghalib was loved as a poet of less austere lives. It was, however, only at Zauq's death in 1854 that Ghalib achieved the prime position as the poet of the Mughal court.

However, by that time rising Muslim fundamentalism and Christian evangelism threatened the *mushairas* of the Mughal court. By 1857, the cataclysm of the Mutiny and the Siege of Delhi would destroy this cultural heritage. The British, pursuing divine vengeance for their humiliation, pursued a policy of cultural extermination: mass murder, rape, destruction of buildings and shrines, looting. They sought to raze Delhi to the ground, perhaps in some reliving of Carthage from their schoolboy history lessons.

Amidst the victims of the looting were Zauq and Ghalib's poetry. Much of their poetry was lost or destroyed by the British. But one poet and critic, Muhammad Husain Azad, survived, fled the troops, and managed to rescue some of Zauq's ghazals. In the evening of 17 September, while sheltering in his house with his whole extended family. He recalled,

> The soldiers of the victorious army suddenly entered the house. They flourished their rifles and shouted: Leave here at once!' The world turned black before my eyes. A whole houseful of goods was before me and I stood petrified: What shall I take with me?' All the jewels and jewellery were locked in a box and were thrown into a well. But my eye fell on the packet of [Zauq's] Ghazals.[77]

Zauq's *Ghazals* were being prepared for a critical edition for publication after Zauq's death in 1854. Muhammad Husain then chose to save the Ghazals, the most precious object in that collapsing city.

> While these exist Zauq lives even after his death; if these are lost his name cannot survive either. So I picked up the packet and tucked it under my arm. Abandoning a well-furnished home, with twenty-two half dead souls I left the house – or rather the city. And the words fell from my lips, 'Hazrat Adam left paradise; and Delhi is paradise too. But if I am Adam's descendant – why shouldn't I leave paradise just as he did.

Much of Ghalib's poetry was lost and destroyed by the British in their looting of Delhi in 1857. He had kept no copies of his verse, and two private libraries where his friends stored his poems were ransacked. But unlike Zauq, Ghalib lived through the Siege of Delhi and witnessed the collapse of the culture he loved so dearly. In a letter to a friend he described how:

> A few days ago a faqir who has a good voice and sings well discovered a ghazal of mine somewhere and got it written down. When he showed it to me, I tell you truly, tears came to my eyes.[78]

---

[77] Dalrymple, *The Last Mughal*, pp. 374-5.
[78] Dalyrmple, *The Last Mughal*, p. 463.

Ghalib would survive another 12 years in the ruined city, in this destroyed cultural paradise. He was one of an estimated one thousand only surviving Muslims. He saw the princes reduced to begging, and the women of the court, after mass rapes by the British, forced into prostitution. He could find no booksellers, no binders, no calligraphers and no poets in the this once vibrant city of learning and culture. His city had become a desert, stripped of its living heritage of language, the Fort, the bazaars and the watercourses.

Ghalib's sadness was deep and memorably expressed. He wrote, "A man cannot quench his thirst with tears". And again:

> You know that when despair reaches its lowest depths, there is nothing left but to resign oneself to God's will. What lower depths can there be than this: that it is the hope of death that keeps me alive?[79]

And finally: "My soul dwells in my body these days as restless as a bird in cage." I am yet to read much of Zauq and Ghalib's poetry, and there is a great gulf between Urdu and English in poetic translation. Yet Ghalib's sadness at his devastated culture and Zauq's miraculous survival from the looters of the British Raj, make them part of the heritage of the *Burning Archive*.

On the history and meaning of the eight hour day

13 May 2018

Today, something a little different. I have been looking over my old digital writing files: fragments, half-done essays, pain-ridden diaries and so on. This lifelong testimony reminded me of the difficulty

---

[79] Dalrymple, *The Last Mughal*, p. 464.

Jeff Rich

I have experienced in becoming the writer who I am.

But amongst all that pain has been some achievement, even if there has been little recognition of those works.

So today I thought I would post the article published from my doctoral thesis on the history of the building industry in nineteenth century Victoria, and the culture that emerged celebrating the eight hour day.[80]

I wrote this article by editing one of the chapters from my PhD thesis, about 14 years after completing the thesis. By that time I had abandoned dreams of working as an academic historian, and was working in the public service. I had passed up the opportunity to rewrite my PhD as a book, despite a half offer from Cambridge University Press. I had no connections and no network of support to make my way in that world, and was struggling to make my way in a new career in government, despite the constant doubts about my purpose and suspicions that I would never belong in this culture. Then, fourteen years later, I got wind of plans to commemorate the 150th anniversary of the eight hour day, in part sponsored by the Victorian Government. I wrote an email to Terry Moran, who was then head of the Victorian Department of Premier and Cabinet, to suggest I could play some role in the celebrations, but I was ignored. But I made contact with the conference organisers, and suggested I give a paper from my thesis.

Editing the chapter of the thesis had its challenges. I had lost touch with the academic world, and felt no affiliation with the clapped out Marxist culture of the Society of Labour History. I no longer inhabited the mental universe, that conceived the thesis, when I combined ideas from Foucault, which saw class as a form of the truth/power, and emotional impulses, inherited from E.P. Thompson, to save these unionists from the condescension of posterity. I also soon found that my digital files of my thesis, written in WordPerfect (does anyone remember that word processing program, with its blue screen and

---

[80] Julie Kimber, Peter Love, *The time of their lives: the eight hour day and working life* (Australian Society for the Study of Labour History, Melbourne, 2007).

flashing cursor?) were corrupt and unreadable after so many years. So, I scanned the pages of my thesis using an OCR photocopier, and slowly corrected all the formatting mistakes and errors transcribing words and footnotes.

I gave the paper at the conference at the University of Melbourne in June 2006. I spoke to a full lecture hall – one of the few occasions when I have performed in this way. I remember I stayed briefly after giving my talk, felt out of place, and returned to work in the afternoon.

The story I told in this article still has resonance for me. It was a story about how, even in the apparently material conditions that defined work and industrial conflict, the meaning of events were inseparable from the striving for recognition and the webs of significance that we, culture-making beings, weave through the time of our lives.

The Slow Death of My History
7 October 2018

Over the last couple of months I have been reading history. Simon Sebag Montefiore, *The Romanovs: 1613-1918*, Orlando Figes, *A People's Tragedy: the Russian Revolution 1891-1924*, and Ian Kershaw, *Rollercoaster: Europe 1950-2017*.

All of this reading has been valuable and fascinating to me. The intricate catastrophes of the Romanov dynasty, the myriad tragedies of the Russian revolutions, and the institutional complexity of the formation of modern Europe. I have stored in a gallery in my mind a thousand portraits of remarkable individuals, twisting events, peculiar psychologies and extravagant cultural expressions.

I suppose this might mean that history for me is the habit of a collector. I store away in my mind a cabinet of curiosities. In the privacy of my study, I open up this cabinet, and have an infinite conversation with my imaginary friends, strangers and enemies. This conversation is precious to me, but how does it help me to act in the world?

I see fewer and fewer companions in the world for this journey into the underworld of our times. History as an academic discipline is in steep decline. Enrollments are falling. Publications are dull. The ideas of the discipline have suffered the strangling of post-modernism and the new tribes of bullying thought. It has turned on itself, and alienated its own practitioners and students. My own attempt to reconnect to this discipline late in my career has been spurned. When I look over the bookshelves carrying my own country's history I am astonished by their poverty: military history, populist history like *Girt*, and a reliance for serious history on the greats of the 1950's to 1970's, such as Manning Clark and Geoffrey Blainey.

And the people I encounter in the bureaucracy are astonishingly ignorant of history. Worse: they have a narcissistic belief that history is an irrelevance in these times of constant change. History in the eyes of the radical manager is a redundant encumbrance, a stuffy pedantry that can be ignored in pushing out the messages of the day. And so they march aimlessly into traps, proclaiming themselves inanely the first, the best, the largest, the fastest ever. They march cruelly to the horizon, blinded by the disappearing sun, while their *grand armée* dies in the deep winter of human frailty.

I long to find other custodians of the sacred past, who believe with Faulkner that the past is not dead; that it is not even past. But where in our decaying culture, do I find companions in the dreaming of ruins?

One place is the words of Felipe Fernández-Armesto. Asked about conservatism in the "Age of Trump", he says let us think a little more about *longue durée*. After all, Trump, like all American Presidents, is a "blip." These words resonated with me after a visit to the bookshop where the shelves were full of books about Trump, and the extraordinary conflation of American domestic politics with the fate of the democratic world.

And another is the cultural adventure – the new ways through the ruins – pioneered by Jordan Peterson. The institutions that have carried history for so long – especially the university – are slowly dying. The last druids of the past might make their way to the sacred grove again, and there through affectionate curiosity for the lives of the dead, re-imagine a true life of the mind.

A year of history: reflections on 2018
16 December 2018

Looking over my posts for the year I am struck by the recurrence of history in my material. I have read more history than literature this year – although, of course, I believe that history is one branch of literature. A quick recap of my year's reading, before some reflections on what all this history means. I read:
- Richard Fidler, *Ghost Empire* about Byzantium and his own discovery of the remnants of this forgotten empire in our lives
- William Dalrymple, *The Return of a King: the battle for Afghanistan* about the first Anglo-Afghanistan war and the sheer folly and bastardry of British colonial rule
- William Dalrymple, *The Last Mughal: the fall of a dynasty.. Delhi 1957* about the ruin of a tainted but marvellous literary culture and the "Indian Mutiny"
- my own writings on the history of the eight hour day
- Kay Redfield Jamison's biography of Robert Lowell
- Andrew Scull, *Madness in Civilisation*
- Taylor Downing, *1983: the world at the brink*

- Christopher Hibbert, *The Borgias and their enemies*
- parts of Burckhardt, *The Civilisation of Renaissance Italy*
- parts of Machiavelli, *The Prince* and *The Discourses on the History of Livy*
- the end of Weber, *The Protestant Ethic and the Spirit of Capitalism*
- samples of Oswald Spengler's *The Decline of the West*
- Orlando Figes, *A People's Tragedy: the Russian Revolution 1891-1924*
- Simon Sebag Montefiore, *The Romanovs: 1613-1918*, which was truly marvellous
- Stephen Platt, *Imperial Twilight: the Opium War and the end of China's last golden age*, and
- I began Ian Kershaw, *Roller-coaster: Europe 1950-2017*.

I also watched television dramas, documentaries and movies, some fictional but glorying in the recreation of past worlds, and not all of which I can recall:

- *The Plague* set in Seville in the 1590s
- *The Medici: Masters of Florence*, about Cosimo de Medici
- The latest version of *War and Peace* by the BBC
- *The Alienist*, portraying an early forensic psychologist or psychiatrist in 1890's New York, and
- *Civilisations* with Simon Schama and Mary Beard.

It has been a history feast this year. I am not sure I have read a single fictional novel, although I have enjoyed fictional television dramas. No, I recall now I did read Proust's *Time Regained*; but that is it for fiction, and that great artwork is somehow almost in a different plane than mundane storytelling. I read a tiny bit of Gerald Murnane, *A history of books*, and Blanchot, *The madness of the day*, again not the usual fiction. I tried reading a couple of H.P. Lovecraft's stories but did not get through more than one or so of the shorter stories.

It is as if I am not willing to take the fictional bargain, the willing suspension of disbelief, and take on the reader's burden, the making together with this text of an imagined world. By contrast, I willingly project myself into past real worlds through empathy, attention and invented dialogue with the figures of the past.

I want to believe that one day I might return to enjoying fiction. I heard Bernard Cornwell, the historical novelist, say that the fascination of reading a novel is to find out what will happen in the end. I remember that feeling, and spending hours immersed in Trollope, Dostoyevsky and many other books. But maybe the fascination of history, that spreads into great literature for which the stories are known and established, is not what will happen in the end, but how and why will they get there, and what twists and turns will there be on the way. And truth is stranger than fiction, and the minds of many that you hear in any well-crafted history are always richer than the single writer's voice of any fiction. The invented is of less interest to me than the discovered. The documented is more compelling than the dramatised.

History, or good history, has a power of insight into the dilemmas of our times that cannot be found in the private micro-troubles of some fictional character, who so often these days is a caricature of identity – or so I suspect, since I read too little contemporary fiction to know. History helps me to orient myself in the world, and to place my own dramas and the melodramas of our republics in distress against a greater story and a more vivid canvass. History teaches the virtue of patience, and the lesson that this too will pass. It teaches that empires fall and rise, and in the spaces of their negligence the life of the mind can flourish and leave an unanticipated legacy. History teaches that culture is an unruly garden, and the schemes of the great to protect their status after death rarely succeed. The worms and the termites of the world eat away at the registers of wealth; the wind and the sand of the desert overtake every fortress of magnificence; memory and the meaning of the past spread like bizarre underground rhizomes in directions no gardener can plan. So Shelley wrote in *Ozymandias*:

> Look on my Works, ye Mighty, and despair!
> Nothing beside remains. Round the decay
> Of that colossal Wreck, boundless and bare
> The lone and level sands stretch far away.

Jeff Rich

Berlin, *Vergangenheitsbewältigung* and finding freedom in the past
19 June 2019

After Prague, we traveled by train to Berlin. There were no preeminent icons of literature – at least fiction and poetry – who I intended to discover or rediscover on this trip to the German capital. It is not because figures from German literature have not been participants in my infinite conversation over the years. I think of Thomas Mann, *Death in Venice, Buddenbrooks* and *The Magic Mountain,* for example, or a more displaced figure like W.G. Sebald. I have sampled but not really gone into the depths of figures like Hölderlin, Goethe, and Brecht. But many of the most influential cultural figures from Berlin or more broadly German culture for me have been in the broader field of history, philosophy and social science: Walter Benjamin, Max Weber, and the great German historical tradition, especially associated with *verstehen*.

So, it was fitting in Berlin I spent less standing in the crypts of great writers, and more time experiencing contemporary Germany's treatment of its history, or, to qualify, Berlin's presentation to its visitors of how it is working through the traumatic past of National Socialism, the Holocaust, the separation of Berlin and the communist authoritarianism of East Germany. Throughout the city, there are markers and monuments, often poetic and powerful, of these times of troubles. In Bebelplatz, in front of Humboldt University, there is an empty underground stained white library representing the site of the burning of books by the Nazis. There are the great voids of the Holocaust Museum, and the deeply affecting shadow city of grey stylae in the Holocaust monument. There is the Topography of Terror museum, which places a strip of explanatory boards over the site of the Gestapo headquarters and remnant of the Berlin wall. There are monuments to victims of the mass killings of the Nazis: homosexuals,

Roma and Cini, and, most important to me of this group, the victims of euthanasia – disabled and mentally ill. Wherever you go in the city, you can find markers, stones, boards, statues and buildings that reflect upon German crimes of twentieth-century history.

The central idea through these monuments, markers and public interpretations is *Vergangenheitsbewältigung*, which is translated as "struggle to overcome the [negatives of the] past" or "working through the past". Germany is rightly commended for the sophistication and openness of its approach to dealing with the moral legacy of its dark twentieth century. It is contrasted to the approach to history in China, or Russia or China, or heavens forbid – America. It has influenced truth and reconciliation commissions throughout the world.

But it is not without its controversies and weaknesses. Theodore Adorno criticised the idea as a mask for false contrition and inattention to fundamental inequalities in social conditions, which were in his blinkered Frankfurt School view, the true cause of fascism. There have been major controversies over whether there is a unique German war guilt, and debates over the inclusion of various groups in the monuments of victims. I know only a little of these debates, but did leave Berlin with the impression that, at least, the tourist experience of German history is trapped within narrow lanes of working through the past – the Nazis and the Berlin Wall.

Please don't misunderstand me. No-one should forget or minimise these experiences. But I wondered if a trite tourist trope has trapped the greater depth and complexity of German culture and history. I stood on Bebelplatz and heard the stories from our guide about culture-hating book-burning Nazis, but I heard no-one comment that here we were standing in front of the university named after Alexander Humboldt, no reference to George Steiner's observation that the intellectuals and universities were part of the crimes of the Nazis (Heidegger burnt no books), and no reference to the book-burning of our times, the de-platforming and social media flaming of the identity radicals. George Steiner had a more acute feeling of this co-habitation of cruelty and culture. As he wrote in *Language and*

Silence,

> We come after. We know now that a man can read Goethe or Rilke in the evening, that he can play Bach and Schubert, and go to his day's work at Auschwitz in the morning. To say that he has read them without understanding or that his ear is gross, is cant. In what way does this knowledge bear on literature and society, on the hope, grown almost axiomatic from the time of Plato to that of Matthew Arnold, that culture is a humanizing force, that the energies of spirit are transferable to those of conduct?[81]

In another way, Checkpoint Charlie and Eastside Gallery struck me as trite renditions of history. It surprised me that more was not made of how Berlin has moved on culturally since 1989, and created its own culture and its own kind of freedom. Overall, there is so much to German history, literature and culture beyond the events of 1932 to 1989, I wondered why we cannot view this city and this country through a different lens. As Steiner wrote,

> It is not the literal past that rules us, save, possibly, in a biological sense. It is images of the past. These are often as highly structured and selective as myths. Images and symbolic constructs of the past are imprinted, almost in the manner of genetic information, on our sensibility. Each new historical era mirrors itself in the picture and active mythology of its past.[82]

---

[81] George Steiner, *Language and Silence* (1967).
[82] George Steiner, *In Bluebeard's Castle* (1971).

My Descriptions of the Northern Peoples
4 August 2019

I am returning today to my notes on my travels, and piecing together the literary and cultural associations prompted by my travels through Stockholm and Uppsala in June.

I began to say that I knew little Swedish or Scandinavian writing or culture as I entered the country, but that was not really true. As we took the train from Copenhagen to Stockholm we, of course, went over the Øresund Bridge, that beautiful vaulting arc which haunts the classic of Nordic Noir, *Bron/Broen/The Bridge*. I had just left Copenhagen and wondered why there were not Nordic Noir tours of this city, which surely would offer a more vital encounter with the contemporary culture than the tired photographs of the mermaid gifted by a philanthropic American. The uncanniness of ordinarily atypical people's struggles with life and crime and duty, and the tragedies hidden in simple affluent modern life – these seemed to be the great themes of Nordic Noir. This gift is perhaps a revival of the Scandinavian dramatic tradition of Strindberg and Ibsen.

And as I look around my study now that I have returned I see fragments of incomplete encounters with Scandinavian literature. I have some poems of Tomas Tranströmer, which I have admired from afar for their privacy, their intermingling of mind and nature. He was criticised, I read, in the 1970's by the then socially radical for being detached from his age, and not making the mandatory social criticisms in his poetry. But surely this is the stance of any enduring poet, even if none of us can know whether our detachment from the age is a step into the infinite conversation or a way to walk your writing life in shadowed oblivion.

Of course, I read Ibsen and Strindberg in my 20's, but the content of those dramas is long gone, except perhaps the breaking apart of social roles, especially those of men and women. And there is a big book which I have started but never got very far into, by the early twentieth-century Norwegian author, Sigrid Undset, *Kristin Lavransdatter*, which portrays, the blurb says, the clash between feudal violence and Christian piety. I also have the great Finnish folk epic, the *Kalevala*, which I have read maybe one-third of.

Even my knowledge of Swedish history was poor and fragmentary. There were a few cameo appearances in my knowledge of other topics: a Swedish invasion of Russia and Northern Europe in the seventeenth century; the attempt to convert the royal family to Catholicism by the sixteenth century Jesuit Papal Nuncio, Antonio Possevino; a noble husband or two with walk-on parts during the French revolution, connected to the great Madame de Staël; the Scandinavian tradition of liquor control through government-controlled shops, that has not transported so well to other cultures; the Social Democrats and the welfare state in the twentieth century; Michel Foucault's brief and tainted sojourn in the great university town of Uppsala; the assassination of Olof Palme; and of course, the Viking and Norse heritage.

But none of it cohered into a story that could walk in my dreams. On our trip to Stockholm, however, we did visit the wonderful Swedish History Museum – Historiska Museet, which features an inspired exhibition with a meandering timeline footpath that takes you through the story of Sweden from the 11th century until today. Of the museums we visited in Europe, the Swedish museums dealt best with the role of women in history. It was through this timeline walk that I learned about the remarkable Queen Margareta of the Kalmar Union (Sweden, Norway and Denmark) in the late 14th century, and the enigmatic Saint Bridget or Birgitta, who I had earlier been introduced to at Roskilde Cathedral. I would recommend this museum to any visitors to Stockholm.

For a bit of fun, you can also use the website of the Swedish History Museum to take a quiz to work out the closest match between your personality and a figure from Norse mythology. When I took the quiz, just now, it reported me as being Heimdall.

Somewhere in that story told at the Swedish History Museum in Stockholm was the great book that I had read about in Felipe Fernández-Armesto's *Civilisations*, but have not read myself, Olaus Magnus, *Description of the Northern Peoples*. This book is, in Fernández-Armesto's judgment, "one of the world's great unacknowledged works of genius", which revelled in the difference, diversity, magic and marvels of the great icy El Dorado this exile set down. Olaus was the titular Archbishop of Uppsala, a Catholic exile in a Lutheran state in the terrible mid-16th century. And it was in the University Library at Uppsala, which we were being shown around during our visit by our son who was on exchange there, that I saw an old edition of the great book on display in a glass case at the entrance to the library.

It was also in this library at Uppsala that Michel Foucault studied for his doctorate that would later become the grand poetic misrepresentation of *The History of Madness*. It was here in Uppsala that Foucault taught French with complete disregard for his students, partied like the privileged brat he was, driving his white jaguar around the small regional town, and submitted his doctoral manuscript to the Swedish scholar, Sten Lindroth. Professor Lindroth was unimpressed, and his judgment on the poor scholarship and history of the young Foucault was, in retrospect, correct. Yet here I stood in the very library hall where was born this strange poetical work that inspired me to read every word of Foucault, and pursue the strange intellectual ambitions of my early life. This was a pilgrimage to the relics of a fallen saint.

Also in Uppsala we happened upon the museum dedicated to the great Swedish botanist, Carl Linnaeus, one person from Sweden who has had truly global impact. This museum contains Linnaeus' old house, his specimen garden and his collections. It sits on one of the main town streets in Uppsala, which also is the seat of the great old Uppsala Cathedral, spiritual home of the Swedish Church, built to replace the old pagan temple of Gamla Uppsala. The garden features plants of every continent of the world, except, of course, from the continent we had travelled from, Australia, which was not known to world botany at this time. Linnaeus, who gave the world its system for the scientific classification of plants, corresponded with botanists across the world, including Joseph Banks after whom are named the banksias in my front garden, which are flowering today as I look out my study window. On the upper floor of the Linnaeus House is a cabinet containing some of the anthropological curiosities collected by Linnaeus. He followed in the footsteps of the exiled Archbishop of Uppsala, Olaus Magnus, in travelling and recording the lives of the people of the North. There in his cabinet are his own notes of his journeys to Lapland, and some of the gifts he received, or he acquired (we can never really know which), from the Sami people: an old boot and a shaman's drum, one of only fifty or so remaining. As Fernández-Armesto tells us,

> The magic of shamans, which harnessed the power of the souls of things and summoned the dead in the service of the living, was communicated by drumbeat, until the late seventeenth or eighteenth century, when Christian evangelism stamped it out. Indeed, the drum was regarded, in some communities, as the shaman's reindeer, on which he rode to the spirit world. Only a few of the great magic drums which accompanied the Sami bear-hunters still survive. Like the books of the Maya, they perished in scores or hundreds at the hands of missionaries. The art of reading their pictographic inscriptions has been lost but that should not be taken to mean that the red figures, traced in alder-bark juice on the reindeer-hide drumskins, did not once recall stories or spells for their shamanic interpreters, or, according to plausible modern attempts at decipherment, display cosmic diagrams or maps of the heavens.[83]

And so, in this unanticipated room in Uppsala, I came across my own fragmentary thoughts on the shaman's drum and the disappearance of stories from the world. And, of course, I realise now that my mind is drenched in the night journeys of the shaman and the stories of Scandinavian literature, that we know as Norse mythology. My daughter is named Freya. I wear a Thor's hammer around my

---

[83] *Civilizations*, p. 47.

neck. I play games full of retold stories of Yggdrassil and the three worlds that surround it. And on my shelves are the Poetic and Prose Eddas, which, through the words of the great *skalds*, like Iceland's Snorri Sturluson, and through the care and discipline of the unfashionable monks and scholars who preserved these stories for centuries in the *Codex Regius,* protected these stories from disappearing from the world or being lost in the snowstorms of the Arctic North.

# Part Six

Social Fragmentation

Life Cycles
20 October 2015

Our culture may lie in ruins; our republics may be distressed; our economies blackjacked by rentier financiers; our societies fissured with conflicts of identity; but at least our lives are longer.

This great achievement of medicine and social development, in harness with its twin, the fertility revolution, has changed the potential of human lives. In Japan today nearly one-third of the population is over 65. Many other countries will see similar shares over the next fifty years. This new demography changes not only societies and cultures. It changes the biological experience of life cycles and populations. There has never before been a human population with these biological and cultural characteristics before. Most people in high and middle income countries can reliably live past sixty in social institutions that provide imperfect but secure and healthy retirement. The life cycle then has more than seven seasons, and a long and blessed Autumn in which great navies of the soul may sail. The holy city of Byzantium is becoming the busiest port of the world.

Time may change me, but I can't change time
19 May 2016

In *How to be a Conservative,* Roger Scruton writes:

> Whatever our religion and our private convictions, we are the collective inheritors of things both excellent and rare, and political life, for us, ought to have one overriding goal, which is

to hold fast to those things, in order to pass them on to our children.

Here Scruton states a fair and elegant summation of a true conservative view, which increasingly I hold dear despite all the social pressure to move with the times. In the task of governing, which Oakeshott compared to steering a ship across a shoreless ocean, this guide is more reliable than any substantial aim, any goal of an enterprise, and any hollow rhetoric about change.

Change is the moral imperative of the consultocratic courtier. It is the restless impatience to make a difference, and then to move onto the next lucrative contract, that is entombing real life in so-called 'system reforms'. Change is touted to conceal the empty slogans, the ignorance of even the quite recent past, and the hustling, bullying promotion of fellow courtiers. Speeches are ornamented, after a search of a quote book, with Benjamin Franklin's "when you are finished changing, then you are finished!" And this piece of all-American bunkum is really meant as a threat. In the same way, Malcolm Turnbull's evocation of the Pentecost in an Armani suit – "there has never been a more exciting time to be alive" – is an advertisement of profound neglect of the human heritage, wrapped in recycled McKinsey powerpoints, and concealing the true, insolent, ceaseless threat to redesign free and responsible lives into agile agitprop. But the snake-charmer's tune of change mesmerises the courtiers so they do not ask the key question: if the only constant is change, will these changes you call for last beyond next summer?

It is all a far cry from the deeper argument about change set out in Felipe Fernández-Armesto's *A foot in the river: why our lives change and the limits of evolution*. Humans, Fernández-Armesto explains with vivacity and wit, are cultural animals; not by any means the only cultural animals, but surely the most splendidly and chaotically various in our ever-shifting cultures. Our faculties of imperfect memory and exceptional anticipation give us gifts greater than hunting in packs, or farming, or the modern curse of the project plan. They give us imagination; and when imagination sets to work on human culture it creates, fissures, imitates, errs, develops: it makes lives change. Driving all this cultural change is a reworking of Girard's theory of mimetic desire and the simple observation that the more opportunities for exchange of errant, new and traditional ideas, the more cultures change. So in today's circumstances of exceptional ease of exchanging ideas, good and bad, there has never been a sustained time of more rapid cultural change.

But unlike the consultocrat courtiers, Fernández-Armesto does not mistake all change for good. Some changes bring blessings; some birth rare and excellent things. But some change brings burdens, losses and a dark tide of sorrow. Change brings excitement, and it brings deep unsettling threats to loved lives and cherished institutions. The quickened pace and chaotic form of change in our times stands opposed to most of human experience, and perhaps frays the edges of our evolved brains and instinctual hearts. So *A Foot in the River* helps us move beyond the cheap tricks of the courtiers and the civic religion of the leadership class.

The excitement of innovation is but one emotion evoked by this annual collapse of the Tower of Babel. Fernández-Armesto writes,

> Within living memory the world seems to have transformed over and over again, inducing 'future shock', fear, bewilderment, and resentment. Meanwhile the increasing urgency of the accelerations of change and the ever more disturbing effects on people's sense of security, well-being, and confidence in the future have glared through the headlines.[84]

Within each of us, there is a restless search for some new kind of kick, but it fights an instinct in favour of the familiar.

> When people feel the threat of change, they reach for security, like a child clenching its grip on a comforter. When they do not understand what is happening to them, they panic. *Grandes peurs* lash society like a flagellant's scourge. Intellectuals take refuge in 'postmodern' strategies: indifference, *anomie*, moral

---

[84] Fernández-Armesto, *A foot in the river: why our lives change and the limits of evolution* (2015).

relativism, scientific indeterminacy, fluid identities, and the embrace of chaos. *Je m'enfoutisme*.[85]

In this more subtle view, being done with change is never finished with; but more like the moon following the sun. These words from a true sage are not a counsel of despair, nor a retreat to the mysterious, as in Heraclitus' runic phrase, 'all things change'. Fernández-Armesto's book helps us to understand change, but does not urge us to stop fearing it, In characteristically wise words, he says that, there are indeed plenty of reasons to fear change. We ought to respond intelligently to all the emotions evoked by change, and do so with the faculty that is the source of change itself, our imagination.

So this history of change shows how time changes me, but I can't change time. Fernández-Armesto might guide those of us who want to govern our communities in ways that preserve those 'rare and excellent things' in our culture, which are cherished by those with affection for civic life, but despised by reformers, change managers and courtiers. Those excellent things can be easily destroyed in a day or a single *diktat*. They are worth fighting to preserve against the depredations of folly and the callow champions of change. Long ago, Heraclitus spoke of them: "People dull their wits with gibberish, and cannot use their ears and eyes".

Is Nothing Sacred?
15 July 2016

One of the surprises of my mid-life has been the admission of a longing for the sacred. In the 1980's, I remember, there was a band,

---

[85] Fernández-Armesto, *A foot in the river*, p. 198.

called 'The Sacred Cowboys', who sang a post-punk dirge, "Is nothing sacred?" The song got under my skin in a way, and it seemed to my youthful mind more of a frenetic statement of the absurd, a rhapsody of disillusion, proud disillusionment, pounded into the ground with thrashing guitars and drug-wild drums beating out any last cinders of hope for transcendence. When I remember the song now, I hear the lament in its rough chorus.

The cowboys buried the sacred all those years ago, but I exhumed its body when I read Jonathan Haidt's book on moral judgment, *The Righteous Mind*. Psychological research has shown that a sense of the sacred is one of the foundations of moral instincts. Haidt calls it the sanctity foundation. It drives emotions of disgust, and has its origins in evolutionary protection from dirt, pathogens and excrement. More so than an aversion to the awful, this foundation supports the beautiful and the common. The psychology of sacredness bind individuals to communities. "When someone in a moral community desecrates one of the sacred pillars supporting the community," Haidt writes "the reaction is sure to be swift, emotional, collective and punitive".[86] A world with no sacred objects is a strange, anomic and difficult world to live in. Is nothing sacred, indeed?

When I read Haidt's book I was surprised to learn, on doing one of his tests, that I scored more highly than the norm on the sanctity foundation. I discovered perhaps some statistical support for my breezy self-description—that I was socially liberal, but culturally conservative. This sense of the sacred was always there, but I had hidden it beneath a dedicated secularism. After all, I was the child of atheists. Before the age of 40, I had only entered a church once or twice in my life. I inherited no tradition of the sacred, but through education and reading I did acquire a rich cultural repertoire – the burning archive of the infinite conversation. Until I read Haidt's book, I confused this lack of a religious tradition with the irrelevance of the sacred. In truth, all my striving to be part of the infinite conversation was a search to commune with holiness.

---

[86] Haidt, *The Righteous Mind* (2012), p. 178.

At the same time, this misunderstanding of the sacred and the role of religion in human lives meant that the full significance of the twentieth century critique of the Death of God and the Death of Man did not really register with me. I remember once a history professor sought to engage me in discussion of one of the essential questions – does God exist? Who cares, I thought. It doesn't matter.

But now I see a more tragic quest for sanctity in our modern lives. Not only is God dead, but perhaps culture is dead too? What is the place of the sacred after the death of the gods and amid the ruins of a decaying culture? Roger Scruton raises this in a discussion of Wagner's ring cycle:

> That is why *The Ring Cycle* is of ever-increasing importance to music-lovers in our times. Its theme is the death of the gods, and what the gods have bequeathed to us, namely, the knowledge of, and longing for, the sacred. Until we recognise sacred moments, Wagner implies in this monumental work, we cannot live fully as free beings. These moments are the foundation of all our attempts to endow human life with significance.[87]

This tragic search for the sacred leaves some of us hanging like Odin from a tree to gain the power of runes. For me especially, culture is the domain of sacred. Some interpreters of suspicion might see my wish for the sacred as a sublimated longing for love, and I cannot say with certainty that it is not a long alienated belief in belonging to a lost tribe that sits at the base of all my yearning for culture. This wish takes others to mysticism and cults, and for some the practice of violence and power is limned with a sacred urging. That very strange book by Roberto Calasso, *The Ruin of Kasch*, is an extended meditation on how the modern world forgot that sacrifice and the sacred lies at the base of all authority, while overthrowing traditional authority with cultish violence. But I pursue a more peaceful path: to care for the monuments of unageing intellect.

---

[87] Scruton, "Richard Wagner and the Valhalla state of mind", *Prospect Magazine* (June 2016)

Poetry: to redeem or to love the world?

22 September 2016

Featured on aldaily.com today is an article from *The Atlantic* with the provocative title of "why (some) people hate poetry". It is a review of a new book by Ben Lerner, called *The Hatred of Poetry*.

Lerner attempts an explanation for the intense dislike that some people express for poetry. He attributes hatred of poetry to the resentments of the ignorant masses. Poetry is life affirming, but the ordinary mass consumers have made too many compromises to avow poetic life. They look on poets with envy and contempt, rather than scrutinise their own shallow shadows. So even if they might admit dallying with poetry when young and romantic, they will despise it as a waste of time in their crowded, retweeted lives now.

I suspect there are two simpler explanations. One. No one thing is loved by all, so why would we be surprised that some people across the spectrum hate poetry? Two. Much modern poetry wants to be despised. It declares bland and obvious political opinions on behalf of some identity. It makes *dada* with words. It mimics scholasticism in short lines. It resumes Joyce's war on language. In its pursuit of the purification of language, it forgets the second half of Mallarme's and Eliot's *aperçu*: to purify the language of the tribe.

Lerner's book contrasts all poetry before the Romantics with all poetry since then, roughly 1800. He creates his own myth of a partition between olden and modern times. In olden times, the tradition believed in natural laws and poetry as a craft. In modern times, poetry became the channeling of the universal powers of creativity. So, poems are lesser to Poetry. The old manners – craft, respect for tradition, love of the forms, and patterns of rhymed verse – are drowned beneath a great tidal wave of unbridled creative force. So Emerson (as quoted by Lerner) writes:

> [it] is not metres, but a metre-making argument, that makes a

poem—a thought so passionate and alive, that, like the spirit of a
plant or an animal, it has an architecture of its own, and *adorns
nature with a new thing*. (my emphasis)

Especially after 1900, Poetry gives birth to Invention, Creative Spirits and the Shock of the New. And the old-fashioned mass audience for poetry whimpered in the back rows, and headed for the exits.

What intrigued me most about Lerner's ideas, however, was his plans or rather visions for the future of poetry. Craft is not enough. Hobby is beneath contempt. Take that, modest Ted Kooser, with your *Poetry Home Repair Manual*. Not even Romantic Invention is enough. Lerner yearns for Redemption through Poetry, and that most peculiar form of redemption associated with cultural Marxism, and, in particular, the strange prophet, Walter Benjamin. Prophetic writings, of course, can stimulate all kinds of imaginations. After all, this blog is inspired, at least in part, by Benjamin's well-known but still mysterious thesis on the philosophy of history that describes the angel of history being blown by a storm:

> But a storm is blowing from Paradise; it has got caught in his wings with such violence that the angel can no longer close them. The storm irresistibly propels him into the future to which his back is turned, while the pile of debris before him grows skyward. This storm is what we call progress.

And am I not looking for some form of redemption too? The word was in the strap line of my blog. But the utopianism of Benjamin and the cultural Marxists has a peculiar blindness to the real suffering of the world – a suffering given a voice in the poetry I love, such as Symborska, Herbert, Milosz. This peculiar world-blindness is both excoriated and understood in Roger Scruton's wonderful *Fools, Frauds and Firebrands: thinkers of the New Left*, which has a grace and empathy rare among leftist thinkers. Clearly, though Lerner has not read Scruton or Leszek Kolakowski or even much history, because he sees poetry rather like an unwritten chapter of Marx's *Das Kapital*, with all its follies of the labour theory of value. He writes (as quoted by the review):

> 'Poetry' is a word for a kind of value no particular poem can realize: the value of persons, the value of a human activity beyond the labor/leisure divide, a value before or beyond price.

Oh deary me, can someone give the man on the left a good book to read, please?

The reviewer is quite savage at the end, and skewers the lofty impoverishment of poetry by Lerner, describing it "as an example of the dead end into which modern poetic theory has been led by its grandiose aspirations". But grandiose might be a little wrong: misdirected is kinder. After all, we do all yearn for redemption in some way – but to confuse redemption with the revolutionary overhaul of human affairs, the total transformation that Lerner and Benjamin and every utopian wishes for, must bring great personal torment. Redemption, to my spirit at least, can more easily be found in the love of the world, *amor mundi*, in all its strangeness and all its diversity. And this love cannot be without loss and sadness because we are losing parts of the world every day, and one day we will be lost to the world too. Poetry, at least in my practice, is less redemption, and more this love of the world. We can find in Wordsworth, who combined tradition and Romance, how poetry can reconcile us to the world as we find it –

> the very world, which is the world
> Of all of us,—the place where, in the end,
> We find our happiness, or not at all.

(William Wordsworth, *Prelude*)

Jeff Rich

Political Emotions
7 September 2016

I am giving a paper at the end of this week at a seminar run by the Centre for the History of Emotions, at the University of Melbourne. It is a second venture for me onto the stage of a more academic kind of writing, although the paper is not especially academic. But it is another step towards a new identity as an author, letting go of imprisonment in silent service to a bureaucratic self-image, and sharing my ideas with the wider world.

The conference is about children's voices in contemporary Australia. My paper looks at how the Royal Commission into Institutional Responses to Child Sexual Abuse in Australia listens to the voices of adults who are giving testimony about childhood abuse, and is called, "The remembered child who speaks of trauma: reflections on the Royal Commission into Institutional Responses to Child Sexual Abuse."

I think the Royal Commission stages public emotions in a remarkable and transformative way. Indeed, it invents an emotional regime – to use a term of the historian William Reddy that refers to an *ensemble* of practices, institutions, forms of expression and expressiveness – that is more compassionate and responsive to victims of trauma, at any age.

In this way, I think the Royal Commission is performing the important role of public staging of political emotions towards creating a just, compassionate society. Martha Nussbaum has described such practices in her works, *Political emotions: why love matters for justice* (2013) and *Hiding from humanity: shame, disgust and the law* (2004). I do not really have the time in my paper at the conference to elaborate on or to document these ideas, so I might just say a few things about them here on my blog.

Political emotions come in many forms. Shame and disgust are among the most important aired at the Commission. Nussbaum writes that a just and good polity cannot live by reason and logic alone, but should develop institutional ways of working with all of these emotions. She writes:

> Such public emotions, frequently intense, have large-scale consequences for the nation's progress toward its goals. They can give the pursuit of those goals new vigor and depth, but they can also derail that pursuit, introducing or reinforcing divisions, hierarchies, and forms of neglect or obtuseness.[88]

So, she argues there are two main tasks of political emotion in liberal societies.

Firstly, political cultures and institutions need to cultivate love and sympathy, and especially develop the strong commitment to worthy projects that are required for communal effort and shared sacrifice. Such emotions have belonged to all sorts of various identities – the nation, the utopia, the struggle, the faith, gender, sexual preference, race and class. In the Royal Commission's case, it needs to cultivate sympathy for victims, and a sense that we all belong to a common traumatised childhood.

Secondly, Nussbaum says political institutions need to hold at bay "tendencies to protect the fragile self by denigrating and subordinating others". There have been so many examples of such forces breaking the bonds of weak political cultures in the past, and leading to disgust, envy, and shaming others. But it seems to me that the Royal Commission has an especially important role of keeping abuse and the shame it brings for victims, perpetrators and bystanders out of the secret shadows. Is it shame that drives the response of institutions to cover up the failures and abuse by their members? Could it be projective disgust that scalds empathy before it can take hold when leaders of the church are confronted by pictures of the suffering of abuse victims?

Political emotions, as much as reasoned justice, are necessary for a common political culture, in which our practices and discussions

---

[88] Nussbaum, *Political Emotions: Why Love Matters for Justice* (2013), p. 2.

reinforce attachment to important norms. In these values, despite all certainty, we have little more than our feelings and our intuitions to support them. These emotions are the foundations of our political arguments, not independent logical analysis nor self-interested utility maximisation.

Here is the great failing of utopian thinking on both the right and the left. Speaking of the transcendent rationalism of America's libertarian heroes (who are inspired by how Ayn Rand shrugged off the burden of the world), Nussbaum writes:

> The libertarian challenge, however, contains a valuable lesson for our project: we must pay attention to the facts of human psychology, insofar as these are at all understood, and we must not ask of people what they cannot deliver, or can deliver only with great strain. ... Striking the right balance between aspiration and acceptance is one of the most difficult and delicate tasks of the political life, as of the personal. But the right balance cannot be one that erases the longing for justice.[89]

Here, in her embrace of "real people as they are", Nussbaum echoes some of the best of conservative thinking, as in Oakeshott or Roger Scruton. Whatever our political projects, they must be made of the crooked timber of humanity, and with compassion for our faults and our frailty, our shame, our fears, our tender cares. Through the emotion of compassion, through the various ways it is realised in our culture and institutions, Nussbaum arrives at the idea of *tragic spectatorship*, which is so important to the remarkable catharsis of the Royal Commission. Nussbaum writes:

> As they mature, citizens must learn, in effect, to be both tragic and comic spectators of the varied predicaments of life. The tragic perspective gives insight into shared vulnerabilities; the comic perspective (or a comic perspective of a particular sort) embraces the unevenness of human existence with flexibility and mercy, rather than hatred.[90]

---

[89] *Political Emotions*, p 117.
[90] *Political Emotions*, p 21.

The Royal Commission into Institutional Response to Child Sexual Abuse is a prime example of a modern liberal democracy enacting such tragic spectatorship, and in the process creating new possibilities to respond to victims of abuse at all ages.

The Great Confinement
20 October 2016

In *Hyperion*, Keats evoked the Great Confinement that the Age of Reason had imposed on madness, or at least as imagined by the Romantic Mind.

> Just at the self-same beat of Time's wide wings
> Hyperion slid into the rustled air,
> And Saturn gain'd with Thea that sad place
> Where Cybele and the bruised Titans mourn'd.
> It was a den where no insulting light
> Could glimmer on their tears; where their own groans
> They felt, but heard not, for the solid roar
> Of thunderous waterfalls and torrents hoarse,
> Pouring a constant bulk, uncertain where.
> Crag jutting forth to crag, and rocks that seem'd
> Ever as if just rising from a sleep,
> Forehead to forehead held their monstrous horns;
> And thus in thousand hugest phantasies
> Made a fit roofing to this nest of woe.

I have taken up again, after a break of two months, Andrew Scull's *Madness in Civilization: a cultural history of insanity*. Here I learn that the archetypal lunatic asylum of the English speaking world, Bedlam or Bethlem Hospital, featured two large statues on plinths at its gates.

These statues were of the figures of melancholy and raving madness. Melancholy madness lay imprisoned and disabled by his sadness. Raving madness, full of impotent torrents, hoarse, lay shackled. These two statues, according to Scull, were alluded to by Keats in his poem of the fall of the titans, Hyperion, which I confess I had not read until prompted by Scull's account. They appear as the bruis'd Titans, who make a fit roofing for this nest of woe.

Whether we know them as asylums or mental hospitals or rehabilitation clinics, these places, which I have known as a visitor, but not a patient, have long been nests of woe. But Scull does a fine job of showing that they can at times be more than that. Beneath the lurid and dark imaginings, the grotesque exploitation, for profit or for poetry, of the insane and the infirm, we can find other motives and other experiences of caring and protection in these places. Of course, he does not minimise the cruelty and the suffering known in these places, but he also sees the compassion of those who cared and offered a place of refuge for their ill family members. With a modern perspective, sees the struggle of families in a world with few supports to take care of their mad members and to protect all who knew them from their worst excesses.

Scull's history is a long response to the myths of radical madness in Michel Foucault's *History of Madness* (also translated as *Madness and Civilization*), one of the pinnacles of the French radical literary tradition of the 20th century. Foucault and this tradition celebrated de Sade as the great libertine whose texts spoke of excess and transgression which defied the law that had sought to confine de Sade with *lettres de cachet*. Indeed, this radical literary tradition, which celebrated de Sade culminated in Foucault's celebration of the remorseless libertine in both his texts and his way of life. By contrast, Scull gives attention to his despairing mother-in-law who saw her daughter lost in de Sade's fantasy world and betrayed by de Sade's dangerous liaisons with her sister and many prostitutes. So Madame de Montreuil lured de Sade with a ruse to Paris, where she confined him in the Chateau de Vincennes and then the Bastille. Every loving family member of a person who has experienced the extremes of psychotic behaviour can understand what she did. There is no need to use Foucault's grand myth of resistance to reason, the Great Confinement.

This myth, Scull shows, was mistaken about the true historical circumstances. Foucault put forward the claim, that there was a Great Confinement of the insane in the seventeenth and eighteenth centuries, made possible by a strange reordering of symbols and discourse in the minds of Western man (Foucault did indeed think in terms of such toxic intellectuality). But Scull judges that, for all its rhetorical grandeur, Foucault's history "vastly overstates the true state of affairs".[91] The insane were a small and secondary population in the great congregations of the broken in the new French general hospitals, such as the *Salpêtrière*. Even more so in rural Europe, most of the mad who were confined were a danger to themselves or others, and most of the mad were dealt with, often inadequately, within families, poor houses or religious institutions.

Still, the image created by Foucault, in that strangely mesmerizing yet unsatisfying book, *Folie et Deraison* (translated as *Madness and Civilization* in English), has an enduring magic. "By a strange act of force, the classical age was to reduce to silence the madness whose voices the Renaissance had liberated, but whose voices it had already tamed," Foucault wrote.[92] I confess this grand gesture of retrieving from confined silence the voices of madness mesmerised me as a young man who encountered the voices of both madness and mind medicine. The poetry made me overlook all the errors of Foucault's argument. The pose of defiance made me pass over the crude recycled Marxism of Foucault's interpretation of the great confinement as an act of power asserting order.

But I cannot overlook this any more. There it is, in his text, the absurd statement that the Hôpital-Général and all the professions of medical care for the insane "had nothing to do with any medical concept. It was an instance of order, of the monarchical and bourgeois

---

[91] Scull, *Madness in Civilization*, p 127.
[92] Foucault, *Madness and Civilization*, p 38.

order being organized in France during this period" that reflected bourgeois capitalist order.[93] Foucault continued,

> Confinement ... is a 'police' matter. Police, in the precise sense that the classical epoch gave to it – that is, the totality of measures which make work possible and necessary for all those who could not live without it.... What made it necessary was an imperative of labor. Our philanthropy prefers to recognize the signs of a benevolence toward sickness where there is only condemnation of idleness.

So Foucault turned all the complex storm of emotions, thought and practice provoked by the still deeply mysterious presence of madness in our lives to an old-fashioned Marxist conspiracy theory that condemned the bourgeois in a stance of radical defiance. As Roger Scruton wrote, Foucault "devoted his work to unmasking the bourgeoisie, and showing that all the given ways of shaping civil society are reducible in the last analysis to forms of domination."[94] In the end, I discovered in my own real life, that Foucault's theories were worthless discards when faced with the real experience of falling into madness or caring for a loved one who is mentally ill.

Scruton also identified the enduring power of Foucault's writings. His essay is a sensitive and remarkable tribute, yet a scathing critique. He writes of Foucault with a generosity and admiration not dispensed to other fools, frauds and firebrands, such as Sartre, Habermas or the entirely despicable Jacques Lacan. "His imagination and intellectual fluency," Scruton wrote, "have generated theories, concepts and insights by the score, and the synthesising poetry of his style rises above the murky sludge of left-wing writing like an eagle over mudflats." He identified that Foucault's great book on madness retold the Hegelian master-slave story as a conflict between reason and madness, and it is perhaps my own experience of struggling to find my way between these two experiences that had led to my long enchantment with Foucault's metaphors and my long search through his radical

---
[93] *Madness and Civilization*, p. 40, 46.
[94] Scruton, *Fools, Frauds and Firebrands: Thinkers of the New Left* (2016), p. 99.

pantheon of mad anti-gods. As Scruton wrote from the revolt of the Romantics and the early modernists through to the twentieth century:

> Madness is out of the cage, and confronting us with *our* truth. At the end of Foucault's drama the gods of the French post-war Olympus enter stage left, to stick out their tongues at the bourgeoisie in the stalls. Goya, de Sade, Hölderlin, Nerval, Van Gogh, Artaud, Nietzsche, all are proof, for Foucault, that the voice of unreason (*déraison*) can no longer be silenced, and that the reign of bourgeois normality is over.[95]

This great, dreamed, titanic struggle between shackled raving madness and its captor, ordinary life, has both sustained me and led me many times astray. Still, I feel Foucault could only have written this great book by knowing the borderlands of madness and reason from the inside, and this experience spoke in the poetry of his style in a way that his drier and more pedantic critics cannot attain, despite all their evidence, prudent judgment and good sense.

Yet today, I let go of this titanic struggle, in the knowledge that the voices of madness have never wholly be silenced nor fully confined. So instead of Keats' epic vision of madness, as much a vision from the outside as the confining, caring doctors in Foucault's own poetic satire, let us recall that even in an asylum, with medical confinement, the voice of John Keats' near contemporary, John Clare, could still speak and break the silence, with a tone quite different to Artaud's obscenity-laden rants, and in a way that reaches to every one who writes, and so asserts their being, however diminished by the vast shipwreck of any life. I turn, instead and in closing, to read John Clare's poem "I am", composed some time between 1842-64 in Northampton General Lunatic Asylum, now St Andrew's Hospital.

---

[95] Scruton, *Fools, Frauds and Firebrands*, p. 102.

Jeff Rich

Ragnarök
21 November 2016

A.S. Byatt has written a short and puzzling book.[96] It is a kind of tribute to the Norse myths that she learned as a child through a gift from her parents of a book, *Asgard and the Gods*. Most of the book is told through the eyes of "the thin child", a reconstructed persona of Byatt as a child, growing up during World War II. Her father was away at the war, never to return, and she was threatened directly by the Germans, whose mythology she read with the fervour of childhood, hooded by a bed sheet at night with a torch lighting her way to Valhalla.

The war destroyed this thin child's world, but the stories of Asgard filled her with a "contrary myth" that she found more sustaining than the pallid Christian stories she was taught at school. This contrary myth sustained a belief in renewal and regeneration that was not possible in linear time, and was so needed in a world set to destroy itself. Now as she moves between the thin girl's innocent dreams and the old writer's bitter knowledge, the power of this myth is waning. She conjures back its magic, but it seems a world that is lost. Even the possibility of thinking in myth seems more alien to the "civilisation that I live in."

Byatt's book is also a meditation on how that civilisation may be facing its own Twilight of the Gods.

> But if you write a version of Ragnarök in the twenty-first century, it is haunted by the imagining of a different end of things. We are a species of animal which is bringing about the end of the world we were born into. Not out of evil or malice, or not mainly, but because of a lopsided mixture of extraordinary cleverness, extraordinary greed, extraordinary proliferation of our own kind, and a biologically built-in short sightedness.[97]

---

[96] *Ragnarök: the end of the gods* (2011).
[97] Byatt, *Ragnarök*, p. 167.

So she "wanted to write the end of our Midgard." In her telling, the destruction of the great ash tree, Yggdrassil, is only too literal. She finds the mythic metaphors only too real in our modern polluted world. The death ship, Naglfar, is, in the *Edda*, made from the fingernails and toenails of the dead; in our world, Byatt finds this ship in the trash vortex, that vast swirling heap of rubbish that forms a corrupted island somewhere in the heart of the Pacific.

It is not only our Midgard of nature that is falling into destruction, but the so too are the realms of culture built by we Aesir. Still, there is the strange persistence of the beautiful stories of lost times. The gift given to Odin, after his trial hanging from the world tree like a dead man, can endure the final judgment of the Gods.

Blessed rage of order
7 November 2016

This morning I read through two more chapters of Andrew Scull's *Madness in Civilization*, which broadly covered the nineteenth century and the gentle transformations from madhouses to asylums to lunatic hospitals, from moral treatment to alienism, from psychological medicine to psychiatry, and from madness to mental illness and, still worse, degeneracy.

The term, psychiatry, was invented by a German doctor, Johann Christian Reil in 1808, and he formed the term from two Greek words for soul (*psykhe*) and medical treatment (*techne iatrike*). These two words wrestled, in Scull's account, for the spirit of psychiatry through the nineteenth century, and beyond.

Unlike my renounced influence, Michel Foucault, Scull sees the compassion and the humanistic hope that motivated reforms of medical treatment of the insane through the nineteenth century. He records the great hope vested in the institution of the asylum, publicly operated by a more benevolent state, infused with moral principles, and regulated by a form of containment that was kinder than the private madhouses that so scandalised many of the moral reformers of the nineteenth century. It was because of these flawed but honest attempts to institutionalise kindness that Queen Victoria's physician called the new institution of the lunatic asylum "the most blessed manifestation of true civilization that the world can present".[98]

Scull differs from Foucault and his followers who condemned moral treatment as a "gigantic moral imprisonment." Scull judges the new asylums to be humane improvements on crowded, abusive, money-making madhouses. He does not shy away from documenting precisely the horrors of even the kindest asylum or the disappointments of the most humane of their keepers. Indeed, the real heroes of Scull's story are not the great doctors and propagandists, like Pinel or Tuke, but the non-medical custodians of the insane who were guided by care, compassion and the assiduous observation of which treatments seemed to help their patients best. So, it is not Pinel's great moral reordering of medicine that Scull foregrounds, but the practical and careful practice of the lay governor of the Bicêtre, Jean-Baptiste Poussin, and his wife, Marguerite. They observed daily the effects of different treatments. It was their compassionately guided experimentation with different forms of care that Pinel later systematised into a grand theory. Foucault mistook the whole process for ideas ordering reality.

Throughout Scull's more grounded account, we meet the rare voices and images that spoke of soul from within the great confinement. Here Scull comments adversely on John Clare's poem, *I Am*. I disagree with Scull that the poem fails, even in its darkest moments of lament, to make a "vigorous assertion of personal autonomy and individuality". We also meet van Gogh, and the kind

---

[98] Scull, *Madness in Civilization*, p. 25.

portrait of his doctor, Felix Rey, who sadly found is portrait horrifying. But by the time van Gogh was painting, doctors and their mad patients were becoming estranged by ideas of degeneracy, and the idea of medical treatment was winning out over the soul in the struggle for the spirit of psychiatry.

Degeneracy was an idea that consumed *fin de siècle* Europe though first powerfully articulated by a French alienist, Benedict-Augustin Morel, in his *Treatise on the Intellectual, Moral and Physical Degeneracy of the Human Race* (1857). But it found its most influential expression in Balzac's fiction and in Max Nordau, *Degeneration* (1895). I recall in my university days being fixated by this period in culture, and have long been preoccupied with similar themes of cultural decay, even though my more ordinary, compassionate heart is repelled by the biological determinism of these theories. By 1900 the mad were an incurable burden, and a frustration to the prestige and good will of their treating doctors. So, Tuke's great grandson, the inheritor of the family tradition of asylums, but a successor who had lost the great reformer's optimism, would say, with all the cruelty of a heartless administrator, that the insane were "an infirm type of humanity… On admission 'no good' is plainly inscribed on their foreheads".[99]

His words reflected a greater pessimism among psychiatrists that mental illness could be cured, and this led to a fateful dalliance with eugenics, which culminated most tragically in the compulsory sterilisation of thousands of the mad and disabled in Germany and their killing in the T-4 operation that was the pilot of the holocaust. But eugenics was not only a German disease. My own country, my own state, went very close to adopting compulsory sterilisation of the insane and idiotic in the 1930s, and eugenics was widely embraced by the prominent and influential, especially in liberal and progressive circles. It is perhaps one more historical reason to be grateful for the persistence of religious sentiment. Faith saved many more lives than reason here. Not just scientific rationalism, but the legal greats of liberalism failed the simple and the frail. Scull quotes Oliver Wendell

---

[99] Scull, *Madness in Civilization*, p. 243.

Holmes, that beloved liberal jurist of the United States Supreme Court, son of a doctor, occasional poet, and yet capable of delivering this cruel 1927 judgement on whether the American constitution prohibited compulsory sterilization:

> It is better for all the world if instead of waiting to execute degenerate offspring for crime, or to let them starve for their imbecility, society can prevent those who are manifestly unfit from continuing their kind. The principle that sustains compulsory vaccination is broad enough to cover cutting Fallopian tubes... Three generations of imbeciles are enough.[100]

All progressive schemes for the improvement of the human condition – especially in the utopias of public health – are tempted by this rage to order the crooked timber of humanity, most perfectly exemplified in the disorders of madness.

In the late nineteenth century, Germany was the unexpected latecomer to asylums due to its late political integration and surging tide of university research. Here psychiatry gave itself over to the rage for order, which yet contained within it a blessed urge for cure. Most German medical research into the mind pursued the dissection of the brain in laboratories; but Emil Kraepelin, was forced, by the accident of his poor eyesight, to pursue the lower-status observational research conducted through direct treatment of the thousands of patients in Germany's new asylums. There, Kraepelin observed the patients before him, and made careful notes on cards, which he then assembled and reassembled into a classificatory scheme for mental illness, which in its essentials still endures today. So developed the first diagnostic manual of psychiatric disorders, derived from clinical observations. So too were born the ideas of bipolar disorder and schizophrenia, which Kraepelin called, as did Jung, *dementia praecox*.

But this scheme for ordering the disorders of the mind cannot be dismissed, in the way Foucault did, as a ruse of power in the form of a grid of surveillance and control. Nor can it be belittled as the assertion of an arrogant profession's power. Kraepelin acted with more

---

[100] Oliver Wendell Holmes, 1927, quoted in Scull, *Madness in Civilization*, p 266.

compassion towards his subjects than many of his less grounded professional colleagues. And does not madness call for disciplined compassion and grounded imagination from us all? Where would we be, after all, without the imagination's blessed rage for order?

The eternal triangle: love, art and work
28 January 2017

Sigmund Freud did not say, despite reports, that the standard of a successful life was *to love and to work*. Erik Erikson once reported Freud saying something along those lines, but the memory of disciples is unreliable. The expression closest to this formula in Freud's voluminous writings, his *Götterdämmerung* of our sex-driven and career-mad times, was this sentence from *Civilization and its Discontents*:

> The communal life of human beings had, therefore, a two-fold foundation: the compulsion to work, which was created by external necessity, and the power of love.

Our common experience today is that work is practised as both love and necessity. Sometimes, we have good days when we dream our careers are our true vocation, and our work can express our life's purpose. Sometimes, we have bad days when work is a time sink that frustrates the realisation of ourselves in an art of living.

We deceive ourselves, and make ourselves miserable in these fantasies. In classical Greek myth, the child of Ananke (necessity) was Adrasteia, and it was she, not her irresistible mother, who distributed, with all the caprice of a nymph, rewards and punishments in this world. Today, by contrast, we compound rewards and necessity, and imagine, with our poor kenning, that our frail attributes will always be rewarded in this world. When we see ourselves rewarded and recognised in our jobs, we see fate and vocation smiling on us. And when they do not, we long for that job that will bring us meaning, recognition and wealth. In truth, Adrasteia hands out both laurels and whip lashes with no regard for what happens in our minds. The uncontrollable goddess-nymph determines the outcomes of our actions, but we cannot escape our bondage to necessity.

We would be more content if we accepted these bonds for what they are – lifelong shackles that we learn to get by with over time. They tie us to our master, but allow us to roam freely in other domains of life. Perhaps it is our Romantic and democratic dreams of a universal aristocracy, where everyone can live like a movie star on their vacation, that makes us so miserable at work. For most of human culture, work has been the servant of the dark Greek god, Ananke. But in our culture today, Work is a three-faced god. One face serves belonging, love, and connection with our true kindred spirits. A second face plays in the studio where we realise our gifts. And the third face brings those gifts and rewards that promise to elevate us to the top of whatever social hierarchy we struggle to climb. In making Work into this free, generous spirit, we overlook Freud's words – that we suffer the *compulsion* to work, created by *external necessity*. We come to believe that we choose to work as an act of *inner freedom*.

But over our long working lives, we slowly learn that work cannot be this three-faced god, except for those few people projected to our screens as role model legends. Work is rather a daily grind. A cruel social lottery. It is a theatre of cruelty and of the absurd. It is a graveyard of disappointments, grand illusions, organisational reforms, and of long, deadly marches through the marshes, driven by the ambitious and the crazed. Yet we must endure it. We have no choice. Ananke stands over our withered bank balances and sends us out to keep the wolf at the door. Still worse, we endure it for a longer time than all of human history. The boom in life expectancy has stretched the term of an unnatural working life into 50 or 60 years. The boom has become a curse of longer years in the office cubicle. But though we endure it, we do not need to succumb. We can resist its illusions, if not its drudgery. We can refuse to confuse necessity with love, even if we must submit to dark Ananke's will to dominate our lives. We endure our working lives by reaching for the other points of the eternal triangle that has long driven human culture. We reach for love and art. They are the deeper veins of living purpose. They are the true lodestars by which we navigate our troubled oceans.

The Revolutionary
24 January 2017

The adjective, "revolutionary", lost all threat sometime after 1968. "Revolutionary" is now just another exaggeration in an advertising-drowned world. But still I have known people within these last five decades who have lived their lives by this creed. The splendidly delusive Australian Maoist historian, Humphrey McQueen, truly believed in the 1970's that The Revolution was imminent, while he wrote in a well-proportioned professorial office in leafy suburban Canberra. He believed his angry denunciations of all that was wrong with this country and culture would bring the day of Revelation closer.

Nothing was further from the truth. The black-clad, intense and hairy revolutionaries of the 1970's have grown old, tired and disappointed. They have fallen behind the pack. Society has passed them by. They are replaced now by pretenders who can attach the concept of "revolutionary" to anything. These technological ephebes celebrate as revolutionary, as "disruptive" of whole economies, the act of hailing a cab with an app, of keeping fares down by paying no tax and ignoring all the rules. The tradition and culture of the Revolutionary – stretching from Nechayev through Lenin to Alinsky - has been trashed.

In the 1970's some revolutionaries still followed Nechayev's creed through to its stated goal. They acted as implacable enemies of Society. They dissembled belonging to this society, but planned in secret cells to destroy it. The Baader Meinhof gang, the Weather Underground, the Red Army Faction, the Japanese Red Army, Action Directe and others drew a following. They fascinated a certain group of young idealists who sought to wage war with simple life. They are portrayed in the great movie by Visconti, *The Conversation Piece* (1974), which captures the mood of the 1970's in Europe, when affluent, lost youths are seduced by the violent, iron-willed purpose of revolutionaries, so much more appealing than the cultural collapse and moral aimlessness of their own lives. These people have not gone away, but they today rarely go by the name of revolutionaries; instead they are hackers, extremists, activists, antifascists, or just plain terrorists.

And the sad siren's song of Nechayev's creed still exerts its charm. It was laid down in *Catechism of a Revolutionary* (1869) by Bakunin and Sergei Nechayev.

> The revolutionary is a lost man; he has no interests of his own, no cause of his own, no feelings, no habits, no belongings, he does not even have a name. Everything in him is absorbed by a single, exclusive interest, a single thought, a single passion – the revolution. In the very depths of his being, not just in words but in deed, he has broken every tie with the civil order, with the educated world and all laws, conventions and generally accepted conditions, and with the ethics of this world. He will be an implacable enemy of this world, and if he continues to live in it, that will only be so as to destroy it the more effectively.

The Revolutionary embraces the doom that faces us all, and seeks to bring this same tragedy down on all our heads. The revolutionary is a weapon of determined steel pointed at the despair of existence. This merciless way of life seems a long way from the brand-conscious pleasure heads who lead the protests of identity politics. Today's 99 per cent protestors borrow the appearance of revolutionaries in their second-hand, hand-me-down clothes, not their creeds of destruction.

But could events and mind-worms turn these peaceful protests to violence? Could radicals turn into Revolutionaries if they are convinced that stronger medicine must cure greater evils? What events? What evils? - an "illegitimate" president of the USA, who in turn treats political conventions as traps for chumps; societies sickened by excess wealth; protests that flood the plains but cannot fill the water tank; national security agencies out of control. Then there are all the nationalists who want to make their country great again, and may respond to violence with violence.

The world seems headed for dark times in which I fear the violence of the revolutionary may make a comeback. If it does, remember this: Nechayev was a murderer. If it does, beware of your implacable enemies down the street. If it does, read Dostoevsky *The Possessed* again. If it does, tend your garden.

Massacres in History
11 January 2017

When the violence and brewing disorder of modern times confronts us, we readily fall for three comforting delusions: our liberal minds have conquered the violent instincts of the human animal; our modern ideologies (Nazism, Marxism, Imperialism, Neo-Conservatism, Neo-Liberalism, or Islamism) are specially drawn to total war; or our powerful nation states have a peculiar talent for blood-curdling murder.

Alas, not one of these modern delusions is true. The pages of history are littered with massacres and community violence. Of course, the reader of history can overlook these stories. History has so many other threads to follow – the glories of great leaders, the diversity of culture, the grandeur of art, the suffering of ordinary people, the struggle for power, the competition for resources, the hierarchy of status, the blooming of beliefs, or the fading of faiths. But in all those threads, blood stains the wattle.

It is difficult to face this squarely. The wound to human pride caused by the repeated violence of our kind is deep, and we naturally seek to numb the pain. Either we turn to more pleasant thoughts, or we develop elaborate denials of the humanity of the perpetrators of violence. Our kin then become dictators, monsters, barbarians or orcs. Or we give a strained nobility to the fight for justice. Then bandits, thugs, or rebel yells become freedom fighters, poetic champions of a noble cause, who cloak violent instincts in mystic illusions, just like Byron setting out to fight for the Greeks.

Violence offends our idea of progress, which accompanies modern culture like an ever-vigilant chaperone. Darker thinkers know this. John Gray's work has long taken apart the modern belief in human progress. In reviewing Pinker's *Better Angels of our Nature*, Gray targets this grand illusion:

> Improvements in civilisation are real enough, but they come and go. While knowledge and invention may grow cumulatively and at an accelerating rate, advances in ethics and politics are erratic, discontinuous and easily lost. Amid the general drift, cycles can be discerned: peace and freedom alternate with war and tyranny, eras of increasing wealth with periods of economic collapse. Instead of becoming ever stronger and more widely spread, civilisation remains inherently fragile and regularly succumbs to barbarism. This view, which was taken for granted until sometime in the mid-18th century, is so threatening to modern hopes that it is now practically incomprehensible.[101]

Gray characterises Pinker as belonging to a modern liberal school of technological optimism that believes in big data and google, rational

---

[101] John Gray, *The Guardian*, 13 March 2015.

enlightenment and science, democracy and the American way of life. But this manner of thinking is, Gray writes, a quasi-religious practice like a Tibetan prayer wheel that is spun to produce reassurance that life has meaning, that history progresses, and that the best part of humanity is unequivocally good. When confronted by the bloodied pages of history that tell of massacres, communal violence and the descent of civilised people of every time and every place into barbarism, Pinker and the liberal optimists spin their wheel and so carefully, mindfully will the problem of violence away.

For whatever fortuitous reason, I came across one such bloodied page of history last night when reading Richard J. Evans, *The Pursuit of Power: Europe 1815-1914*. The page told the story of the struggle for Greek independence, their fight for freedom and release from the "cruel yoke of Ottoman power" in the 1820s. The Greeks held a national assembly at Epidauras in 1822 where they declared, despite the fractious rumblings within their own ranks, a "holy war" against the Muslim Ottoman overlords, who had ruled since 1453. Like many holy wars, the Greeks' fight for a separate, Christian nation soon justified massacres. A British observer, George Finlay, recoiled at the violence of the rebels when they killed the local Muslim population:

> Women and children were frequently tortured before they were murdered. After the Greeks had been in possession of the city for forty-eight hours, they deliberately collected together about two thousand persons of every age and sex, but principally women and children, and led them to a ravine in the nearest mountain where they murdered every soul.[102]

The Ottoman rulers and the Muslim local population responded with massacres of their own. The Orthodox Patriarch of Istanbul was hanged on his cathedral's gate. At Salonica local crowds massacred the Christian population turning the city into a "boundless slaughterhouse". On the island of Chios, Greek rebels besieged an Ottoman garrison, which itself held hostage many of the wealthy Greek Christian merchants of the island. When Ottoman troops and

---

[102] George Finlay, quoted in Evans, *Pursuit of Power (2016)*, p 55.

boats arrived to reinforce the garrison, the balance of the siege turned. The Ottoman soldiers tortured their hostages to reveal the hidden locations of their treasures, and then massacred them. The Chios streets were littered with corpses, and the island's buildings burned to the ground. Nearly 30 000 Christians were killed. Others were sold into slavery. The island's population fell from 120 000 to 30 000.

Yet this next link in the chain of communal violence inspired a humanitarian response to fight to defend the birthplace of Western civilisation. Eugene Delacroix's *The Massacre at Chios* (1824) rallied the educated classes of Europe, who were steeped in the love of classical Greek culture. Across Europe, idealistic young men were inspired by glorious illusions, and went to fight for the divided and compromised Greek rebels. They believed they were on the front line of a struggle for justice and civilised Europe itself. One observer noted that, "All came expecting to find the Peloponnesus filled with Plutarch's men and all returned thinking the inhabitants of Newgate [London's main prison] more moral".

Of course one of the famous foreign fighters was that mad, bad and dangerous to know poet, Lord Byron. He left behind the ravages of his incestuous and treacherous relationships in England, and dedicated himself to his great Cause, a greater delusion. He confided in his aristocratic friend, Marguerite, Countess of Blessington, who kept a journal of her conversations. Byron told her "he who is only a poet has done little for mankind," and so by fighting for the Glory of Greece he would "endeavour to prove in his own person that a poet may be a soldier".[103] He died there at Missolonghi in April 1824. And the myth of the Romantic nationalist martyr rose from his 36-year-old corpse. Today he is considered a national hero in Greece. The phenomenon of young men and women fighting and dying uselessly in a civilisational struggle, drunk on dreams of justice and glory and romance and martyrdom, is older than the Islamic rebels of ISIS.

---

[103] Quoted in Evans, *The Pursuit of Power*.

From the Burning Archive

The recurring reproach to reason
15 April 2017

Today, I finished reading Andrew Scull's *Madness in Civilization: a cultural history of insanity*. The book ends with a series of falls from grace of modern ways of thinking about madness: psychoanalysis becomes stranded with its limitation to a small elite, and there learns it is irrelevant to the suffering of most severely mentally ill people; then the great disappointments of the evacuation of the asylum, which became a shameful symbol of the enemy of freedom, that proceeded without any conscientious attention to the community care of the most unwell; and finally, the descent into confusion and denial of the Diagnostic and Statistical Manual (DSM) itself, which in its fifth edition, was abjured by Robert Spitzer and Allen Frances, the architects of its earlier editions.

Out of the collapse of the great encyclopaedia of the disordered mind, there emerged a new project – to anchor all mental illness in biological causes. Led by the Institute of Mental Health in the USA the new scientists of the brain disavowed the DSM's study of symptoms to search for more fundamental biological mechanisms. Thomas Insel said, "As long as the research community takes the DSM to be a bible, we'll never make progress. People think everything has to match DSM criteria, but you know what? Biology never read that book".[104]

Rather than a descriptive symptomatology, the new neuroscientists believed they could build a diagnostic system on firm biological foundations. But they were to be disappointed. Despite the flashy images of the brain in action, they came no closer to understanding the mysteries of the disordered mind. Discoveries were limited to mundane routines of the orderly mind. Why? Both the human mind and madness, which is the most potent expression of that mind, is one part biology, two parts culture.

---

[104] quoted Scull, *Madness in Civilization*, p 408.

Modern psychiatry made two metaphysical wagers – that madness is an illness and that it can be explained by the body alone. But the wager has not paid off. Our cures need to be neither solely mental nor merely medical. They must embrace the cultures that temper, limit and excite the voices of madness within us. It is not that the pills or biological explanations will not play some role. "But," Scull asks, "will madness, that most solitary of afflictions and social of maladies, be reducible at last to biology and nothing but biology?" Scull answers his own questions:

> The social and cultural dimensions of mental disorders, so indispensable a part of the story of madness in civilization over the centuries, are unlikely to melt away, or prove to be nothing more than epiphenomenal features of so universal a feature of human existence. Madness indeed has its meanings, elusive and evanescent as our attempts to capture them have been. It remains a fundamental puzzle, a reproach to reason, inescapably part and parcel of civilization itself.[105]

Madness is in an infinite conversation with our ordinary selves. It is the reproach to reason that we must live with and dream from.

Turn and face the strange

11 April 2017

About a year ago I wrote a post, *Time might change me, but I can't change time*. It was prompted by Felipe Fernández-Armesto's *A foot in the river: why our lives change and the limits of evolution,* and frustration with a dose of bland management rhetoric about change. Today I

---
[105] Scull, *Madness in Civilization*, p 411.

finished rereading Fernández-Armesto's book, again prompted to reflect more deeply on change by a defiant reaction to urgings from senior bureaucrats to change with change. I also learned that I had misheard the refrain from Bowie's song, and substituted one "change" for the more mysterious "trace". What more might I say about change beyond the slightly dyspeptic remarks of a year ago?

Fernández-Armesto's book is valuable because it is a deep reflection on what change really means, and how change happens, especially in the realm of culture. Organic change occurs through evolution, selection and inheritance, but cultures do not evolve so that the mental model of cultural change can borrow from but not be limited to biology. The changes that occur in cultures follow no uniform pattern of descent, progress, or adaptation for survival. There are many such stock metaphors of cultural change, but Fernández-Armesto replaces these tropes with an image of culture as a chaotic, pluralistic world, in which vectors of change shoot in every direction.

He does agree, however, with our bureaucratic friends that the speed of change has quickened in today's societies when compared to most human history, but with a twist. The great successful cultures, he remarks, are those that have endured with little change for thousands of years. There have been examples of cultures that have run furiously after the lure of change and so brought on their own collapse. Perhaps the speed of change today may test the limits of our social engines. Today's innovation could be tomorrow's ruin. So he speculates the pace of change may slow or even cease. Events, dear boy, events.

These reflections emerge from a deep reflection on biology and culture, and an attempt to think across those disciplines, so long divided. He presents the now well-established evidence that culture is not a uniquely human treasure. Other creatures have culture, especially our fellow primates. No other species has yet, however, imagined such a bewildering diversity of cultures. And to differentiate in culture is to change cultures.

Fernández-Armesto sets down a chain of propositions at the outset of his book.

1. "Culture is a by-product of faculties of memory and anticipation evolved in some species"
2. "Those faculties predispose cultures to change"
3. "Humans' faculty of anticipation is exceptionally developed and contributes to making them highly imaginative"
4. "Humans are the most mutable of cultural creatures because in their case peculiar features of memory and imagination make them fertile in ideas (which I understand as ways of re-imagining the world)"
5. "Ideas are the main motors of change in human cultures"
6. "The pace of change is a function of the mutual accessibility of ideas: the more that ideas are exchanged, the more new ideas ensue; and cultural instability increases accordingly."

The biology of our brains bestows on us a faculty of imagination; and with that imagination we unleash the dogs of change on the world. Imagination feeds on its own artifacts, its mistakes, its deceits, its delusions, its random deviations. Change is not a driver. It is not the final cause of external reality. It is culture's wild child.

> Culture stimulates imagination further still, partly by rewarding it and partly by enhancing it with psychotropic behaviour. We praise the bard, pay the piper, fear the shaman, obey the priest, revere the artist. We unlock visions with dance and drums and music and alcohol and excitants and narcotics.

Change is not an external necessity, to which we must loyally submit, but the coils of the "imaginative animal." Fernández-Armesto writes:

> Imagination is the motor of culture. We look around us. We see the world. In our mind's eye we see it differently – improved or made more conformable to some imagined model, pattern or ideal of order; or, if our taste so inclines us, we envision its destruction or reduction to chaos. Either way, we recraft our world imaginatively. We act to realise the world we have re-imagined. That is how and why cultures change.

So we come to a more genial response to the stern lectures from managers on changing with the change. These demands for organisational changes are so often so petty, and yet insisted upon like a martinet commander who demands conformity with some new marching order. But they are but one imaginative reordering of the world. I choose another dream with less fury, less tempest, and deeper roots in the great world-tree.

On tyranny or terror
31 May 2017

The American historian of Eastern Europe, Timothy Snyder, has delivered a strange best-seller in *On Tyranny: 20 lessons of the twentieth century*. Its special sauce is made by mixing seemingly wise apothegms – 'be as courageous as you can', 'be calm when the unthinkable arrives' – with a wailing cry for help from the soul of liberal America in despair at the triumph of Trump.

His warnings that the USA may slide into totalitarianism under Trump have delivered him an audience on talk shows and business magazines. I bought his little book out of love for the great East European dissidents under communism like Havel and Kolakowski, quoted liberally in this little lament for a broken liberal consensus. Some early ideas were intriguing, but ultimately I put this work, which can be read in barely an hour, back on the shelf in disappointment.

The essay is an extended implied comparison between the unfolding phenomenon of Donald Trump and tyranny, ancient and modern, but most of all its Nazi manifestation. If we believe Professor Snyder, we are at the beginning of the end of democracy. All the signs show an accelerating slide into tyranny: the condemnation of the media, the contempt for the educated elite, the search for new partners, such as Russia (god forbid), in the fight against terror. Snyder even compares the burning of the *Reichstag* with our contemporary responses to repeated attacks of terror.

Now I am no ingénue about the quality of our democracy or political leadership in a disintegrating culture obsessed with shallow spectacles. Nor am I bedazzled by that impresario of shallow spectacle, Donald Trump. I predicted on my blog in July 2016 that Trump would both win the Presidential election and then fail as President. But to equate Trump's administration with Hitler's or Stalin's reflects a loss of bearings by Professor Snyder. So too I cannot agree that the response to terrorism has no real grounds or that it is a scare campaign by conniving political leaders to usher in dark tyranny.

It does seem that Professor Snyder has allowed Trump to get under his skin, and to distort his better judgment. The madness of twitter overwhelmed the good Professor when he tweeted, in the hours after the Manchester terrorist bombing, that Trump's health care reforms in just four hours would claim the same number of lives as the bombing. Twitter can make idiots of even the most intelligent people.

Professor Snyder would do still better to reassess his level of concern with terror over tyranny. Islamic State, after all, operates both. Democratic states need to defend their citizens against both. It is true that democratic states need urgently to repair their political institutions and stop the rot in their democratic culture. But that task must be done together with action against the dark terrors that reach into our lives every week. We must defeat the tyranny of terror. That is at least one lesson so far of the 21st century. That is a lesson better learned from Michael Burleigh than from Timothy Snyder.

From the Burning Archive

The Hope of None
3 May 2017

In reading Max Sebald's *Austerlitz* last night, I stumbled on the passage that reports the memories of the character, Austerlitz, when he ambled into the strangely desolate town in which lay the ruins from which he had averted his attention for four decades. Here he found the reason for his long avoidance of his personal and national history. Here he recovered the fate from which he fled as a Jewish child on a train. Here he knew again the loss, the unbearable trauma, that none of his family survived.

There he saw the gate of Theresienstadt, with its slogan in wrought iron decorating its upper border: *Arbeit Mach Frei*. None who entered believed this slogan of the powerful, this siren song of productivity. Only the eerie freedom of death, if it can be known, was delivered here. But we have forgotten. Again, we are led to believe that work will set us free.

We need to remember, like Austerlitz, and to turn and face the great destructiveness at the heart of our modern society – this turning of the necessity of work first into a compulsion, and then into a vocation. Creative destruction? Innovative disruption? None truly believe that surely? It is not work, but simpler perceptions that can give us all hope, that may set us free. So says Zbigniew Herbert in "The Envoy of Mr Cogito":

>Beware of dryness of heart love the morning spring the bird
>with an unknown name the winter oak
>light on a wall the splendour of the sky
>they don't need your warm breath
>they are there to say: none will console you.

This post was composed in response to the prompt 'none' and was accompanied by a photograph of the gate of Theresienstadt in the Czech Republic, former German concentration camp.

Jeff Rich

Fragile Identities, Fragile Memories
8 September 2017

> It is justice which extracts from traumatizing remembrances their exemplary value, turns memory into a project, and it is this project of justice that gives the form of the future and of imperativeness to the duty of memory. (Paul Ricoeur, *Memory, History, Forgetting*)

Some years ago I was asked to prepare one of those profiles of myself that serve to introduce your more elusive character traits to colleagues in the workplace through a series of questions about life outside of work and reflections on work. The Proust questionnaire had questions like: 'what were my memories of childhood?' and 'which movies had changed my life?' I replied 'none', but several books had, including *A la récherche du temps perdu*. It also asked 'what kind of workplace did I want to work in?' I replied in an instant, with a flash of intuition – "one that respects human frailty".

No one ever really asked me about this statement of philosophy. I do not know if many read my profile. A few said "great profile" to me over the weeks my "Get to Know" profile featured on the employee of the month board. But none of the revelations in this profile, hinted though they may have been – my years of drinking, the fragility of my mind, my poetic stirrings, the madness of my parents and childhood, not even my declared philosophy of the workplace – none of these hints at the broken shards of my identity ever led to an approach towards greater intimacy.

Still, even though this poem of the everyday dates from ten or so years ago, that orientation still defines who I am at work. We are all frail, and our projects tragically fail many times. Yet still we can move towards a good life, a just life if we live together as neighbours in each other's frailty.

The French philosopher, Paul Ricoeur, once described a little ethics to guide the cohabitation of the divided self in a troubled world. This little ethics – perhaps another way to describe ordinary virtues as I name them – was "aiming at a good life lived with and for others in just institutions".[106]

It is a simple statement, yet an enduring challenge. Its modesty is welcome in these days when identity politics is loud and proud, and forgets that it is both fragile and only ever lived through institutions. Yes, those much denounced, treacherous and ever so frail institutions.

How do we bridge the gaps between our frail identities, our limited capabilities, which always melt in the sun like Icarus' wings, and our hopes for more just institutions? I make my way in one of these institutions, government, and try to live a good life with and for others within it; but is the institution just? And if it is not just, what can I do about it? Poor, limited, frail and incapable me?

Only by practising, in Ricouer's phrase, a little ethics of small intentions, or in my own terms, the ordinary virtues, can I bridge the gap between my private dreams of good government and the public poverty of the unjust institutions of government today, with rampant clientilism and patronage, the competitive control of rival gangs, a surrender to vacuousness, a loss of public spirit and shared high culture, a fragmentation into a thousand hard brittle shards of shrill politicking.

And only by knowing that we are all frail – both self and other, both governed and governing, both oppressed and oppressor, both conqueror and vanquished – can we transcend the murky politics of both populism and identity politics. Only by knowing we are all frail, all potential victims at the sacrifice, can we avoid fusing identities with deadly beliefs about history.

Elsewhere in *Memory, History, Forgetting*, Ricoeur writes:

> A third cause of fragility is the legacy of founding violence. It is a fact that no historic community exists which does not have its origins in war. ... The same events, therefore, signify glory for some, but humiliation for others. One side's rejoicing

---
[106] *Oneself as Another* (1992) p. 172.

corresponds to the other's execration. This is how real and symbolic wounds are stored in the archives of collective memory.

There is enough war in history; we do not need history wars and culture wars that both consecrate and desecrate public memory. We need rather to practise humility in asserting and nurturing our mercurial identities, while kindly forgiving, if not forgetting, the sins that lie in all of our pasts.

The return of sacred violence
3 September 2017

> Central to both torture and terror is the political psychology of degradation. (Paul Kahn, *Sacred violence: torture, terror and sovereignty*)

> Violent imitation, which makes adversaries more and more alike, is at the root of all myths and cultures. (René Girard, *Battling to the End*)

It is a characteristic of our time that while political authority disintegrates, political violence for a cause is resurgent.

This is a troubling phenomenon, but its difficulty should not lead us to avert our eyes.

Its most obvious form is in the appeal of Islamist terror to a small group of Western Muslims.

But we have also seen acts of extremist violence from across the political spectrum. On one side, we see Antifa and its violent protests, a Bernie Sanders supporter shooting Republicans at a charity baseball match, and a comedian pictured holding the severed head of a democratically elected President as a fake trophy. On the other side, we see the spectre of white supremacy, nostalgic for the confederacy, shouting "Jews won't replace us," and then driving a vehicle, the mobile weapon of choice in these times, into a crowd of leftist demonstrators.

Identity politics, in all its forms, from the rainbow coalition to the white supremacists shouting "you won't replace us", lives on the edge of violence. By asserting one identity, this mode of politics begins to degrade those who differ in their identity. Tolerance and respect are not important values for identity politics. The ardent radicals sneer at these condescending gestures of a collapsing hegemony. Authority – the essential attribute for the effective exercise of governing power – is despised. Yet authority alone can constrain violence.

Is the return of sacred violence across our world closely related to cultural decay? Here, in closing this brief fragment, are the thoughts of René Girard in *Battling to the End*:

> I began to see the end of war as a subject in itself. The last days of an institution whose purpose was to control and restrain violence corroborates my central hypothesis, namely that for three centuries all rituals and institutions have been crumbling. War, through its rules and orders, also helped to create meaning by establishing new equilibria over an ever growing geographical area. It has generally ceased to play this role since the end of World War II. How did the system suddenly disintegrate? How has political rationality finally become powerless?

Jeff Rich

On Revenge
3 December 2017

All visible objects, man, are but as pasteboard masks. But in each event – in the living act, the undoubted deed – there, some unknown but still reasoning thing puts forth the mouldings of its features from behind the unreasoning mask. If man will strike, strike through the mask! How can the prisoner reach outside except by thrusting through the wall? To me, the white whale is that wall, shoved near to me. Sometimes I think there's naught beyond. But 'tis enough. He tasks me; he heaps me; I see in him outrageous strength, with an inscrutable malice sinewing it. That inscrutable thing is chiefly what I hate; and be the white whale agent, or be the white whale principal, I will wreak that hate upon him. (Captain Ahab in Hermann Melville, *Moby Dick*)

I will have such revenges on you both,
That all the world shall – I will do such things –
What they are, yet I know not: but they shall be
The terrors of the earth.
Shakespeare, *King Lear*

At times, thoughts of revenge have driven me mad. Thoughts, but I do not act on them. The thoughts pool like dirty water in my mind. They become a home to disease, and plots to inflict the terrors of the earth on my enemies. But these plots find no actors, know no conspiracies, and drop into the fetid water like mere bitter letters.

I have borne enough insult, humiliation and loss in my wanderings across the seas of power to dream on revenge. The modern office is a company of strangers, where tragic drama is frowned upon and cynical detachment is preferred. But decisions on jobs and titles and projects and favours are as fateful for soul-making as the adventures of a whaling ship.

Once, after many years of being passed over for promotion, I was subjected by a boss to the silent treatment for weeks on end. It was only broken by a suggestion that I go to some other part of the organisation, where I could be completely forgotten by him. For a few weeks I discussed this exile with the area, but I was unwilling to go because the job did not suit my skills; the new manager I knew I could not work for; and I believed surely I deserved better. At some point, when I still believed I was negotiating the arrangements, I learned from this new manager that I had already been transferred. The paperwork had been signed by my old boss two weeks before, and no-one had even told me. I later learned the new manager had told all her staff months before, before the idea was even put to me, that I would be working there. The plot to use me for their purposes had been hatched without me. The basic dignity afforded to anyone to be involved in decisions about their own work was denied me. I had been traded like a chattel in this black bureaucratic market.

This humiliation broke my identity as a professional public servant. It smashed my sense of self. It led to thoughts of suicide and deep depression. The world seemed like a great wall of inscrutable malice, seeking to destroy me. The depression was a war within myself between my own letters of the underworld and an instinct for another life-affirming response. As in Dostoevsky's *Letters from the Underworld*, I immersed myself in a "state of cold, malignant, perpetual rancour" in which I would taunt and worry myself with my own fancies.

> Of those fancies it will be ashamed, yet it will nevertheless remember them all, exaggerate them all, and even imagine to itself things which have never happened, on the mere pretext that one day it may obtain its revenge, and that therefore it must, in the meanwhile, forget nothing.

Dostoevsky also anticipated the impotence of my dreams of revenge:

> Or perhaps it will actually embark upon a scheme of revenge; but if it does so the thing will be done only by fits and starts, and from behind a stone, and incognito, and in a manner which makes it clear that the mouse distrusts alike its right to wreak

vengeance and the ultimate success of its scheme, since it knows in advance that its poor attempts at retribution will bring upon its own head a hundred times more suffering than will fall to the lot of the person against whom the vengeance is aimed, but upon whom not so much as a scratch is inflicted.[107]

It seemed to me that the injury done to me was too great to fight back, and so I withdrew into a dark night of the soul. Machiavelli said that "Men should be either treated generously or destroyed because they take revenge for slight injuries – for heavy ones they cannot." So, I was both destroyed and unable to take revenge. I only dreamt on the bitter root.

> Revenge is barren of itself: it is the dreadful food it feeds on; its delight is murder; its end is despair. (Friedrich Schiller)

As the months passed the bitter fancies receded. Writing, and not power, would be my salvation. My redemption lay in literature and culture, and not the petty prizes of office politics. Rather than dwell on revenge, I began to mourn the life and the dreams I had lost. I could not give up my life in the oceans of power, but sailed them not in the *Pequod*, but in *The Flying Dutchman*.

---

[107] Dostoevsky, *Letters from the Underworld*, p. 7.

Persistence, Terror and *Das Schloss* – 2017 Reflections
17 December 2017

Persistence

Twelve months ago I was approaching Christmas and the end of a liberating period of long service leave. It was a period of leave that rejuvenated my writing and my living. It returned a sense of adventure and courage to my cultural life. I found a way, through this blog, to weave together my personal experiences, my observations of the greater world, the visitations of mine terrible angels, and the life of my mind.

But Christmas came with a terror for what the new year of work would bring. The Castle had, some years before, cast me adrift, stolen my life jacket, and turned its back on me. The lordly castellans had hoped I would drown, and now, as I clambered back to the ship, they spurned and insulted me as a cur, not worthy of any enduring position of honour in the Castle.

Still, I lived and still I wrote. I was assigned to pump water from the listing ship, and at night I wrote here. Here dignity, compassion and the life of the mind endured. Here I could leave behind the humiliations of the day. Here I scratched into the paneling of the cursed ship something of beauty, if not every day, then at least most weeks.

Here, I raised my lyre to sing infinite praise.

Terror

The acts of terror and mass violence across the world this year have cast a long shadow. In my home city, Melbourne in the southeastern corner of Australia, so distant from the war zones of the world, we have witnessed a string of incidents: the Bourke Street vehicular attack, an incident on a plane in which a man with mental illness claimed he had a bomb, and the luring of police to a hostage trap by an ex-prisoner associated with terror plots. And, of course, across the world a never-ending chorus of the damned has reported terrors in London, Los Angeles, Manila, New York, Paris, Stockholm, and Afghanistan, Bangladesh, Canada, Egypt, Germany, India, Iraq, Israel, Russia, Somalia, Syria, and Turkey. I have read of feral cities and failing states, and been shocked by the espousal of violence by claimants of social justice like Antifa.

This year I had to confront personally the meaning of terror since it became part of my job. What could my minor provincial government do to prevent and respond to acts of violence, such as the Bourke Street car attack of January 2017? I learned about the motives of mass killers, lone actor terrorists, and group terrorists. I studied grievance-fueled violence and its relationship to extremism and mental health. I met and discussed responses with an Expert Panel on Terrorism and Violent Extremism, composed of a former Police Commissioner and a former Supreme Court judge. I contemplated whether religion provides a salve of peace to counter violent extremism or an ark of the covenant that stores in the culture grievance, hatred and the will both to die and to kill as a martyr.

I remember the moment of September 11, 2001. I was watching the television series, *The West Wing*, when some news broke that a plane had flown into one of the twin towers. My partner and I watched uneasily the news coverage, and saw live to air the second plane fly into the second tower. There have been many incidents since in the new era of pessimism and fear ushered in by that attack. But it has not truly been until this year that I have truly recognised the gravity and depth of the threat posed by the monster of sacred violence that sleeps in all of our hearts.

> He who fights with monsters should look to it that he himself does not become a monster. And if you gaze long into an abyss, the abyss also gazes into you. (Nietzsche, *Beyond Good and Evil*)

Das Schloss

> K. constantly expected the road to turn in the direction of the castle at last, surely it would, and it was only because he expected it that he kept going. (Franz Kafka, *The Castle [Das Schloss]*)

Eighteen months ago I was prepared to give away my long search for the gates of the Castle. I had sought a return to the ivory tower of my youth, where I could study history, and leave behind the court and practical affairs. But the keepers of this tower spurned me too. So on the last day of my work before my long service leave I disconnected my work phone, copied onto a flash drive the few documents that would remind me of my most important personal achievements in the bureaucracy, and packed up the few personal belongings on the desk that I would never return to again. I walked out the door about 3 pm, and, on the eve of an election for a national government, went to watch a live-to-air radio show in my local shopping centre where they talked about political affairs and the looming verdict.

I was not sure I would ever come back, but I had no plans to find another career. A year earlier, I had been in a deep depression. I had fled my work in humiliation and fear. Now I was walking into a deeper and truer life, but a life without security or status or power unless I chose to return. I threw myself into poetry, history, and the meaning of a simpler life. But I remained dependent for a living on the organisation that seemed to despise me.

In January this year I did choose to return to life as a bureaucrat, and I renewed my search for admission to *Das Schloss*. Every month I have written to some minor lord of the Castle, and pleaded to be considered worthy, to be admitted to the orders that busy themselves with the business of the court, there in the mists, beyond my vision, at the end of the twisting road. Twenty times, at least, they have said no, and not once, as I have walked this long twisting road, have I caught a glimpse of the true Castle I have searched so long for.

Now at the end of a year in which I have tried to live in truth, to write my own thoughts as authentically as I can and to act in the world in a way that approaches my values, I still stand as an outcast beyond the reaches of *Das Schloss*. Which way do I walk next year? To the Castle and back, or do I turn my back on this great civil dream, and wander alone like a grey wolf into the Great Dark Forest?

> go for only thus will you be admitted into the company of cold skulls
> to the company of your forefathers: Gilgamesh Hector Roland
> the defenders of the kingdom without bounds and the city of ashes
> Be faithful Go

Zbigniew Herbert, *The Envoy of Mr Cogito*

Borderlands of Madness

10 June 2018

Demi-fous. Mazeland. Dazeland. Driftland. Incipient lunatics. Hysterics. Neurotics. Carriers of latent brain disease. Neurasthenia. Sufferers of high-prevalence disorders. People with shattered nerves. Stressed out kittens. The traumatised. The burnt ones. Melancholics. The worried well.

There are so many names designating those who prowl in the borderlands between madness and reason. Some of these names are drawn from Andrew Scull's *Madness in Civilization*. Scull gives some account of the emergence of concern with this class of people during the nineteenth century. Numbers in the asylums swelled during the nineteenth century for two reasons. First, the general rise in life expectancy lengthened the lives of asylum patients too. Second, the asylum's cures did not work so well for many of the inhabitants, so length of stay stretched out. Third, more people were drawn into the asylum, with the less extreme, less disturbed forms of illness. Simple enough, but still there is debate on what lay behind this growth in numbers. Was it a real secular trend, possibly in response to forms of virus? Was it merely an expanding diagnostic category that swept more and more into a category of concern? Another possibility that Scull does not consider is that perhaps it was a response to changing mental conditions through the nineteenth century, which placed a new strain and new premium on the soundness of the mind.

In any case, the culture and the world of medicine responded to the growth in numbers by devising new forms of treatment that would separate the severe and the moderate or even the mild. They developed sanitoria, which Thomas Mann portrayed so ironically in *The Magic Mountain*, and rest cures, which the great Virginia Woolf was put on, and ultimately Freud's own psychoanalysis for the hysterics and neurotics, who "suffer mainly from reminiscences" (Freud and Breuer, *Studies on Hysteria*). They also raised a permanent mental wall, at least in the mind of many health practitioners, between the experiences of the severely ill, those with "serious" mental illness, in the phrase that is still reserved for the psychotic, and those with low-prevalence disorders or the troubled waifs who are worried, anxious, but do not have an "organic" problem.

Scull does not succeed in telling us about the experience of those banished from serious madness, always to wander the world uncertain of the name, the profundity, or the seriousness of their troubles. He tends, on my reading, to attribute the rise in diagnosis to the interests of the new profession, and behind that there is the old, odd implication of malingering weakness for the half-mad. Too weak to cope with life, they find a form of redemption in the false promises of cures from a new breed of therapies. Still, he does see that Freud's enormous cultural impact did not grow from the specifics of his theories or the mixed success of his treatments, which were only ever accessible to a few. Rather, in Scull's view, Freud:

> denied that madness was simply the problem of the Other. It

lurked, it would seem, in all of us, at least to some degree. The same forces that led one to mental invalidism allowed another to produce accomplishments of surpassing cultural importance. Civilization and its discontents Freud proclaimed, were inevitably and irretrievably locked in an indissoluble embrace.[108]

Madness and reason exist together in a misty fog of war. I was going to say they exist along a continuum, but I do not think they are so neatly arrayed, nor that anyone can be very certain at what degree of latitude their madness sits. And it is perhaps the scientific will to explain that keeps us from best knowing the borderlands of insanity, where roamed those *demi-fous* and hysterics "who crowded their waiting rooms [of the neurologists, who preferred serious cases] … but [were] hard to pin down."

The will-to-explain breeds determinism, and all kinds of determinism have a difficult time with the uncertainty of madness. Freud's determinism drove him to find a royal road to the unconscious, and to invent an increasingly fanciful set of theories that pinned psychic life down to its earliest memories. Biological determinism has sought all sorts of organic explanations of the defective constitutions of the mad, and generated a murder of cruel treatments – lobotomies, insulin comas, leucotomies, teeth extractions and so on. Neuroscientific determinism, currently fashionable, mistakes its pretty pictures of the brain for fixed events in a chain of causation. Social determinism finds all kinds of excuses in the social determinants of health, but only ends up nagging the poor mad to give up smoking in their cells.

So chance and indeterminacy are the madman's friend. They do, after all, relieve the terrible burden of the genetic curse, and so free the self to live as if it were not who it is told and fears it must be.

---

[108] Scull, *Madness in Civilization*, p 289.

Could the culture wars descend into civil wars?
21 October 2018

Over at the online magazine *Quillette*, a Shakespeare scholar at a minor English university, Neerna Parvini, raised a very dire prospect, prompted by that turmoil of identity politics fueled by partisan cynicism, the Brett Kavanaugh US Supreme Court appointment hearing.

> If I was being pessimistic, I'd say it was a moment in which the left chose a nuclear option that threatens to turn the culture wars into a civil war.

That dire prediction resonated with my Spenglerian pessimism just a little, and so let us consider a few of the reasons to take this point of view seriously, and then some reasons perhaps to set it aside.

Parvini quotes with approval Douglas Murray's *The Strange Death of Europe*, in which Murray invokes earlier prophets of civilisational decline, such as Spengler and Stefan Zweig. Murray writes that Europe has "lost faith in its beliefs, traditions and legitimacy". I would add Europe has lost faith in its institutions, which are of great importance as a defence against civil war. This loss of faith springs, in part, from the loss of the "tragic sense of history." As Murray writes:

> They have lost what Zweig and his generation so painfully learnt: that everything you love, even the greatest and most cultured civilisations in history, can be swept away by people who are unworthy of them. Other than simply ignoring it, one of the few ways to avoid this tragic sense of life is to push it away through a belief in the tide of human progress.[109]

It is through this disavowal of its deepest culture that, Murray argues, "Europe is committing suicide". It no longer mounts a defence against its own acts of self-harm. Without those defences, can violence be that far away? We already see some forms of early violence which

---

[109] Murray, *The Strange Death of Europe* (2017), p. 3.

our institutions are too pusillanimous to protect themselves from. Activists and protesters de-platform and intimidate people whose ideas they disagree with. The police then demand a fee from the harassed organisers of the talk. Antifa protesters in masks confront alt-right demonstrators in balaclavas, and scuffle on the streets. On twitter, armies of trolls dehumanise their enemies, and call for their symbolic death. A few fixated individuals take it further, and shoot their enemies.

These scuffles and cells of fanatical tweets are a long way from civil war; but we are deluding ourselves if we do not hear dark trembles beneath these events. Social media is the feral city of our culture. It is dominated by warlords and vicious tribal loyalties, and it unleashes a spirit of murder into the speech of our times. The culture wars are already the beginning of civil war. However minor this violence may be now, the signs of cultural decay are real, and without strong institutions that shelter respectful civil disagreement, where will the resistance to civil war come from?

The defence of a cultured peace will not come from the political elites. Their studied indifference to their own traditions was on display during the Kavanaugh affair, and many other scandals in political institutions outside of the United States of America. The new *nomenklatura* of political professionals have become parasites feeding on the institutions of government they purport to lead. No institution, no convention, no tradition of importance is safe from the conduct of a political stunt. The drive to like and to subscribe leads erstwhile intelligent people into the repeated performance of stupidity on social media. As Oswald Spengler wrote: "Through money democracy becomes its own destroyer, after money has destroyed intellect."

Indeed, the culture wars are a form of intra-elite competition that if it becomes more intense could lead to civil war. Peter Turchin, the historian and practitioner of vast cliometrics, has argued that elite overproduction in the US has driven up the intensity of intra-elite competition. Escalating political competition is seen in the increased total cost of election for congressional races, and the breakdown of social norms regulating political discourse so evident since the 2016 presidential election. Turchin's analysis of past societies predicts an outbreak of political violence, or even "a state collapse, a revolution, or a civil war (or all of the above)."

I want to temper these reflections on the descent into civil war and cultural destruction with some grounds for hope. But it is a hope warded by Spengler's aphorism that optimism is cowardice. I do not wish hope to be craven, but that does not mean fear will not crawl between the cracks. Already our societies seem ungovernable. Our political and democratic institutions are in decline. Our disputes are more acrimonious. Our settlements through civil discourse are more spurious. Identity has asserted itself over all other values, and identity does not brook difference. What weak reeds then are these grounds for hope? As Oswald Spengler wrote,

> There is a vast difference, which most people will never comprehend, between viewing future history as it will be and viewing it as one might like it to be. Peace is a desire, war is a fact; and history has never paid heed to human desires and ideals.

Still, there is some antidote in knowing that our culture is not American, and that the militant enthusiasms of identity politics leave most people cold. We may quietly succumb to grief, rather than die a bloodied, horrible death in war. We might also rescue from the ruins enough fragments of the culture that sustained our best institutions, and those relics may keep the infinite conversation alive for another generation or even another era.

Jeff Rich

Not Belonging—Reflections on 2018
23 December 2018

This year has seen the mass formation of stories of belonging in defiance to an imagined social order of cultural dominance. Here are some examples: #metoo, people of color, it's OK to be white, neurodiversity, gender diversity, identity politics, alt-right, intellectual dark web, and majority-minority. These new claims of belonging, of strength through identity, oppose the powers that be, and dictate a militant speech of cultural war. They propose a claim of displacement and vengeful dispossession of belonging: those who are not like us have been dominant for too long, and have enjoyed possession of the terms of belonging too easily. It is time to shout them down, one way or another; to denounce their exclusions, to tear down their fences and to expose the lies that are spoken in their clubs; and to march into their places, and to burn down their homes.

The culture wars lay claim to belonging itself. They weaponise belonging. Terms such as "people of colour" recycle the epithets of high nineteenth century racism – "colored people" – as a battle-standard that obliterates all cultural subtlety and all weak ties between people other than the index of domination by biological markers. This reversed intimidation demands a new kind of Maoist self-criticism from those who cannot belong, or else. It demands a confused self-identification as someone *you are not* by those *who know they are,* but *wish they were not,* part of the historical oppressor class. So we see phenomenon such as Rachel Anne Doležal, of white ancestry yet identifying as black, of moderate wealth yet claiming to be poor and reliant on welfare. Or the new spiritualism of gender fluidity, and its belief in the wholly cultural nature of the self-assignment of gender (that justifies rather biological treatments of surgery and hormonal medication). Or the use by some alt-right heroes, such as Ben Shapiro, of bullying polemic against bullying ideological zealots in a downward spiral of violent belonging that ends in a degraded public square.

And yet despite all these armies of belonging and identity on the march, I belong nowhere. The world of politics is in disarray with the collapse of liberal delusions, the breakdown of the American empire, and democracies in decay. The world of civil speech has become a vicious guerrilla war of competing identities, with which I do not identify. The world of bureaucracy, in which I have so long dwelled, has become a stage to display the latest beneficiaries of patronage and the new politics of belonging. I exclude myself from both. Every stage of literary culture is wracked by professions of belonging, and a fascination with ideas that are not likely to persist. Only in the quiet possession of the infinite conversation do I find a safe space to share my terrible sonnets and black paintings of the vision of our cultural collapse.

On the Rescue of Society
13 January 2019

Writing in the *New York Times*, David Brooks proposes the "remoralization of the market" as the correct response to economic populism. In an America besieged by Trumpism and Never-Trumpism, by identity politics and MAGA caps, by mass shooters and a permanent war faction in its political elite, by declining life expectancy amidst a mass opioid crisis and by Randian wealth apartheid imposed by its super-wealthy, Brooks looks to the moral fibre of the all-American firm of the 1950s and 1960s to restore a society where "it's easier to be a good person".

It was, in Brooks' telling, oddly political decisions that led to this unleashing of immoral behaviour in the market. In the 1970's President Jimmy Carter began tentative programs of deregulation and tax cuts. In the 1980's President Ronald Reagan accelerated this new model of starving the beast of government. "As a matter of policy," he writes, "we privileged economics and then eventually no longer could even see that there could be other priorities." Still, this political climate endorsed closing "the moral lens" in firms. Companies now valued only their shareholders, not their stakeholders. 'Anything you could do to make money' now became OK. Massive tax evasion through overseas havens became the norm. Society was demoralised by a "secession of the successful" that erased the sheen of material prosperity. In summary, he writes:

> A deadly combination of right-wing free-market fundamentalism and left-wing moral relativism led to a withering away of moral norms and shared codes of decent conduct. We ripped the market out of its moral and social context and let it operate purely by its own rules. We made the market its own priest and confessor. Society came to be seen as an atomized collection of individual economic units pursuing self-interest. Selfishness was normalized.[110]

It is an argument with a lot of sense. Although Brooks writes with the usual American journalistic narcissism (the belief that the world begins and ends in the USA), his observations of the demoralisation of society hold true to my own experience in the Great Southern Land. Some time in the 1970's, the economics profession was installed as the mercenary eunuchs who governed on behalf of the merchant elite. Society was abolished and in its place was placed the icon of the market. Government was re-conceived as a failing family business, which should submit to high-priced lawyers and consultants stripping assets, minimising tax, redirecting revenues to the new private owners of formerly proudly public infrastructure, and lobbying a newly supine political class to ease all rules and obligations on the wealthy elite.

---

[110] Brooks, *New York Times*, 10 January 2019.

Still, we did not end up with quite so bad a society as America the Brave. We kept a functional health care system. We preserved and strengthened a targeted social welfare system that, at least in its payments, if not in its services, works as well as anywhere. Thanks largely to the boon of commodity supplies to China, we have enjoyed a prosperity in which both the poor, the middle class and the rich have all got richer. Social cohesion has been strained at times, but yet has managed ongoing large migration, with minimal friction and fuss. We have never indulged or celebrated the celebrity and super-rich class as much as America, and the few grandiose miners and media moguls who pretend to such status are pilloried, rather than privileged. Philanthropy in our country is more the helping hand of a neighbour when fire or flood or emergency strikes, than the aggrandised pseudo-government of the Open Society Foundation or the Bill and Melinda Gates Foundation.

Australia has not done so well in culture and our political institutions, even though our problems are not as deep as the Americans. Our culture too is in decay. Its roots have been over-watered by bad education, supplied by universities that have decided their core business is not the pursuit of wisdom, but the export of education to overseas students and the commercialisation of knowledge with industry. Our culture's leaf canopy has been deprived of light by liquid modernity and its relentless search for a clickable meme. There remain now few gardeners who know the ancient traditions that sustain the old tree of knowledge. There are many wonderful new plants blooming around us, including the pleasures of this golden age of television drama. But how will this garden grow? What shade and seclusion will it offer against the glowering sun, when the grand old tree at its heart withers and dies?

Our political institutions are decayed too, if not in the state of rotten crisis of that failed state, the USA. In the decade following John Howard, with its many leadership changes, we have displaced Italy in international rankings of the instability of political leadership. We entertain the BBC, eager for distractions from the failure of

Westminster, with stories of being the 'coup capital' of the world. Our political parties have hollowed out, and become shells controlled by a *condottiere* class of political mercenaries, who look to the debauched electoral politics of America for the latest trends, techniques and treachery towards citizens. Our parliaments do not function as deliberative assemblies. They do not debate the great issues of the time. They are not chambers of elevated rhetoric that dignifies the moral conflicts of our society, unlike the language of Disraeli or Gladstone or Lincoln. Now we endure endless dumb social media posts, tatty little scandals of personal indulgences, and repackaged virtue signalling aimed at micro-targeted groups of the electorate. Our bureaucracies – once a bulwark against patronage and client politics – have been thrown open to a spoils system run by this degraded political elite.

Many people within the national media and leadership circles still look back mistily to the great "era of reform" between 1984 and 2006 when Prime Ministers Hawke and Howard, with Treasurers Keating and Costello, led a series of economic reforms that opened up the country's trade with the world and laid the foundations for the great period of prosperity we have enjoyed. How many years is it now since we last had a recession? 27? What greater achievement could we ask for from our political leaders? And how far have they have fallen since? The high priests of market fundamentalism in the bureaucracy look on the current state of politics and cry. Ken Henry, former head of the Treasury, takes aim at this degraded spectacle of political mercenaries turning parliament into a social media pile-on.

> Our politicians have dug themselves into deep trenches from which they fire insults designed merely to cause political embarrassment. Populism supplies the munitions. And the whole spectacle — the whole dreadful spectacle — is broadcast live via multimedia, 24/7. The country that Australians want cannot even be imagined from these trenches.[111]

Ah, but he without sin should cast the first stone. Henry was the

---

[111] Ken Henry, National Press Club via *The Australian*, 23 February 2017.

advocate of the view that the one great reform the country needs is changes to tax rates (not a joke). But Ken Henry's stern moral views seemed to melt into thin air, when as Chair of the National Australia Bank, he appeared before the Banking Royal Commission. When tested on what his response was to immoral, criminal conduct by the banking executives he employed and supervised, Henry shrugged his shoulders and said, "sure we paid them bonuses, what else would we do… sack them all?" He tells the Banking Royal Commission, in the indulgent phrases of a philosopher-bureaucrat who has grown too used to admiration in the shadows, that:

> The capitalist model is that businesses have no responsibility other than to maximise profits for shareholders. A lot of people who have participated in this debate over the past 12 months have said that's all that you should hold boards accountable for, is that they are focused on the maximisation of profits for shareholders. …. It's open, obviously, to the commission to enter into this rather important debate. It could play a valuable role by doing so. But anyway, for what it's worth, NAB's view clearly today is that incentives should be aligned with customer experience.[112]

So, we are back to Brooks' observation that morally hollow business leaders, stimulated by the celebration of the free market, have brought us to a social crisis, that requires a re-moralization of business as an antidote to populism. It is as if the Dostoevsky fable of the Grand Inquisitor was misapplied by some ambitious economic student without fear of the consequences. Yes, everything in the market should be allowed, and all old traditions and virtues pushed aside before the great wave of reform. But what we see in Henry's answer is that the mind that despises populism and engineers economic reform is the same mind that cannot apply standards of common decency to the operation of a business.

But we are also at the heart of a paradox with Brooks' observation. The initiator of the change in society in Brooks' tale is government. It is

---

[112] Ken Henry, quoted in *Australian Financial Review*, 27 November 2018.

the Presidents who change the rules, and the ideologies – free market fundamentalism and moral relativism – that reshaped the culture. But after that catalyst, government retreats from Brooks' story. And it is not *in government* where Brooks for a cure for this republic in distress. Rather, Brooks looks to a re-moralisation *in the market*, and a restitution of moral virtues – the "old-fashioned norms around loyalty, cooperation, honesty, equality, fairness and compassion."

But one cannot hope to rescue society from the market by making the market be more like society. Rather, we all must try to live more of our lives outside the modern prisons of market, consumption and celebrity. And in the political realm, we need an insurrection of virtue that restores to the ordinary acts of governing the essential character of dignity, compassion, truth-telling and humility. In so doing we might leave behind this era of rule by the market, its amoral merchant elite and their political *condottiere*. We might create or better still repair public institutions so that they can provide sustaining ways of life.

The Victorious Hermit in Copenhagen
21 June 2019

I was only in Copenhagen for a day; in which time I strolled down Strøget; ate some excellent pickled herring in Nyhaven; enjoyed the excellent cinnamon and cardamon buns of Danish bakeries; relaxed on a cruise boat around the harbour during which the guide was openly contemptuous of the tourist obsession with the little mermaid statue; and spent hours in Tivoli Gardens which offered a carnival of free entertainment for all generations and many tastes.

Tivoli Gardens was the greatest surprise, and gave the key to the famed tolerance of the Danes. This large Garden in central Copenhagen is much more than an amusement park. It offered stylish vegetarian dining at the top restaurant, *Nimb Gemyse*; modern ballet performed to the music of John Adams at the pantomime theatre; a rock concert of a leading Danish Muslim singer at which people aged from 12 to 60+ stood, danced and enjoyed the music together; and gentle mingling of many generations and cultures.

In the afternoon we took a break from the urban centre and took a train to nearby Roskilde, which I learned is an ancient site of Danish history, once the trade route hub for the Vikings. It was founded somewhere between the 7th and 9th century. Roskilde means "Ro's Spring", and indeed we walked past the spring on our way from visiting the remarkable, world heritage Roskilde Cathedral, dating from 1275, to the Viking Boat Museum, which unfortunately we were too late to enter. Roskilde provided an insight into some deep roots of Danish culture: the Viking heritage, Christianity, the Danish Protestant Church, and the enduring monarchy. Here at Roskilde Cathedral are buried 39 Danish monarchs, and a tomb is being prepared for the current long-serving queen, Margrethe II, monarch since 1972. This tomb is remarkable for its beauty, and there is a small exhibit on how the current Queen's tomb is being crafted. The tomb will appear as clear glass, and the Queen's wrapped remains will be held in an impressed centre. It is quite exquisite as both applied art and a symbol of the Danish open society.

When we were in Copenhagen the Danish elections were under way, with the count held a few days after we left the city. I watched the results come in subsequently on Swedish television from our hostel room in Stockholm. The Danes claimed to reverse the trend towards right-wing populism. The Danish nationalist, right-wing party lost ground, in part due to its involvement in some scandals over the misuse of public funds. Retrenchments in some public services and a decline in the quality and reliability of public health services also led to a loss of votes for the centre right/liberal governing coalition party. So, it led to a new government forming from a small majority for the 'red bloc'.

I was not in Denmark long enough to learn more about the great enigmatic victorious hermit of existentialism, Søren Kierkegaard. A statue of Kierkegaard stands in front of the Danish Royal Library, where his unusual writings are held, but I was unable to visit either/or indeed come to grips with the fragmentary, pseudonymous texts. Like Kafka, Kierkegaard was unable to establish kind, familiar, intimate relationships. He broke off an engagement with a woman, and separated himself into his literary and philosophical hell. He is another father of fragments and confused identities. Despite his troubled personality, he had a remarkable influence on philosophy, literature and many aspects of culture, including on the great traditions of humanistic psychology, such as Binswanger, Rollo May and Carl Rogers, which has done so much good for the world.

I have read a little Kierkegaard, but the depth of this influential enigma awaits me; like the depths of Denmark and Copenhagen they invite me to further interpretation, insight and curiosity. The pseudonym used by Kierkegaard for his first major work – *Either/Or* – was (translated from Latin) "Victorious Hermit." Let that be an inspiration to me.

Forgiveness and the madness of crowds

13 October 2019

Douglas Murray places this remark from G.K. Chesterton in the epigram of his *The madness of crowds: gender, race, identity*: "The special mark of the modern world is not that it is sceptical, but that it is dogmatic without knowing it".

His book is a restrained testing of the absurdities of identity politics, social justice and intersectionality. He highlights the extreme cases of the excommunication from their identity of Germaine Greer (no longer a feminist), Kanye West (no longer black), and Peter Thiel (no longer gay). But he also speaks compassionately of the objects of sacrifice in the virtue-signaling cults, such as a 17 year old woman who posted on instagram a photo of herself in a Chinese-themed prom dress and was then pilloried worldwide as a 'casual racist'. He enlivens the real experience of the people beneath the categorical claims of identities, such as the suicidal subjects of unsuccessful gender reassignment operations, or the people with the difficult dilemma of inter-sex status. He restores the old account by Jan Morris of her experience transitioning from man to woman over the 1960's and 1970's. His attention to Jan Morris is a kindly reminder of Murray's broader theme that the past knew more than the social justice warriors care to acknowledge.

Murray has courageously written the thoughts, doubts, and uncomfortable truths that are on many minds, and yet are sometimes bullied into silence by inter-sectional manias. He reasonably urges people who claim terrible injustices and oppressions, to stop a moment, and ask, 'Compared to what?' The equalities debate has paradoxically become most extreme when the real achievements of equality are at an historical high.

He urges restraints on the incited crowds, who bray revolution in the name of a declared identity and clamour to tear the house down. Be careful, Murray says. The world is delicate, fragile and unknowable, more so than your slogans admit. The crowds could easily have their way, tear the house down, and then discover there is nothing left to replace this home. Still worse, the demolition job could create a sink hole.

Murray invokes Hannah Arendt on moral decisions in an affluent society. In 1964, Arendt argued in a lecture to newly affluent and all-powerful Americans that the actions taken by humans over the course of their lives have unbounded, limitless consequences. Arendt described this condition as the "frailty and unreliability of human affairs." In this frail, unreliable web of relationships, we humans learn that:

> every action touches off not only a reaction but a chain reaction... every process is the cause of unpredictable new processes... [and as a consequence] we can never really know what we are doing.[113]

Murray follows Arendt in seeing society through this veil of frailty. It led the great student of totalitarianism to make all claims of knowledge modest, and to advocate one ordinary virtue above others, that is, forgiveness. In the *Human Condition*, Arendt wrote:

> Without being forgiven, released from the consequences of what we have done, our capacity to act would, as it were, be confined to one single deed from which we could never recover; we would remain the victim of its consequences forever, not unlike the sorcerer's apprentice who lacked the magic formula to break the spell.[114]

Unfortunately, Murray comments, forgiveness is the last thing on the mind of the frenzied crowd. To forgive, the crowd today must get control of the whirligig social media engine, and let go of its retributive, punishing attitude to the past. It must adopt some sentiments of conservation towards our flawed and fallen former fellows. Murray writes:

> We live in this world where everyone is at risk... of having to spend the rest of their lives living with our worst joke. ... A world in which one of the greatest exertions of 'power' is constantly exerted – the power to stand in judgement over, and potentially ruin, the life of another human being for reasons which may or may not be sincere.[115]

Hannah Arendt made a case in *The Human Condition* that a moral stance in politics can be based on forgiveness and respect. Such a

---

[113] Arendt, "Labour, Work, Action" (1964).
[114] Arendt, *The Human Condition* (1958), p. 237.
[115] Murray, *The Madness of Crowds: Gender, Race and Identity* (2019).

politics would form a kind of friendship towards strangers and neighbours, rather than a blind affirmation of membership of self-identifying, self-chosen groups. This kind of politics would be more aware of its limits. It would not aim, as much radical identity politics does,

> to politicize absolutely everything. To turn every aspect of human interaction into a matter of politics. To interpret every action and relationship in our lives along lines which are alleged to have been carved out by political actions.

Murray calls instead for some blessed relief from politics in central domains of our lives. He reverses the core mantra that the personal is political. Some aspects of our personal lives just are not that political. Some aspects of our political actions should just not be that personal. He observes how empty lives and personalities devoted to politics can be:

> But of all the ways in which people can find meaning in their lives, politics – let alone politics on such a scale – is one of the unhappiest. Politics may be an important aspect of our lives, but as a source of personal meaning it is disastrous.

I have known this disaster personally. When my long search for recognition, status and adventure in the political world collapsed and failed recently I contemplated the renunciation of the political world. Murray does not prescribe monastic isolation from the political world, but he encourages us to rely less on politics as a source of meaning. "The call should be," Murray writes, "for people to simplify their lives and not to mislead themselves by devoting their lives to a theory that answers no questions, makes no predictions and is easily falsifiable."

This advice is flexible. It prescribes an aversion to ideology and crowds, but allows for many responses to those temptations. Murray dissuades us from a politics of performance and expression, and prods us towards a politics of responsible action within a shared commons of governing. Murray's wards help us hold fanatics at bay, even if they do not provide ready-made solutions to rebuild our virtues and institutions. That, after all, is the work we must do together with our fellow citizens in a spirit of intelligent civility and open inquiry. It is that spirit that Murray demonstrates so excellently by example.

Emmanuel Todd's Lineages of Modernity
16 February 2020

> Never have human groups of such a size been so rich, so old, so educated, so devoid of collective beliefs. (Emmanuel Todd, *Lineages Of Modernity.*)

Emmanuel Todd, *Lineages of Modernity* is a sweeping re-conception of both global history and our moment of political crisis[116].

Todd offers to explain the crumbling of the liberal global project of universal rights and limitless commerce. Why did Trump, Brexit, and the other populist, traditionalist, nationalist revolts against the liberal world order occur? Why are we experiencing endemic and escalating conflict about culture – to the point of violence – between the rainbow guards of identity politics and the guys in MAGA hats, between the quiet Australians and the elites who perform in politics/media? Why has liberal democracy failed? Why have we entered a fragmented post-democratic society?

Todd goes beyond the elevated arena of politics and looks to deep strands of culture, family and demography. He is a demographer, anthropologist and sociologist. He notoriously predicted in the 1970s the collapse of the Soviet Union on the basis of foreign trade statistics and falling birth rates. His deepest speciality is family systems, and a large part of *Lineages of Modernity* outlines the characteristic, distinct

---

[116] Todd, *Lineages of Modernity: a history of humanity from the Stone Age to Homo Americanus* (2019).

family structures that shape the society of the Anglosphere (the launching pad of globalist dreams) and other societies. These family structures generate underlying values expressed in cultural, social and political orders. Todd explains our moment of crisis with these fundamental anthropological facts, and shows how cultural fragmentation, not liberal global convergence, is the deepest problem our politics must respond to.

The quote at the head of this post points to major social facts that make our era distinctive. Durkheim defined social facts as, "manners of acting, thinking and feeling external to the individual, which are invested with a coercive power by virtue of which they exercise control over him". Here are some of the social facts Todd traces in modernity.

First, never have human groups been so rich. The percentage of people in the world who live in extreme poverty has fallen from over 80 per cent in 1820 to 10 per cent or less today. This rate has fallen from over 55 per cent since 1945. The level of ordinary wealth distributed across the world has increased. This is the rise of the "global middle class" that the globalists see as a vast homogeneous market for i-commerce, but, in truth, if we take Todd's view, is the fertile soil for divergence, driven by differing values and family systems.

Second, never have human groups been so old. This fact is well known but little considered for its profound reorientation of our basic values and modes of living, including our ordinary experiences of family, culture, the inheritance of tradition, and the living together of multiple generations. The profound transformation can be visualised by looking at a graph of the demography of the Word Population from 1950 to 2100 – a graph of the population pyramid. The graph changes from a narrow, sharp-pointed triangle in 1950, to a wide near flat-topped bell today, even more flat-topped in 2100.

Third, never have human groups been so educated. Literacy rates globally exceed 90 per cent. Years of schooling and post-school education are greater than ever. There has been an enormous growth of "human capital" since 1970, with the conscious expansion of mass higher education. Even in my lifetime I can recall the rates of completing 12 years of schooling in Australia increasing from about 30 per cent to an effective maximum of over 80 per cent.

But there is a constraint and a paradox hidden in this growth of formal education. The constraint is a decline in the quality of education. More years of education have a different impact if that education is of lower quality. The canon has collapsed while the university has exploded. When credentials have increased in advanced societies, the rate of reading has decreased. Given the known neurological effects of intensive reading of long texts, increased education does not mean increased cognitive performance, for all the years and the costs. The mass university of the 20th century may be a less beneficial cultural phenomenon than the printing press of the 15th century.

The paradox is that growth in education levels has also led to education becoming central to new systems of social stratification. There have been decades of progressive calls for investment in education as an antidote to rigid social hierarchies and a stimulant to social mobility and economic growth. But despite mass participation, advanced societies are in a state of educational stagnation. Can we really escape the bounds of human cognition? If we flood the markets with degrees, do not degrees become less valuable?

Todd identifies that stratified education levels have now become the most efficient explanation of political cleavages. "The question of higher education," Todd writes, is essential "to understand the new stratification of advanced societies and the disintegration of the body of citizens". So, this profound change in social practice, overlain with the deep demographic change (the social role of young people and patterns of family formation), has undemocratic consequences. Those adverse consequences are real even though more education is advocated by progressives and generally seen as aligned with democracy.

> The destruction of educational homogeneity, which fostered egalitarian sentiment and democracy, explains, as we have seen, the emergence in advanced societies of an inegalitarian and anti-

democratic subconscious. But it was the Left that desired mass education, including higher education. It is thus the Left that has unknowingly guided society towards inequality. The historical and ideological link between the Left and education undoubtedly enables us to understand why and how the inegalitarian drift of the educational system has dragged the Left along with it, transforming it into a new kind of Right, although it will never, ever admit it. And this has occurred in the three major Western democracies.[117]

Fourth, never have human groups been so devoid of collective beliefs. Todd identifies the divergence of advanced societies, and the collapse of the unifying cultures of those societies. The cultures of Russia and America are diverging, contrary to the liberal hypothesis of convergence through globalisation. But each culture is not diverging down a single path. The cultures of each country or each civilization are fragmented. Globalisation breaks up the common ground of each society through changes to family systems, national symbols, religions, and cultural canons. It is creating a plurality in every single society.

Cultural fragmentation is at the heart of our modern political experience. As I have written elsewhere, one thing we have lost amidst our cultural fragmentation, and which I encounter most days in my day job as a government bureaucrat, is a civic culture of governing. Our political communities have been shattered. We are riven by identity politics and hyper-partisanship. We fight culture wars and proclaim fluid fissured identities that separate us from traditions of civil dialogue. We have lost the art of talking to strangers, and working across the aisle.

Todd clarifies how this fragmentation is connected to social stratification based on education, and the paradoxically anti-democratic sentiment of the new, degraded academy. Academia is "a world that thinks it is on the left but is actually organizing inequality and conformism [as seen] in the crystallization of ideological alignments in the England of Brexit and the America of Donald

---

[117] Todd, *Lineages of Modernity*, p 249.

Trump".[118]

'Trump derangement syndrome' is a reaction to this cultural conflict. The ongoing derangement of many patricians of the American republic stems from a failure to look at society as it is. Todd comments on Trump's election victory in an interview:[119]

> Looking at the election as a historian, what happened was an expected outcome. Over the past 15 years, the quality of life of Americans has fallen and the mortality rate for whites between 45 and 54 has increased. Moreover, whites make up three-quarters of U.S. voters. The people now understand that free trade and immigration have thrown all workers around the world into global competition and that has resulted in inequality and stagnation. The voters simply chose the candidate who focused on those two issues so they acted in a very rational way.
>
> What is odd is that everyone seems surprised by the result. The real question is why did the elite, the mass media and university scholars fail to see the reality of society. During the campaign, there was a heated exchange in lies about the candidates as individuals. However, when it came to talk about the society, it was Trump who spoke the truth. He said that things were not going well in the United States. That is true. He also said the United States was no longer respected by the world. He saw that allies were no longer following in the footsteps of the United States. In that area as well, he was speaking the truth.
>
> Clinton reminded me of those people who said "I am Charlie" after the French weekly newspaper Charlie Hebdo was attacked by terrorists. These are the people who said their own society was a wonderful one which held an extraordinary set of values. That was nothing but a religious confession totally detached from reality. With the election of Trump, the United States and the world have been brought back down to reality. It is easier to deal with various issues when one has returned to reality rather than be mired in fantasy.

---

[118] *Lineages of Modernity*, p. 218.
[119] Emmanuel Todd, "Trump Was Speaking The Truth About State of U.S. Society", November 2016.

The fantasy persists, even until today with the hysterical responses to Trump draining the swamp. Todd comments on the fantasies of sufferers of Trump Derangement Syndrome. As Todd writes: "The establishment media have portrayed Trump as vulgar, aberrant, evil or insane; the voters, suffering but rational, have expressed their desire to take America back to its foundations."[120]

The new elites of our post-democratic society are opposed to democracy, and the roots of that opposition grow in the deep social facts observed by Emmanuel Todd. I am not sure that a democratic revival is possible. Perhaps only a republic of virtue can be revived? Perhaps a revival is only possible through constraint of global lawlessness by some form of nationalist populism? But what is certain is that a democratic revival requires a bounded polity. A market without borders, matched to an over-extended empire, is, by contrast, where oligarchy thrives.

> A democracy is a specific people organized, for its own ends, on its own territory. This group defends its border. It is not an abstract collective, deciding for humankind in general. If we accept this historical evidence of a dark, ethnic national component in the original form of democracy, we can manage to see, and understand why the resistance to oligarchy and the democratic revival affecting Western 'democracies' one by one, disorganized as these are by the new educational stratification and free trade, are inevitably tinged with xenophobia. Democracy is being reborn, but against the Mexicans in America and the Poles in England.[121]

Reading *Lineages of Modernity* opens new paths of understanding. Where they take us is unknown, but they will reveal a deeper cultural history of our world.

---

[120] Todd, *Lineages of Modernity*, p. 241.
[121] Todd, *Lineages of Modernity*, p. 256.

Jeff Rich

Notes on a Balinese Cockfight
1 March 2020 (Written near Ubud, Bali, Indonesia)

I am in Bali, staying for a short-stay luxury escape at Padma Resort, Ubud, which is actually at a small village, Payangan, about 45 minutes drive north of Ubud. It is a marketing sleight-of-hand by the resort, but no matter. For the cost of minor distance from the well-known Ubud, connected by a regular shuttle bus, we are rewarded with a guarded palace, perched on the hills, that overlooks rain forest, rural life, and the sensual glory of the 'world's most instagrammable pool'. One spectacularly beautiful Estonian influencer was posing in the hotel's infinity pool as I swam there yesterday. She is a paid guest of the hotel, part of the mirage of social media success and the i-economy. Instagram and its influencers were, however, not on my mind as we were driven by our courteous English-speaking butler from Denpasar airport to this princely five-star resort.

From the confined view of the back seat of a modern black sedan, I peered out at the sides of the streets. I saw modern highways signposted for all the world the same as back home. I saw congested yet orderly traffic, including many motor-cyclists, local and expatriate. I saw temples and houses with shrines. I saw petrol stations laid out for all the world like the same stores in Melbourne. I saw roller-door shop-fronts, with their owners peering out on the passing world. I saw guru medicine franchises advertised on billboards, and countless stone carving shops, with Buddhas, Ramas and dancing girls, all turned out, I assume, for the tourist market. Plants grew luxuriantly everywhere, threatening to overwhelm this commercial civilization, just like Borobudur. And I saw, newly carved from the ancient epics told in those old ruins, magnificent new public statuary that depicted scenes of Arjuna fighting the Kauravas in the *Mahabharata*. So my mind turned to my memories of Peter Brook's great dramatization of the *Mahabharata* (1985-9), which inspired me in my early 20's, and the great essay by Clifford Geertz, *Deep Play: Notes on a Balinese cockfight*.

I had read Geertz's seminal essay at university in the 1980's when I studied both history and social theory. Geertz had taught Greg Dening, who was the head of department for a while, and practised a kind of anthropological history. Dening never taught me, though his wife and collaborator Donna Merwick did, and it was Dening who awarded me the prize for best history student in my final honours year at Melbourne. What surprised me about my recollection of the essay was that I could recall only fragments of theory, abstract thoughts on the significance of culture, perhaps gleaned from other Geertz essays. Geertz had written a virtuoso thick description of the Balinese culture he observed in the 1950's and 1960's, but I could recall none of the carefully chosen detail of this artful essay. Now that I was in that very Balinese culture Geertz described, I could not recall anything about the actual Balinese cockfight.

So I pulled up 'Notes on a Balinese Cockfight' on the internet, and began to read. Even as I noted the correct title, I realised how much I had misremembered this great essay. I had forgotten all the details of the cockfight itself. I had forgotten Geertz's artful story within a story: how he accidentally got caught up in a group escaping from the then Muslim authorities' raid on this cockfight, and how this flight from the official and the everyday began his induction to understanding Bali, and set him on a spiral fall into a deeper interpretation of culture. I had even forgotten the presence of 'Deep Play' in the title.

Deep play was central to Geertz's ideas. Deep play was at the heart of how Geertz interpreted culture as text, performance, social theatre and the investiture of meaning in life. Geertz also played deeply when writing his texts. With an awareness of play and risk, Geertz he first articulated the idea of 'deep play', by drawing on some marginal notes in a text by Jeremy Bentham, the Utilitarian Prime. He countered Benthamite play with the thoughts of Max Weber, as if to demonstrate there is more to deep play than is dreamt of in the philosophy of the utility-maximisers. Deep play challenges all functionalist, materialist, economistic or Marxist ideas of society. Geertz uses 'deep play to free his field of anthropology from materialist dominion, and to bring it into the theatre of culture.

Deep play is the realm of the cockfight, and the cockfight is a theatre of culture and of life itself. Despite a ban by the authorities on the cockfight and its lowly status among scholars, Geertz looked to the cockfight to find his interpretation of Balinese culture. It was there, in the forbidden, quotidian, but profoundly theatrical, and not in the high arts that culture played at its deepest. The cockfight occurs in the realm of deep play, where stories are performed of how the world might be; where the mundane counting of bets measure the great risks of life; and where social status is but a secondary prop in a more glorious theatre. Deep Play is also the realm of poetry, and Geertz quoted (in part) Auden, from his elegy for Yeats:

> For poetry makes nothing happen: it survives
> In the valley of its making where executives
> Would never want to tamper, flows on south
> From ranches of isolation and the busy griefs,
> Raw towns that we believe and die in; it survives,
> A way of happening, a mouth.

W. H. Auden *In Memory of W. B. Yeats*

So it is for the cockfight. It makes nothing happen: men go on humiliating, and being humiliated, but status does not change. But the cockfight displays and survives as a way of happening that may be called art, that spins webs of significance for people.

> The cockfight is 'really real' only to the cocks – it does not kill anyone, castrate anyone, reduce anyone to animal status, alter the hierarchical relationships among people nor refashion the hierarchy; it does not even redistribute income in any significant way. What it does is what, for other people with other temperaments and conventions, *Lear* and *Crime and Punishment* do; it catches up these themes – death, masculinity, rage, pride, loss, beneficence, chance – and ordering them into an encompassing structure, presents them in such a way as to throw into relief their essential nature.... An image, fiction, a model, a metaphor, the cockfight is a means of expression; its function is neither to assuage social passions nor heighten them (though in its play-by-fire way it does a bit of both) but in a

medium of feathers, blood, crowds and money, to display them.

Geertz concluded his great essay with one of those *obiter dicta* that I did not forget, that never left me, and that oriented me in the infinite conversation:

> The culture of a people is an ensemble of texts, themselves ensembles, which the anthropologist strains to read over the shoulders of those to whom they properly belong... Societies, like lives, contain their own interpretation. One has only to learn how to gain access to them.

These words have for more than 30 years made up part of the ensemble of texts in my life, not as an anthropologist, but as an outcast participant in the infinite conversation. But today I wonder if the cultures that produced both Geertz (a certain form of the Academy that money, functionalism, reform and the Woke have progressively destroyed over that same 30 years) and the Balinese cockfight (that uniquely poised culture of Bali that Geertz studied with such care) are in irreversible decay.

Are there still Balinese cockfights or *tajen*? It seems so, but they are less common. They remain illegal, but have they receded in significance? They are reported in the digital press, and tolerated for ceremonial purposes; but are they becoming more marginal? Are they being replaced with the jejune memes of global culture? I cannot say since they are not part of my brief packaged luxury stay in Bali.

Today, we read Geertz's initiation into the deep play of the cockfight after 50 years of globalization. The enterprise of anthropology, as Geertz understood his cultural anthropology, itself seems remote. These last 50 years have seen growing cultural interchange and diversity of expression produce paradoxical impacts. This phenomenon of globalization has been one of the great transitions of my times, and making sense of its history is part of the task I perform in the *Burning Archive*. As Fernández-Armesto wrote in his history of ideas,

> Paradoxically, one of the effects of globalization will be diminished exchange, because in a perfectly globalised world,

cultural interchange will erode difference and make all cultures increasingly like each other. By the late twentieth century, globalization was so intense that it was almost impossible for any community to opt out.[122]

In the resulting global culture, I come to Bali and find an Estonian Instagram influencer and the ghost of Clifford Geertz, but not one sign of a cockfight.

Degeneration

8 March 2020

A generation after the commissars left the scene, positive freedom is more difficult to attain, and the West is populated by people who are less and less capable of an agency free from the banalities of the marketplace, the media, and mass opinion. It is not clear that our institutions can survive without a free people, or at least a plurality capable of self-command. The challenge of the next decade will be to break the ideological monopoly of liberalism so that thick views of the self can guide the education of future generations. Unless we succeed, we will lack the men of character we need to defend and renew the institutions that secure freedom in the West." (Ryszard Legutko[123])

An abiding theme of this blog is cultural decay. I have had this concern for a long time. I recall at university being intrigued by the phenomenon of late 19th century reaction against social trends celebrated by some as progress, but abhorred by Nietzsche as the acts of the herd. I read the early studies of mass group psychology, such as

---

[122] *Out Of Our Minds: What We Think and How We Came to Think It* (2019)
[123] 'Why I Am Not A Liberal', *First Things* (March 2020).

From the Burning Archive

Gustave Le Bon, and the extraordinary conservative condemnation of cultural and social progress found in Max Nordau, *Degeneration* (1892). Nordau applied early concepts of psychopathology, as pioneered in the prisons and lunatic asylums of nineteenth century Europe, and applied it to the artists, intellectuals and cultural mimics of *fin-de-siècle* Europe.

Nordau was a doctor who had a clinically authoritarian distaste for the pathological subjects he observed. I did not share Nordau's horror when I looked at this *fin-de-siècle* Europe, but rather viewed it with fondness. This era of early modernism – roughly 1890 to 1930 – gave me my cultural traditions, perhaps more so than any other period of history. This era saw the works of Proust, Joyce, Mallarme, Kafka, Stravinsky, Jarry, Rilke, Yeats, Kandinsky, Chagall, Picasso and so many more. I compared this era of degeneration with my own life-world becoming adult towards the end of the twentieth century, and wondered whether I too was a witness to some kind of civilisational collapse or some kind of *Götterdämmerung*. As Nordau wrote in *Degeneration*:

> But however silly a term *fin-de-siècle* may be, the mental constitution which it indicates is actually present in influential circles. The disposition of the times is curiously confused, a compound of feverish restlessness and blunted discouragement, of fearful presage and hang-dog renunciation. The prevalent feeling is that of imminent perdition and extinction. *Fin-de-siècle* is at once a confession and a complaint. The old Northern faith contained the fearsome doctrine of the Dusk of the Gods. In our days there have arisen in more highly-developed minds vague qualms of a Dusk of the Nations, in which all suns and all stars are gradually waning, and mankind with all its institutions and creations is perishing in the midst of a dying world.

The same question hangs over us today. Our institutions, our social arrangements, our culture and our planet appear in terminal decay. We struggle to produce vital, authentic and courageous affirmations of the human spirit. We have degenerated into polarisation and identity politics, into crud culture, crass marketing and the careerist academy. The words with which which Nordau heralded epochal decline 128 years ago ring true today:

> One epoch of history is unmistakably in its decline, and another is announcing its approach. There is a sound of rending in every tradition, and it is as though the morrow would not link itself with to-day. Things as they are totter and plunge, and they are suffered to reel and fall, because man is weary, and there is no faith that it is worth an effort to uphold them. Views that have hitherto governed minds are dead or driven hence like disenthroned kings, and for their inheritance they that hold the titles and they that would usurp are locked in struggle. Meanwhile interregnum in all its terrors prevails; there is confusion among the powers that be; the million, robbed of its leaders, knows not where to turn; the strong work their will; false prophets arise, and dominion is divided amongst those whose rod is the heavier because their time is short.

In these circumstances people evoke chaos. Then Nordau asked whether art and some terrible new beauty offered a way out of this chaos. He asked, what shall inspire us? But true art is not to be found in a degenerate public sphere, full of cheap vendors, clowns and hucksters, let alone the crud, crass and careerism of today.

> So rings the question from the thousand voices of the people, and where a market-vendor sets up his booth and claims to give an answer, where a fool or a knave suddenly begins to prophesy in verse or prose, in sound or colour, or professes to practise his art otherwise than his predecessors and competitors, there gathers a great concourse, crowding around him to seek in what he has wrought, as in oracles of the Pythia, some meaning to be divined and interpreted. And the more vague and insignificant they are, the more they seem to convey of the future to the poor gaping souls gasping for revelations, and the more greedily and passionately are they expounded.

The market-vendors, fools and knaves take different forms today. These characters appear on panel shows, and grind out their repeated lines to the disappointment of the poor gaping souls in today's crowds.

But the paradox is that these crowds have never been richer, healthier or better educated. This cultural collapse is occurring amidst affluence and mass higher education. It makes it stranger still.

Ross Douthat – a journalist at the *New York Times*, not a promising sign – has written an account of this modern degeneration, *The Decadent Society: How We Became the Victims of Our Own Success*, which I have only accessed through a review and a discussion on a podcast. According to the review, he breaks decadence into four components,: stagnation (technological and economic mediocrity), sterility (declining birth rates), sclerosis (institutional failure), and repetition (cultural exhaustion).

His argument on repetition is interesting. This is the degeneration of the endless remake, the self-parodic redo, the umpteenth movie made from the *Marvel* comics. What his argument seems to neglect is the destructiveness of degeneration. After all, it is only a very narrow strand of the culture that is repeated. So much more risks being lost in the infinity of the burning archive's digital flames, as this blog and my poetry evokes.

His argument on sclerosis also takes us back to the quotation with which I began this post. This institutional failure is the political decay of Francis Fukuyama. It is abundantly clear everywhere, perhaps nowhere more clearly in the presentation by the Democratic Party of the United States of America of Joe Biden as a candidate for President. By this move surely America has descended into the political gerontocracy of the Soviet Union of the 1970's and the 1980's. But, as Peter Thiel observes in his review of *The Decadent Society*, Douthat offers no real solution to this sclerosis beyond a religious revival, which will mean little to me, and technological fantasies, such as interstellar travel. These pipe dreams, however, ask nothing of the citizen but prayer and a ticket-to-ride. Ordinary citizens should be offered some reasonable, moderate and motivating goal if there is to be a Renaissance in political institutions and the whole culture.

> For statesmen, that means deconstructing the corrupt institutions that have falsely claimed to pursue those goals on

our behalf. It is a paradox of our time that the path to radical progress begins with moderation. Extreme optimism and fatalistic pessimism may seem to be stark opposites, but they both end in apathy. If things were sure to improve or bound to collapse, then our actions would not matter one way or the other.[124]

Our actions, our ordinary virtues do matter, and that takes us back to the prefatory quotation. This quotation comes from the conservative Polish philosopher and politician, Ryszard Legutko, a member of the Law and Justice party. I cannot speak for anything about what he has said but for the one piece that I have read, 'Why I am not a Liberal'. But surely he is right to propose that the antidote to degeneration is to cultivate deep character, not shallow identities. This way gives us hope that we can rebuild vital institutions that express human flourishing.

On Living not by Lies

7 February 2021

2020 has taught us through bitter experience that our societies are not vaccinated against totalitarianism, and certainly not the mutant strain of "soft totalitarianism" described in Rod Dreher, *Live Not by Lies: a Manual for Christian Dissidents* (2020).

The last year has seen lockdowns, curfews and bans on the most fundamental human relationships. In the service of public health rule, we have banned attendance at funerals and births, walking in a park with two friends, a death vigil for an elderly relative or spouse, and children playing on the swings. This year has seen oligarchs in

---

[124] Peter Thiel, "Back To The Future," *First Things*, March 2020.

America conspire to elect their man by hook or by crook, and to excuse China as a kind of democracy that 'listens to people', and certainly knows how to implement harsh public health measures. It has seen Red Guards in the streets, demanding displays of loyalty to the Authorities of the New, intimidating and even executing opponents, practising an iconoclasm that tears down any impure statue, purges all the 'olds', and cancels the infinite conversation that has transcended narrow identities for millenia. It has seen parliaments suspended; states of emergency declared; basic freedoms of assembly, worship, thought and movement denied; calls for the citizenry to act like new *stasi*; reporting of facts suppressed by the cartels in Big Tech and legacy media; openly authoritarian calls for "reality czars" (i.e. an Orwellian Ministry of Truth), reeducation camps, deplatforming, and deprogramming; counter-terrorist tactics were deployed against domestic opponents; and the authorities denied speech, travel and economic rights of the new dissidents. Symbolically, the new administration in the imperial capital of Washington DC was installed in a new forbidden city guarded by 30 000 troops, with a perimeter fencing of ribbon wire, and a fog of misinformation from the mainstream media.

We have descended into a post-democratic society, led by a collapsing imperial elite whose instincts are to manipulate mirages, not to encounter reality. And all these events have largely happened after Rod Dreher wrote his book on the coming soft totalitarianism or at least while it was being prepared for publication. The earlier insight of *Live Not by Lies* proved correct.

> Today's totalitarianism demands allegiance to a set of progressive beliefs, many of which are incompatible with logic... Compliance is forced less by the state than by elites who form public opinion, and by private corporations that, thanks to technology, control our lives far more than we would like to admit.... Today in our societies, dissenters from the woke party line find their businesses, careers, and reputations destroyed. They are pushed out of the public square, stigmatized, canceled, and demonized as racists, sexists, homophobes, and the like.

And they are afraid to resist, because they are confident that no one will join them or defend them.[125]

Vaclav Havel and Alexander Solzhenitsyn both appear in Dreher's book. From the grave, from the burning archive, they both call us to live in truth. Both authors have served as moral examples to me for decades, and appear many times in my texts. I am, however, more drawn to the enigmatic humanist, Havel, rather than the stern Orthodox Christian, Solzhenitsyn, who is Dreher's principal teacher. From Havel I learned, from a speech in 2010, of the moral malaise that corrupts our social order, especially the elites who believe they can know and control reality.

> Not only a globally spreading short-sightedness, but also the swollen self-consciousness of this civilisation, whose basic attributes include the supercilious idea that we know everything and what we don't yet know we'll soon find out, because we know how to go about it. We are convinced that this supposed omniscience of ours which proclaims the staggering progress of science and technology and rational knowledge in general, permits us to serve anything that is demonstrably useful, or that is simply a source of measurable profit, anything that induces growth and more growth and still more growth, including the growth of agglomerations. But with the cult of measurable profit, proven progress and visible usefulness there disappears respect for mystery and along with it humble reverence for everything we shall never measure and know, not to mention the vexed question of the infinite and eternal, which were until recently the most important horizons of our actions. We have totally forgotten what all previous civilisations knew: that nothing is self-evident.[126]

These ideas have been a resource for resistance to cultural decay. Now Dreher's book gives me the courage to resist the creeping authoritarianism that I dare name as such. I stand with the former East European dissidents who survived Soviet totalitarianism and then

---

[125] Rod Dreher, *Live Not By Lies* (2020), pp. 8-9.
[126] Vaclav Havel, Speech At Forum 2000, 2010.

witnessed its rebirth in the contemporary American Empire.

And for me the second part of Dreher's book is the partial beginning of a new Benedictine rule, a set of rules for enduring the suffering of the post-democratic society, cultural decay and the *diktats* of our beclouded elites. I have already adapted them in part. I cannot change the fact that my character was formed not by religion, but by the infinite conversation of inherited cultural traditions. The seven rules that Dreher sets out are, in my adaptation:

1. Value nothing more than truth
2. Cultivate cultural memory
3. Families are resistance cells
4. The Infinite Conversation (in Dreher's version, Religion) is the bedrock of resistance
5. Standing in Solidarity of the Shattered (including Jan Patočka's phrase the solidarity of the shattered)
6. The Gift of Suffering
7. Live not by Lies.

For me, this blog is very much a practice of rules 1, 2, and 4.

On reading Dreher's book I am inspired to pursue small groups of others who may also wish to live not by lies in this cultural dystopia that our political, scientific, commercial and imperial elites have made. Dreher spoke of both Sir Roger Scruton's and Jacques Derrida's work with the Czech resistance.

> Sir Roger Scruton, who helped Czech allies build the intellectual resistance, emphasizes the importance today of dissidents creating and committing to small groups… The point is to find something to draw you out of yourself, to discover your own worth in relation to others, and to learn how to accept the discipline that comes through accountability to others and a shared purpose.[127]

I am too isolated, and need to find some kind of fellowship, not only in my imaginary dialogues with the infinite conversation, but in simple solidarity with others.

---

[127] Dreher, *Live Not By Lies*, p. 179.

> We desperately need to throw off the chains of solitude and find the freedom that awaits us in fellowship... Only in solidarity with others can we find the spiritual and communal strength to resist.... the blessing of our own freedom from loneliness, suspicion and defeat.[128]

Fellowship is my medicine for the loneliness and locked down persecution of our new soft totalitarian times. I can only hope that this blog, and the soon-to-come other channels, will help build strong cells of resistance amid the ruins of our post-democratic world.

---

[128] Dreher, *Live Not By Lies*, p. 181.

Part Seven

Unravelling Empires

Jeff Rich

Donald Trump and America's Wounded Pride
22 July 2016

Today I watched live the speech made by Donald Trump to accept the Republican nomination for the presidency of the United States of America. I watched as a detached and curious observer since this was the first and only time I have observed a full Trump performance, rather than edited excerpts in the news.

His speech was energetic and extroverted. He was calm before the audience and surprisingly in tune with its moods. Every now and then he would join in the chant of the crowd, "USA! USA!" Another time, after Trump declared that he would deliver on one of his vague but triumphant promises – restoring safety, law and order, making America great again – the crowd chanted back to him, "Yes, you will" in a seeming improvisation that taunted Obama's wishful rhetoric of "Yes, we can." And he set himself up as the outsider who is hated by the elites because they benefit from a rigged system he defies; the truth-teller who will lay out the facts of violent crime, poverty and international security failures; and the leader who gets grand things done, despite the censors, critics and cynics who oppose his great visions.

I can claim no knowledge of the American mind or American popular sentiment. How Trump's performance will play out in opinion polls, I do not know. There is no doubt that the policy content – the real plans to justify the overwhelming promises – were absent. I listened out for how, when he said he would outline his plan to restore jobs and prosperity, but I was disappointed. I paid attention when he began to say what he would do from day one to stop civil disorder and gun crime, but the rhetoric turned back on itself. I hoped to learn just how American diplomacy would proceed in a more multi-polar and insecure world when the USA! puts itself first, rips up trade agreements, accuses other countries of cheating, and demands allies pay their way for the *Pax Americana*. I fear that I will just have to wait with trepidation in the months ahead to see new American Greatness is realised.

Despite these doubts Trump's speech impressed me with two intuitive predictions. First, Trump will win. Second, Trump will not be able to do what he has promised.

The emotional torrents channeled by Trump are powerful. Although it is a conventional idea to denounce Trump as an ignorant and irresponsible 'demagogue'. Perhaps we need a new word to describe a political leader whose power derives not from oratory before crowds, but celebrity in television and media? The fact remains that the sentiments he stirs are powerful and authentic. People love their country. People want safety. Americans cannot believe they should be anything but number one. They feel left out, and let down. They want desperately to fix things and to fix things fast, in the way that Trump echoed back to them. They sense the sneers and the contempt of the educated elite for the ordinary people left behind by the financial, media and political stars. Hilary Clinton has been typecast as that sneer, and people want to throw her out, or, as the crowd chanted, to 'lock her up'. Trump's speech stained her as corrupt, unpatriotic, soft on violence, and scornful of the poor, uneducated and struggling. Trump was ruthless in his exploitation of the fears, anger and insecurity provoked by street violence, especially by the recent killings of police officers. These emotions will surge over all the doubts about Trump the man. These doubts about Trump's character, his fitness for the presidency, the grand folly of his ideas will not withstand the emotions of the people who want America to be great again. All the attacks on Trump's character ignore his plea that "I am your voice" to a country that believes its leaders betrayed its greatness.

But those weaknesses of Trump will strand his presidency in a disordered society, broken political system, and hostile, suspicious world. I hear over the radio, as I write this post, that one newspaper said he "conjured up chaos and promised overnight solutions." He will get things done, but the world will respond. He will build his wall, but at what cost and with what impact on central America? He will rile China and accuse it of currency manipulation, but will this provoke the final crisis for the USA dollar as the reserve currency? He will empower law and order, and provoke more violence, more rage, more desperation. He will cut taxes and search desperately to cut programs, but will wreck further the weak capability of the executive state in America. He will banish the elites and the opponents, and be fooled and befuddled by the Svengalis and amateurs who replace him. He will bring to white heat a burning political system. He will fail.

And then what for America? The country is in decay, and it is lashing out like a wounded giant. But the giant is in an iron cage of its own making – all the declamations of pride, all the wild gestures, the threats, the desperation make no difference, and only damage the giant more. This wild, violent, bleeding, insulting and falling giant is what scares the world. But I suspect the world will do well as American falls, even if its desperate pride provokes more conflicts in the world. Trump will truly bring America into its darkest hour.

The Unravelling of Empires
10 January 2017

A divided, inward-looking and mismanaged west is likely to become highly destabilising. ... By succumbing to the lure of false solutions, born of disillusion and rage, the west might even destroy the intellectual and institutional pillars on which the postwar global economic and political order has rested. It is easy to understand those emotions, while rejecting such simplistic responses. The west will not heal itself by ignoring the lessons of its history. But it could well create havoc in the attempt. (Martin Wolf, *Financial Times*, 6 January 2017)

A (southern) summer spent reading the magisterial histories of John Darwin – *After Tamerlane* and *Unfinished Empire* – has inoculated me against the false lessons of history pronounced by journalistic oracles, such as the distinguished Martin Wolf from the *Financial Times*. He is not alone in brooding on the dark omens that have filled our contemporary skies. Across the Atlantic, Robert Samuelson from the *Washington Post*, issues a similar warning. The question of the year, he states, is "whether we're witnessing the gradual decay of the post-World War II international order, dominated by the economic and military power of the United States."[129] He in turn summons the old Svengali of American statecraft, Henry Kissinger, who warns that when the international order is moving from one system to another, then:

> Restraints disappear, and the field is open to the most expansive claims and the most implacable actors... Chaos follows until a new system of order is established. (Kissinger, *World Order*)

Are we entering the death of one order, and the chaos in which a new world order will be reborn? Here our prophetic pundits would do well to read Darwin's work deeply rather than stay within the cocoon of their false assumptions about the "pillars" of the post-war international order.

Darwin provides a world-weary, realistic, yet scholarly overview of world history since 1400, when Tamerlane aspired to rule the world. By the time of Tamerlane's death in 1405, he had conquered most of the world island of Eurasia but still had not imposed a single political order amid competing empires. Tamerlane becomes Darwin's governing metaphor. There has been no single international order, no common vision or shared liberal intellectual assumptions between competing empires. Those empires have risen and fallen, waxed and waned, imploded and recovered in response to fickle, changeable circumstances, and in ways that only with the blind hindsight seem to be a story of progress or the rise of the West.

---

[129] "2017: Welcome to the new world order," *TRTWorld*, 3 Jan 2017

Darwin assumes also that empires are the most common form of political order through all of human history. Empire is not a European original sin, as in nationalistic histories of colonial imperialists (something I observed commonly in the history museums of Vietnam). It is not only the *ancien régime* of Roman or European aristocrats imposing themselves on the Third World. Rather, it is rooted in some fundamental human characteristics.

As Darwin explains, "the exchange of information, knowledge, beliefs and ideas – sometimes over enormous distances – has been just as typical of human societies as the eagerness to acquire, useful, prestigious or exotic goods by trade or by barter."[130] When those goods and ideas, which serve both the dogs of war and the icons of faiths, have circulated between societies, they have:

> upset the cohesion of some societies much more than others, making them vulnerable to internal breakdown, and to takeover by others. So a second propensity in human communities has been the accumulation of power on an extensive scale: the building of empires. Indeed the difficulty of forming autonomous states on an ethnic basis, against the gravitational pull of cultural or economic attraction (as well as disparities of military force) has been so great that *empire (where different ethnic communities fall under the same ruler) has been the default mode of political organisation throughout most of history.* Imperial power has usually been the rule of the road.[131] [my emphasis]

These assumptions lead into a remarkable narrative of contending empires competing with different resources and visions of "modernity". This story is very different from the accounts of the rise of the West that dominate the economics schools of the world, and seep into the accounts of the globalised world and post-war international order by journalists. Darwin's story is remarkable for making clear how open the future was to these contending empires, and in a way how late the moment of European domination came. In contrast to complacent assumptions about the pillars of Western

---

[130] *After Tamerlane*, p. 22.
[131] *After Tamerlane*, p. 23.

thought or the genius apps of Western civilisation (Niall Ferguson), Darwin tells how:

> In practice, and for reasons that we are far from understanding fully, for almost two centuries after 1750 it was North West European societies (and their transatlantic offspring) that mobilised [resources and people] fastest and also coped best with the social and political strains that being mobile imposed. Far-flung empires, and a global economy shaped to their interests, were to be their reward.[132]

But that reward was not a permanent prize, not a pillared temple of Western vigour and superior intelligence. One of those far-flung empires, the British Empire, was made of private enterprise, of commerce, Christianity and civilization. Its dominance in the nineteenth century was powered by cotton, coal and capital. And it would discover in the 1950s and 1960s that it was no longer a world power on a par with the USA and the USSR. It had been eclipsed by its transatlantic offspring and old continental enemy in the bipolar world of the post-war international order.

Another of the far-flung empires – the United States – would draw some stranger lessons from the history of empires. Like a millennarian visionary, it would believe that it had made a decisive break from this tainted history of imperial rule. Darwin is not fooled. Empires are still empires when they are not ruled as the Romans did, nor as the Europeans. Darwin relates the bare facts – the commercial presence, the cultural influence of global media, and more than 700 military bases in over 130 countries of the world. The post-1945 American system of international order was thus imperial in all but name. It was the empire that dared not speak its name, and yet believed itself to be the 'indispensable nation'.

Like its imperial ancestors and rivals, the American order owed to chance and conflicts its decades of dominance.

> It was the Second World War that made the United States not just the world's largest economy, but also its strongest. It was

---

[132] *After Tamerlane*, p. 27.

the global cold war that made it the world's greatest military power. These were the assets with which American entered the 'globalized' world at the end of the century.[133]

Darwin concludes his great book with some very different reflections on our globalised world than the gospel-preachers of the international financial order. The economic regime of the post-Cold War era is the great exception in the history of the global economy. Darwin writes, "It was produced by an earthquake as dramatic as anything in the world's modern history."[134]

The geopolitical collapse of Soviet power and China's embrace under Deng Xiaoping of a capitalist economy created massive new markets. At the same time, dramatic changes in transport (air travel and the container revolution) and communications (the Internet and digital communications) created conditions for remarkable growth and integration of economies worldwide. It redistributed wealth across the world.

> The great divergence in wealth and economic performance between the Euro-Atlantic West and most of the rest of Eurasia has given way instead to the 'great convergence', which should if it continues restore the balance to the rough equilibrium of half a millennium ago in the next fifty years.

But economic integration is not a bulwark against the building of empires, states and cultures with distinctive values, attitudes, institutions and ideologies. These long-standing human propensities may well surge back in response to the free movement of goods and the dominance of commercial elites. Since I take a long view of the molding of human cultures and empires, my money is on these deeper drives making a comeback and remolding our international order in ways that we cannot yet predict.

And is it not this resurgence of difference and diversity that we are seeing unfold in the unpredicted events of 2016? We see this in the expression of divergence from the views of the Washington consensus,

---

[133] *After Tamerlane*, p. 504.
[134] *After Tamerlane*, p. 504.

the Hollywood celebrities, and the European technocrats. We see these surging sentiments used by Brexit, Trump, a more assertive China, a more assertive Russia, and the resurgent caliphate of ISIS. Contrary to Wolf then, a reading of *After Tamerlane* will open the future to possibilities, both good and bad, but certainly not to one international order, to one remedy to cure the ills of the West.

Darwin concludes his great book, by finally making clear the precise meaning of *After Tamerlane*. In a final section entitled *Tamerlane's Shadow*, he makes these sober judgments on the constant breaking apart of dreams of a new world order.

> Perhaps this is the point. It might well be true that we are on the brink of a great transformation – in geopolitics, economics and culture – at least as far-reaching as the Eurasian Revolution of the late eighteenth century. If this is so, it can hardly be doubted that its impacts in different parts of the world will vary enormously.[135]

Rather than a fairytale story of ascendant beliefs in liberal democracy and globalisation, Darwin offers a deep historical understanding of how our world came to be as it is in its confusing disordered state. It emerges from an exceptionally complex kaleidoscope that Darwin helps the general reader to peer through. Through this glass we see fractals of trade and conquest, diaspora and migration, changing maps and dynamic regions, interwoven cultures and internecine politics. It is a vision that engenders scepticism towards the apostles of the market and pop culture.

> Their effect has been not to homogenise the world, but to keep it diverse. By contrast, the magnetic force of the global economy has been too erratic thus far, and too unevenly felt, to impose the cooperative behaviour and cultural fusion to which theorists of free trade have often looked forward to.

So Darwin sees some similar discontents to those identified by Martin Woolf, but he explains them in a broader, deeper perspective than the hand-wringing of the liberal press.

---

[135] Darwin, After Tamerlane, p. 505.

What we call globalization today might be candidly seen as flowing from a set of recent agreements , some tacit, some formal, between the four great economic 'empires' of the contemporary world: America, Europe, Japan and China. For them and for all other states and societies, the challenge will be to reconcile their internal cohesion with the disturbing effects of free competition. The strain will be great; the outcome uncertain. But if there is one continuity that we should be able to glean from a long view of the past, it is Eurasia's resistance to a uniform system, a single great ruler, or one set of rules. In that sense we still live in Tamerlane's shadow – or perhaps more precisely – in the shadow of his failure.[136]

The havoc that we see about us is not caused by "false solutions, born of disillusion and rage," but the unraveling of empires adrift in the great historical tides of convergence and divergence.

Reflections on a Multi-Polar World
27 December 2017

I was asked the other day in conversation with a friend, what was the best thing about this year? She had earlier said the best thing was the collapse of Donald Trump's opinion poll ratings. After a little thought, I said, perhaps perversely, the best thing about the year was Donald Trump's presidency because it has led to a steep decline in American prestige – or as people like to say today, soft power. Its fall has led to the reemergence of a multi-polar world.

In July 2016 I predicted Donald Trump's election victory and his diplomatic defeat. In "Donald Trump and America's Wounded Pride",

---
[136] *After Tamerlane*, pp. 505-6.

I wrote:

> The country is in decay, and it is lashing out like a wounded giant. But the giant is in an iron cage of its own making – all the declamations of pride, all the wild gestures, the threats, the desperation make no difference, and only damage the giant more. This wild, violent, bleeding, insulting and falling giant is what scares the world. But I suspect the world will do well as American falls, even if its desperate pride provokes more conflicts in the world. Trump will truly bring America into its darkest hour.

Perhaps this vision was too pessimistic. The American economy appears to be rebounding, and that may renew American confidence and American leadership, but the institutional weaknesses of America are too great. This late blooming may repeat Eliot's line that "April is the cruellest month." Indeed, the wild erratic conduct of Trump as President is the epitome of those weak institutions. Trump only confirms that America is an unravelling empire.

So, what have we seen in 2017 that suggests the reemergence of a multi-polar world? Obviously, China has grown in wealth, power and assertiveness. Xi Jinping has launched diplomatic and economic initiatives that look a lot like a new form of empire: the One Road initiative, the Asian Infrastructure Investment Bank, and the beachhead islands of the South China Sea. It has strengthened ties with countries of South East Asia, like Cambodia and The Philippines, that have reasons to resent the American Empire. It has even emerged as a spokesperson for an alternative form of international order with a changed system of global economic governance. Speaking to the World Economic Forum, Xi Jinping said,

> we should develop a model of fair and equitable governance in keeping with the trend of the times. As the Chinese saying goes, people with petty shrewdness attend to trivial matters, while people with vision attend to governance of institutions. There is a growing call from the international community for reforming the global economic governance system, which is a pressing task for us. Only when it adapts to new dynamics in the international

economic architecture can the global governance system sustain global growth.[137]

China opens its arms and welcomes others aboard the "express train" of China's development; America turns inward and surly, muttering how the rules are not fair, and it must make itself great again.

In Syria and Iraq, Islamic State has been defeated territorially; and surely the decisive player in this defeat has been Russia in its backing of Assad and its preparedness to act when America cowered. It was in Munich in 2007 – ten years ago – that Vladimir Putin spoke out against the unipolar globalised world, dominated by American law, firms and culture, and became a single voice galvanising the rebirth of other centres of power.

> We are seeing a greater and greater disdain for the basic principles of international law. And independent legal norms are, as a matter of fact, coming increasingly closer to one state's legal system. One state and, of course, first and foremost the United States, has overstepped its national borders in every way. This is visible in the economic, political, cultural and educational policies it imposes on other nations. Well, who likes this? Who is happy about this?

In 2015 Putin went on to challenge the conceit of American foreign policy – that America is the World's Policeman, the Indispensable Nation, the Great Alchemist of its model, whatever the consequences. In a speech to the United Nations, Putin asked:

> I cannot help asking those who have caused the situation, do you realize now what you've done? But I am afraid no one is going to answer that. Indeed, policies based on self-conceit and belief in one's exceptionality and impunity have never been abandoned.

Is it any wonder that the American foreign policy and security establishment are in hysterical overdrive about the threat that Russia poses to America? The Secretary of Defence and other top officials

---

[137] Xi Jinping, Speech at Davos, January 2017.

claim Russia is the greatest threat to US security.[138] In truth, America is engaged in a heated ideological war against the power that declares an end to Uncle Sam's unipolar vision of security.

Putin and Jinping do not espouse the same model of development. Their countries pursue different policies and cultural preferences. Their allied assertiveness together, however, tolls the death knell of Western dominance. They are not alone. We have also seen more diplomatically assertive European countries. As Britain collapses into nostalgia for the empire on which the sun would never set, Germany and France have shown more diplomatic initiative. Chancellor Merkel took responsibility for the Syrian refugee crisis in a way that shamed America's conceited, insular inaction. President Macron has maneuvered France into the position of peace broker in the Middle East, following Trump's recent petulant, bear-baiting assertion of unilateral diplomacy: the relocation of the US embassy to Jerusalem.

There are no doubt many more examples. But I am no expert in international affairs. I only believe that a multi-polar world is a better, safer place to live in, even though, of course, it still carries many risks. It is surely the most profound shift in politics and culture that I have observed this year, and it recalls the book I read at the outset of the year, John Darwin's *After Tamerlane*. Darwin's history is an antidote to the globalisation fantasy that all nations will transform into an integrated culture. The history of Eurasia, which he so masterfully recounts, shows that the diffusion of so many social and cultural practices across its many states "failed to induce a common view of modernity or of what it was to be 'modern.'"[139] Darwin summed up the grand illusions of globalization. Its effect "has been not to homogenize the world, but to keep it diverse." America, and its dreams of itself as the indispensable nation, have fallen, like so many empires of the past, into the shadow of Tamerlane's failure.

---

[138] https://www.newsweek.com/russia-not-north-korea-greatest-threat-us-pentagons-top-military-officer-640926

[139] Darwin, *After Tamerlane*, p. 505.

Jeff Rich

The End of History Revisited (Reflections on 2017)
29 December 2017

In 2017 Francis Fukuyama published two podcasts providing a retrospective account of his essay, "The End of History" (1989) which was later published in more extended form as the book, *The End of History and the Last Man*, in 1992, 25 years ago.[140]

I had bought Fukuyama's book, back in the early 1990's, when I was a lowly junior bureaucrat, still finding my way in the world, but with vaulting intellectual ambitions, fostered by my years as a graduate student. I was drawn to Fukuyama since the orthodoxies of radical academic thought were crumbling. Although I do not recall his book in much specific detail, I do associate it with other cultural encounters of that time that liberated me from radical, Foucauldian thinking traps. His book was one of many that led me to a more open encounter with the world, a long odyssey through the world of governing. Around the same time, I read Simon Schama's *Citizens*, with its devastating account of the myth of the French Revolution, and watched Andrzey Wajda's films, *The Possessed* and *Danton*. These books and films amplified the shock waves of the world historical events of the collapse of communism in Europe and Russia, and the crushing of dissent in China, symbolised by Tiananmen Square. Every day in the office, closer to home, I observed the disappointments of social democracy, and the radical reworking of the government I served through a strange mix of a charismatic strong leader and liberal contractarianism, inspired by public choice theory.

The years passed. Children came, my perspective on the world changed. The confidence of my university years was delivered increasing blows. My career stalled since I chose to look after my children and my writing, and stubbornly refused to affix myself to any single powerful network. Opportunities passed me by; and I became

---
[140] https://soundcloud.com/user-5799528/francis-fukuyama-end-of-history-revisited

more of an outsider in the institutions in which I worked. But I was an attentive, well-read observer, who, unlike so many of the successful careerists who passed me by, interpreted the events around me with the insights of Clio. And what I observed was a slow decay in political institutions.

I became convinced, as I wrote privately in 2014, that:

> the quality of government and democracy has deteriorated, reflecting the wearing out of a model for governing born in the 1980's. This deterioration underlies poor performance of governments of both sides of politics in recent years.

I wrote this in a secret plea for something better; forging my ideas from a book by the Norwegian sociologist and author on democracy, Stein Ringen. It made me feel like Machiavelli, who Ringen himself invoked[141]. I submitted manuscripts to the powerful patrons who ignored my pleas, just as the Medici ignored Machiavelli's arguments for *virtù*. Like Machiavelli, I believed that:

> For, to judge aright, one should esteem men because they are generous, not because they have the power to be generous; and, in like manner, should admire those who know how to govern a kingdom, not those who, without knowing how, actually govern one.[142]

So my mind was prepared to listen again to Francis Fukuyama when he published the second volume of his global history of political institutions, *Political Order and Political Decay: from the Industrial Revolution to the Globalization of Democracy*. In this book, Fukuyama reworked the account he gave of the end of history back in the exhilaration of the end of the Cold War. He turned from fever about freedom to more sober discussion of the fundamentals of order and authority. Crucially, he focussed in the later book on the formation of an effective state, a system of political order, and strong political institutions. The economic system pursued by a country did not determine its fate. Mere beliefs in freedom and democracy were not

---

[141] Ringen, *Nation of Devils: Democratic Leadership and the Problem of Obedience* (2013).
[142] Machiavelli, from "Dedication" to *The Discourses*.

enough. A form of order had to be established. Rule had to be conducted with authority, and this authority had to impose a form of political order against powerful human social tendencies – reciprocal altruism and kinship affiliation or, more generally, homophily. You scratch my back and I'll scratch yours. Birds of a feather flock together.

In *Political Order and Political Decay*, the state is not a cancerous growth on society, but a difficult and profound achievement of culture, that curbed inherited tendencies of the human animal. This focus on the importance of the state and its way of governing, was in contrast to fashionable anti-statist ideas that suffuse much thinking on both the left and the right. Fukuyama insisted that the state was not a beast to be contained, but a garden to be nurtured. Most of all, it was crucial for political order, including for democratic political order, that the state should be effective. He proposed a triad of political order – accountability, the rule of law, and executive capability.

Executive capability was my world, the world of bureaucracy. It was the decline of executive capability that I observed around me, and that conditioned my mind to support Fukuyama's hypothesis. I have continued to see it throughout this year, both in the outer world of reported politics across the world, and in my observed world of insider politics in the minor provincial bureaucracy in which I serve. Good governments continue to lose their way, as Julia Gillard observed of her own. Too often this weakness is seen as a problem of trust, with executive governments betrayed by a fickle public, incited to rapid mood changes by a feckless media. I see it as a problem of authority, of political order, and the failure of political leaders and bureaucratic elites to practise *virtù*, which I rename the ordinary virtues of governing well.

Fukuyama is a mordant critic of Donald Trump who represents a populist resurgence of a form of accountability, but without the liberal spirit of the rule of law, and completely lacking in effective executive capability. In an interview he says of Trump:

> You know, he gets the democracy point. He loves going to these rallies where people adulate him. He doesn't get the liberal part

so well, which is that you've got this set of rules that constrain power and force you to play by the rules.[143]

Fukuyama went on to analyse the conditions for the rise of Trump in "the institutional shortcomings and the socio-economic impacts of globalization." Trump is also typical of one of the diseases of modern political institutions that Fukuyama diagnoses in *Political Order and Political Decay* – repatrimonialisation. This describes the recruitment of friends and family to offices of the state, and the reorientation of the state to the personal service to the governing leader or, in less corrupt forms, the governing party.

I have seen repatrimonialisation up close in my own bureaucracy. Patronage, not merit, now rules the court. It has a devastating effect on the conduct of elites and the executive capability that is essential to both political order and effective democracy. I wonder, as the year closes, if it is possible to launch an effective resistance to this trend. It has happened in the past, and Fukuyama's account of the emergence of law-based and merit-based bureaucracies in Germany, United Kingdom and the United States (all quite different histories) should be essential reading for any public official. The world I see around me day to day is that of the patrimonial system:

> elites build power through the management of patronage chains by which clients follow patrons in pursuit of individual rewards. All of this is reinforced by ritual, religion and ideas legitimising a particular form of elite rule.[144]

We have turned our back on the culture and institutions that reformed the "patronage-ridden bureaucracies" of the nineteenth-century. The Chief Castellan of my bureaucracy, who espouses a view of public trust that confuses public order with a circle of trust between patrons and clients, would do well to read Fukuyama and his account of the pathway different states took from patrimonialism towards

---

[143] https://www.npr.org/2017/04/04/522554630/francis-fukuyama-on-why-liberal-democracy-is-in-trouble

[144] Fukuyama, *Political Order and Political Decay*, p. 199.

modern government.[145]

Can we turn again, and begin to rebuild new foundations for a better form of political order? Fukuyama's analysis in *Political Order and Political Decay* identifies two principal spurs to the removal of patronage-politics from the institutions of the state.

The first spur was military competition, which prompted the forging of the Prussian bureaucratic state, China's civil examination system, and not least the often misunderstood Northcote-Trevelyan reforms of mid-nineteenth century Britain. The last was, in part, a response to catastrophic elite failure in the Crimean War. Perhaps failure in war may ultimately be a spur to reform of American political institutions, but I can only hope that will not be so in my own minor province, far from the battlefronts of the world.

The second spur may offer more promise to my society. In Fukuyama's account, it was "a process of peaceful political reform, based on the formation of a coalition of social groups interested in having an efficient, uncorrupt government." This process was supported by economic development, growth of education, and specialisation of social roles, leading to the formation of many new social actors who "have no strong stake in the existing patrimonial system." This was the critical process in the United States and Britain, where "economic modernization drove social mobilization, which in turn created the conditions for the elimination of patronage and clientilism."

But it was never a perfect victory, and never a uniform pathway. Different institutional arrangements, social patterns, and congeries of interests, with more or less motive to retain forms of patronage and clientilism, put down deep roots in the new political order. Some aspects of high-minded culture strengthened the new meritocracy; but no culture remains vital for ever. Over the last thirty years we have witnessed more economic and social changes that have watered these old deep roots of patronage and clientilism, and the withering of a culture of living in truth. The human social tendencies Fukuyama

---

[145] https://www.themandarin.com.au/82512-chris-eccles-governing-era-distrust/

identified at the outset of *Political Order and Political Decay* have refused to die.

> The modern impersonal state forces us to act in ways that are deeply in conflict with our own natures and is therefore constantly at risk of erosion and backsliding. Elites in any society will seek to use their superior access to the political system to further entrench themselves, their families, and their friends unless explicitly prevented from doing so by other organized forces in the political system.[146]

Against these forces appeals to merit and an increasingly jejune ideal of democracy are weak reeds. I wish I could find a way to form a social coalition for a better way to govern. But that is not my skill. The best I can do is give voice to my thoughts, and hope that some others may heed the call and have the know-how to put it into action.

It reminds me of the pessimistic, but not defeated, conclusion of another of the books I studied closely this year, *Breaking Democracy's Spell*, by the distinguished political theorist John Dunn. He hoped the great universities might rise to the challenges to apprehend the scale and connectedness of the vast challenges we face. I have lost much faith in those institutions, as I have in the bureaucracies of the world; but perhaps some reinvented university might take on the responsibility Dunn assigned to them. If no-one does, then we will face a terrible future.

> Could human beings do any better in the face of the chaos they have made together? The answer to that can only be yes. Will they do any better, and, above all, will they do better enough? Quite probably not. But that is not a conclusion that it makes any practical sense to anticipate. A species facing self-extermination, even at a relatively sedate pace, has reasons for altering its behaviour. But it will still be the species that chose to acts in the ways that created that risk. How far can human beings learn? In the end they will find out.[147]

---

[146] Fukuyama, *Political Order and Political Decay*, p. 208.
[147] Dunn, *Breaking Democracy's Spell* (2014).

It is as if, 25 years on, we are remembering Nietzsche's Last Man, from the title of Fukuyama's book on the end of history. Still, I hear in Dunn's closing notes, the ominous opening of *Das Rheingold*, and:

> Dr Cogito hears *Das Rheingold*'s opening note,
> And so the story goes:
> We still dig from deep water's mud:
> The ring, the ring, the ring.[148]

Fukuyama is a more dispassionate thinker than I; he is a less portentous philosopher than Dunn; but still he hears a bell tolling for all our democracies in the state of politics in 2017:

> Well, as you know, as a citizen, I feel that it's a little bit too exciting. Every day, you wake up and you really read something you thought was not possible in terms of American politics. As a dispassionate social scientist, I actually think that it's quite interesting, you know, because we have these theories about institutions and how they're supposed to work. And it's going to be a test. I think we're all in for an interesting test of the stability of our democratic institutions, how legitimate they are, whether they can actually self-correct. We political scientists tend to believe this. But, you know, you have to meet reality.[149]

We all must humbly meet reality.

Three Lessons of Impeachment

27 January 2020

Somewhat to my surprise, I have been engrossed over the last few months by the impeachment of President Trump, and its entanglement

---

[148] From my poem "The State of Politics" in Rich, *Gathering Flowers of the Mind*
[149] "Francis Fukuyama on why liberal democracy is in trouble," npr.org (2017)

with the corrosion of the political institutions of the declining American Empire. It has been something of a rabbit hole of discovery, not just about American politics, which I have largely ignored over the years, except for casual and inescapable tuning into the news, but also about my own navigation through the political dilemmas of our time.

I cannot quite recall what triggered the interest. I think at some point I thought, what is going on here? Something is not quite right. It may have been the absurd, hysterical, hostile rhetoric towards Russia which has been embraced by the American Democratic party. It may have been a few bouts of insomnia that led me for some reason to watch on Youtube some of the earliest public hearings of the House Intelligence Committee investigation. Almost immediately I sensed that there was not due process and reasonable interrogation of the facts going on here. At some point I decided to listen to the perspectives of the other side, and not merely to turn sceptical but covered eyes away from the field.

That was how I discovered Stephen K Bannon's podcast, *Warroom: Impeachment*. Here were people I had never turned my ears toward before, and whose views I knew only through retail media glosses. Stephen K. Bannon was the "alt-right" populist strategist of the Trump campaign, who had appeared to flame out early in the Trump presidency. Raheem Kassam was introduced to me by the podcast as the communications architect of Nigel Farrage's Brexit campaign. Jason Miller was a communications strategist for the Trump campaign. I had never closed my my mind to such perspectives, but nor had I ever approached them as if I could learn something from them. Until now I would have assumed they were bilious ranters with suspicious attitudes, and surfers of dangerously nationalist sentiment.

Soon, these old assumptions were proved wrong. The podcast revealed intelligent, inquiring and intriguing hosts. The hosts brought to the show fighters, but also distinguished constitutional lawyers and high class political leaders. And day by day, through tuning into show, I was convinced that there was at least some truth in their hyperbolic claim that the impeachment itself was the 'crime of the century'. The podcast compiled reasons to doubt the story presented in more conventional outlets. There were detailed assessments of the transcripts and hearings and other writing on the impeachment. There were true stories about the RussiaGate hoax. There were exposés of unconvincing remonstrations of Democratic politicians and progressive activist 'scholars'. Each day the podcast seemed to overturn my perceptions of the events of the impeachment, which seemed plausibly understood indeed as an outrageous defrocking of the presidency by the new *nomenklatura* of the administrative state, intelligence apparatus and corporate media.

It was not really a conclusion I ever expected to reach; and I am still in a flux of perplexity, considering what it means for my thoughts on political institutions. I found myself forming new judgments about political actors and political institutions. The lesson of impeachment was not the lazy assumption of the left that Donald Trump is a cocktail of incompetence and dictatorship. Rather, at least today as an interim judgment in my perplexity, here are the three lessons of impeachment.

Lesson 1: The corporate media and its celebrity journalists play at being political actors, but with no legitimate authority. The misrepresentations of the facts of the case on outlets like CNN and MSNBC are truly shocking, and there is not even a mirage of even-handedness or open inquiry. The same may be said even of the Australian national public broadcaster, the ABC, that presents an extremely partial perspective on Trump and impeachment. Key journalists have inserted themselves into the proceedings, under the spell of a belief that they are actors in this drama. Rachel Maddow of MSNBC clearly worked with the Democratic impeachment team on the release of very fuzzy evidence by Lev Parnis. There are too many ex-political operatives who masquerade as neutral reporters, and there is too much co-dependence between these journalists and the politicians who rely on them for air time. So, alternative media is subverting these 'mainstream' voices.

Lesson 2: The FBI's and CIA's alleged activities impacting in the 2016 election and Trump's Presidency deserve investigation. The appalling nature of the abuse of basic legal, constitutional and democratic principles by the FBI, and likely the CIA, beggars belief. The *Report of the Inspector-General on FISA Abuse and the CrossFire Hurricane investigation* is damning. I bought James Comey's book, but I was never fully convinced. It always struck me as odd that he should react so extremely, shrinking as if from an internal fear, to President Trump's comment to him that he 'expects loyalty'. All political leaders expect loyalty. America's security state has become a Kraken in its democratic waters. It is entangled with political operatives, the media and the policy community and the commercial interests of both the war machine, the American oligarchs and the media. It must be confronted to restore decent political institutions and conduct in America.

Lesson 3: Restoration of the American republic – and democracy around the world – requires the retrenchment of the American Empire. To confront that Kraken of the American security state – as much a cancer on democracy as those bogeymen, the Chinese Communist Party and Vladimir Putin – will require the retrenchment of the American Empire. In John Darwin's magnificent and magisterial *After Tamerlane: The Rise and Fall of Global Empires 1400-2000*, he demonstrates clearly the absurdity of any argument that America is anything but an imperial power, with its 700 or more military bases around the world. And he says "as the costs of greatness rise, and its benefits fall, the American taxpayer might come to resent the burden of empire and lose heart in the effort to preserve American power in its lonely preeminence." This turning is surely part of the story of both Trump and the resistance to him. He was the candidate to stop the endless wars, to drain the swamp of those who argued for them, and yet also he rode the tiger of a belligerent commercial nationalism. *Make America Great Again* was a movement of resurgent pride, but always risked being the lashing out of a wounded elephant. The impeachment – with its bizarre echoes of Joseph McCarthy when Adam Schiff made the unhinged comment that "we fight Russia over there so we don't have to fight Russia over here" – showed just how far the security state and its compliant partners will go to maintain the American Empire. One

Democratic candidate directly challenged that Empire, and argued to bring troops home so America could fix its domestic problems – Tulsi Gabbard. In response, Hilary Clinton slurred Gabbard as a 'Russian asset'. Only by retrenching the American Empire can the American republic be saved.

The impeachment curse
3 February 2020 and 2 February 2021

The final forced impeachment of Donald Trump has ended in the result that should never happen in a show trial. The sacrificial victim of the authorities' spite was acquitted.

Jonathan Turley is a reasoned and moderate legal scholar who writes widely on constitutional issues in the United States of America. He has yet to post his assessment of the verdict, but his judgment while waiting for the vote to be counted is:

> former president Donald Trump bears responsibility in the tragedy that unfolded due to his reckless rhetoric. Yet, there was a glaring omission in the substance of the House arguments. The managers did not lay out what the standard should be in convicting a former president for incitement of an insurrection and only briefly touched on proving any "state of mind" needed for such a conviction. That is why I have referred to their case as more emotive than probative. It lacked direct evidence to support the claim that Trump wanted to incite an actual insurrection or rebellion against the United States, as alleged in the article of impeachment. I do not believe that an acquittal was inevitable in this case, but it was all but assured by critical decisions made by the House in this impeachment. The unforced

errors discussed below raise the question of whether the Democrats "tanked" the trial.[150]

Perhaps? But more likely it was never really meant as a trial – since there was no evidence, no due process, no strong legal argument. It was merely an occasion to screen Hollywood propaganda and scream out the frenzy of the impeachment curse.

Will this failure end the mesmerising effect of the impeachment curse? The American political elite may now need to confront their own failures – but that is likely to mean they will continue to avoid their weakness in pursuing a revenge killing of the political movement that challenged them and exposed their weakness. They could not even run a show trial successfully. The impeachment curse has struck again.

On 2 February, 2020 – a year and a fortnight ago, I posted on the failure of the first Trump impeachment trial. I also wrote a post on "Three lessons of impeachment," in which I articulated the third lesson as: Restoration of the American republic – and democracy around the world – requires the retrenchment of the American Empire.

That retrenchment seems unlikely with President Biden-Brezhnev weakly presiding over the demented Imperial War Faction, hunting down domestic enemies of their own imagining. Let us hope some American political leaders can exorcise the impeachment curse.

The Impeachment Curse

2 February 2020

The third impeachment of an American President in my living memory is now drawing to a close: Nixon in 1973-74, Clinton in 1998-99, and Trump in 2019-20. Nixon used government agents to break into the offices of his political opponents, to install bugs to spy on them, and then to cover up the crime. Clinton's rampant sexual appetite drew him into intimidation, coercion and perjury, and he too, against a

---

[150] https://jonathanturley.org/2021/02/12/did-the-democrats-tank-the-second-trump-trial/

background scent of ruthless operations, tried to cover it up. Trump took a short relationship-building phone call with a neophyte Ukrainian President during which he asked a perhaps indelicate, but perfectly reasonable question about suspicious, possibly corrupt conduct in office of his political opponent, a former American Vice-President, who allegedly exerted influence over poor corrupt Ukraine. He made the mistake of having rats in the ship of his National Security Council. They blew the whistle on 'foreign interference'. Unlike his predecessors, Trump did not cover it up, but actually released the innocent transcripts of his calls.

The old adage – first from Hegel, then amplified in Marx – applies: history appears first as tragedy, and then as farce. Farce, sham, hoax, fiasco – all these words apply to this last, most dishonourable of impeachments. I wish other words would be applied now: collapse, fizzle, walk of shame. But I suspect the sanctimonious Chair of the House Intelligence Committee, Adam Schiff, will stand over the dead bodies of the Democrat army, and shout *Charge! Subpoena! Attack Russia!* yet again. Somewhere in the distance, Nancy Pelosi is praying for the Constitution and muttering incoherently about the law.

Failure does not count for this forever Trump impeachment crusade that began even before the Bad Orange Man took office. Democrats, liberals, progressives have been infected with a curse – the curse of impeachment. The curse has a long history.

Let us look at the famous impeachment of Warren Hastings, the head of the East India Company, beginning in February 1788 (within a month, I note in my antipodean home, of the British settlement at Sydney Cove).[151] This case was directly considered by the Framers of the USA Constitution when they debated the impeachment clause. Like Trump's case, with Schiff striving to be renowned as the Pericles of Los Angeles, it was marked by high rhetoric from truly great practitioners, Edmund Burke and the playwright/prosecutor, Richard Sheridan (perhaps Adam Schiff's role model, since Schiff aspired when

---

[151] The following account is drawn from William Dalrymple, *The Anarchy: the relentless rise of the East India Company* (2019)

young to be a screenwriter). Huge crowds and all of high society came to Westminster to watch this great trial. In his opening speech, Burke thundered:

> We have brought before you the head, the Captain General of Iniquity – one whom in all the frauds, all the peculations, all the violence, all the tyranny in India are embodied.

Burke spoke for four days, and was followed by the theatrical Sheridan. As William Dalrymple tells the story:

> His speech was widely regarded as one of the greatest feats of oratory of his day. Even the Speaker was rendered speechless. At the end of his impassioned performance, Sheridan whispered, 'My lords, I have done', and swooned backwards, landing in Burke's arms. 'The whole house – the members, peers, strangers – involuntarily joined in a tumult of applause… There were few dry eyes in the assembly.' Gibbon [the historian Edward Gibbon], alarmed at his friend's condition, went around the following day to check if Sheridan was all right: 'He is perfectly well,' he noted in his diary. 'A good actor.[152]'

The trial gave birth to theories of human rights, and began the slow process of containment of the East India Company within conventional imperial rule, but it was founded on one faulty premise. They impeached the wrong man. Worse, the prosecutors fell victim to the revenge, hate and "obsessional passion" of a bitter and more questionable character, Philip Francis, who had been exposed by Hastings as corrupt, incompetent and contemptible of the cultures of India. Francis had even fought a duel with Hastings, and lost ineptly. After the duel, he returned to England as a bitter, vengeful and twisted man. Elected to a rotten borough in Parliament, he poured poison into the ear of his fellow members, Edmund Burke and others. So began the eighteenth century's most famous impeachment hoax.

In fact, Hastings had, in Dalrymple's words, "probably done more than any other Company official to rein in the worst excesses of its rule." He genuinely loved India, perhaps even more than England to

---

[152] Dalrymple, *The Anarchy*, p. 311.

which he was an orphaned stranger. He routinely expressed outrage at the unprincipled exploitation of the Indians by Company officials. He rebuilt justice, peace and the economy within Bengal, and was the most popular of all the British officials in India, 'positively beloved of the people'.

In an uncanny preview of the Trump impeachment, the bitter curse that infected Philip Francis and the prosecutors of Warren Hastings drove a conspiracy that undermined the truth of their case.

> As a result of Francis's influence, the Articles of Impeachment were full of demonstrable fantasies and distortions, which traded on the ignorance of the audience about the issues and personalities involved. They were also badly drafted and lacked the necessary legal detail. Many of the entertaining speeches were little better than *ad hominem* rants, mixing falsified history and unproved innuendo... It took Hastings' defence many weeks even to begin correcting the multiple errors of basic facts which the prosecution had laid out. If anything, the Impeachment demonstrated above all the sheer ignorance of the British about the subcontinent they had been looting so comprehensively, and profitably, for thirty years.[153]

So by extension, the real truth exposed by the proceedings in Trump's trial is the corrupted export of American crony capitalism to countries like Ukraine that the American political and commercial elite have "been looting so comprehensively, and profitably, for thirty years."

The impeachment of Warren Hastings failed, although it took seven years to reach this conclusion. The last years of Hastings were blighted by the injustice perpetrated on him, and the misfired conspiracy did not help India. For Hastings was replaced not by a man of his sparse habits and admiration for Indian culture, but by a failed general with a deep humiliation to overcome, the same general expelled by the founders and framers of the American constitution, General Lord Charles Cornwallis.

---

[153] Dalrymple, *The Anarchy*, p. 313.

This curse of impeachment appears again in the main American trials. Jackson is impeached, but not removed from office, for breaking a law that is later found to be unconstitutional. Clinton's impeachment exposed an over-zealous case that, because it was not rooted in high crimes, backfired against the prosecutors. Clinton rose in popularity, despite his character flaws and unethical conduct, and the Republican power structures collapsed, leading to the resignation of Newt Gingrich as Speaker of the House.

And now the curse of impeachment has struck again. Despite warnings to forsake the obsession with impeachment by columnists and candidates, the Democrats marched into the Valley of Death, led by their warrior-priest Schiff and their ancient queen Pelosi. Despite the complete collapse of the RussiaGate hoax, they pursued another cooked-up charge by the intelligence community, who appear to be governed by no basic code of public sector conduct, no basic decency, no loyalty to democratic authority. Despite the exposure of the falsity of the "whistleblower" claims, they pressed on, and got caught in a web of their own lies about not knowing his or her identity. Despite complicity in perpetrating the extraordinary injustices exposed by the Inspector General in relation to the FBI, CrossFire Hurricane and the Foreign Intelligence Surveillance court, they pushed forward with another case of bad process and prosecutorial misconduct. Despite the endless claims that 'no-one is above the law', they claim the right to conduct impeachment without constraint by the law. Despite insisting they wanted a fair trial, they put on a show trial, and then everyone saw through it.

Al Green, Democratic Congressman, admitted that the impeachment process began before Trump was even elected. From the first protests of "Not my President" to today's bizarre claims that "This is no acquittal", the impeachment curse has driven the Democrats and the Resistance into a world of constitutional and political fantasy. Now Mara Gay from the *New York Times* editorial board – no doubt a recipient of numerous leaks from political officers – says America is in a "very scary moment in its history a capstone in a total collapse in faith in American institutions" because the Senate essentially dismisses the charges against President Trump as unproven, unconstitutional and unlawful. She did not say the same thing when the FBI was exposed as lying to the courts and allegedly spying on a domestic Presidential campaign, and indeed the same President in office.

Sadly, the curse of impeachment has deranged American democracy. For this deadly virus to be cleared from the democratic heart, I expect it will take Trump's re-election, a Republican victory in the House, a concerted purge and rebuilding of American government officials, a reckoning with bias and political alliances in media corporations, and and a return to the ordinary virtues, traditions and rule of law of the constitutional republic. It might take a few years. It might take a few prosecutions from the Durham investigation. It will witness much melodrama and a few flame-outs. It will require constraint on the part of the many institutions and political actors who have been abused by this crusade. Indeed, it will require the very restraint and return to traditions of decent deliberation that just over half of the US Senate has displayed in bringing this miscarriage of justice to an end. There lies the hope.

An Open Letter to America

23 February 2020

To the citizens, office-holders and advocates of the United States of America,

Your republic is breaking.

Yet your empire holds on.

And so collapses the conceit of manifest destiny as the primal democracy, the greatest country on earth, and the envy of the world.

Indeed, the stubborn protagonists of your empire – whether John Bolton or John Brennan – are breaking your republic. Endless wars and 800 military bases around the world have spawned a bloated political military and a sprawling intelligence community, who now have been exposed in multiple Inspector-General's report as colluding against the democracy that empowers them.[154]

Your elites in Washington DC, Wall St and Hollywood fail, but never feel the consequence of failure. Washington's political, legal, and media elites succumbed to the absurd RussiaGate hoax, and descended into a McCarthyist breakdown of basic principles of justice; but did they admit and apologise for their failure when the true facts were exposed? Corruption is exposed, and the corrupt are preemptively exonerated, and indeed the constitution of the republic is abused during the impeachment curse to hide the corruption.[155] The financial oligarchs failed, and were bailed out, at the expense of the 'deplorables' they despise. Actors and starlets from Hollywood throw out smokescreens to hide their moral failures – whether it is turning a blind eye to sexual crimes or living in luxury – while they condemn ordinary citizens for burning the world with their lowly consumption habits. Actors and celebrities espouse sentimental Marxism that has no effect on their privilege. The journalists and commentators (many of whom are recycled political hacks and members of the intelligence community) of the *New York Times*, the *Washington Post*, CNN, MSNBC collude in perpetrating a hoax, publish made-up stories as political hit-jobs, report fallacies without blushing, advocate elites deciding elections rather than voters, and then have the gall to call for censorship of real reporting.[156] In summary, as Tucker Carlson has said, the incompetence of a ruling class has squandered the legacy of

---

[154] https://irp.fas.org/agency/doj/oig/product.htm, Lee Smith, *Plot Against the President*, 2019.

[155] Schweizer, *Profiles in Corruption*

[156] *Washington Examiner*, 20 Feb 2020, *Washington Post*, 22 Feb 2020, *The Intercept*, 21 Jan 2019.

American greatness.[157]

Yet you persist in the demented assertion of greatness, as if the American empire was represented by Joe Biden's gerontocratic campaign for president. Your journals and think tanks say the USA cannot afford to relinquish its global hegemony.[158] Your progressives screech with absurd fantasies about fighting Russia in Ukraine so that Russia does not invade the homeland, and define as an impeachable offence any questioning of the intelligence community's assessment. Reasonable patriotic people – even serving military officers running for President such as Tulsi Gabbard – are slandered by the intelligence community, rival politicians and the media as traitors. Your President Trump has made the slogan of his movement into a foreign policy to make American great again. The rest of the world respects the restoration of pride among the ordinary people of the flyover states, but shudders at the prospect of this wounded giant stumbling and lashing out in pain.

The world sees this cancer in your divided government and this derangement in the American mind, and the world knows your rule is coming to an end. The world knows you are not who you pretend you are. The world knows you are no longer a beacon of democracy and freedom in the world. The world knows you are not the home of the brave and the land of the free. The world knows you are a decaying empire in disguise. The world knows you are not the indispensable nation.

It is time to wake up, America. It is time to shed your illusions. It is time to clean your own house. It is time to make America humble again.

---

[157] Tucker Carlson, 'Ruling class incompetence', YouTube, 22 Feb 2020.
[158] Robert Kagan, *Brookings Blog*, 25 April 2016.

The persistence of the Mahabharata
5 March 2020

My trip to Bali – now over, since I am returned from the tropical paradise to the dry urban refuge of my home in Melbourne – reminded me not only of Clifford Geertz, but also of the great Indian epic, the Mahabharata.

As we drove through Denpasar, we saw massive modern statues depicting scenes from the Mahabharata, featuring one of the culminating battles between Ghatodkacha and Karna and another of Arjuna. The driver pointed out another statue from the Ramayana, which I confessed to him I had not read, although I had read some of the Mahabharata.

I took from these glimpses into Balinese culture, for little reason really, that the two great Indian epics, the Mahabharata and Ramayana, persist today as vital, living organs of the culture. I could be wrong, but there are many signs of the living presence of the epics in contemporary popular culture in the Indo-South-East Asian world, such as successful television series and comic books. One Indian, Chindu Sreedharan, launched in 2009 a retelling of the 90 000 verse epic one tweet at a time – the venture still goes on. Reportedly, the Pandava brothers still offer character cut-outs for Indian politicians to cast their tired narratives against at each election, and Professor Shubha Tiwari writes:

> *The Mahabharata* is the bedrock of Indian consciousness. It is an important building block of the collective social psyche of India. Since it has become a part of the social mind, Indians forever try to interpret contemporary political and social scenes in terms of *The Mahabharata*.[159]

Is it still the kind of canon that functions like a fruitful, graceful

---

[159] Shubha Tiwari, *Presence of The Mahabharata in Contemporary Political Narration and Literature* (2015).

tree, not like the burned down stump of the Western canon? Is it a sign of decadence in 'the West', or the American *imperium*, that such a canon has been attacked repeatedly by its own elites, who possess no resources for powerful social imagery besides *Marvel* comics? Does the Mahabharata still guide the thinking, judgment and values of the Indo-Hindu world in a vital, creative way – as Spengler or Toynbee might have put it – that the West does not? Is it protected from the Burning Archive?

K.T. McFarland's Revolution in Tamerlane's Shadow
24 May 2020

Over the last week I have read K.T. (Kathleen Troia) McFarland's *Revolution: Trump, Washington and 'We the People'* (2020). I was led to this book by the remarkable case of injustice perpetrated on General Michael Flynn.[160] K.T. McFarland was Michael Flynn's deputy, Deputy National Security Adviser in the first months of Trump's presidency, and was herself subjected to the persecutory prosecution of James Comey's FBI as part of what increasingly appears to be an organised resistance to the new administration by the security agencies in collaboration with political operatives.

I saw McFarland interviewed about her experience, when she endured days of harassing questioning and bogus threats aimed at intimidating her into a guilty plea for a process crime. The aim of this intimidation was clearly to further the resistance and to derail the new Trump administration. The effect on Flynn and McFarland was

---

[160] https://thehill.com/opinion/criminal-justice/495405-michael-flynn-case-should-be-dismissed-to-preserve-justice/

profound. McFarland resigned or was forced out over the concocted legal and media scandal. Flynn has been subjected to persecutory justice in the form of a judge who seems to want to make himself both prosecutor and arbiter, as well as protector of the Obama legacy.[161]

In the interview, McFarland talked about how she had to leave the country for a time, and spent the time writing this book to make sense of her experience. Only now, with the recent disclosures of the documented truth about the Flynn case has she begun to speak again on the panel shows and news programs.

The account of this experience in her book is haunting. Surely the liberal mind is shocked that such Kafkaesque trials occur in the great merchant empire of democracy. McFarland writes that her experience with the FBI, Office of Special Counsel (Mueller) investigation and related Congressional investigations:

> illustrates how dangerously perverted the system has become... these politically-motivated investigations have unintended consequences. They shove our very real problems to the sidelines while those inside the Beltway remain obsessed with scandals that the rest of the country doesn't really care about. But they also cast doubt and suspicion on our governmental institutions when some powerful people in the Washington Establishment attempt what amounts to reversing election outcomes if they don't like the results. Investigation after investigation, impeachment effort after impeachment effort serve to paralyze our elected officials. They also gnaw away at our people's faith in the democratic system itself. Furthermore, they put our national security at risk, as our adversaries exploit the madness of our internal divisions and political paralysis to their own advantage.[162]

It is a damning and revealing judgment from an exceptionally insightful insider of the American national security state. McFarland's career stretched back to Kissinger and Nixon, and included periods as a minor official in the Reagan administration, as a mother and carer, as

---

[161] *Wall Street Journal*, 13 May 2020.
[162] McFarland's *Revolution: Trump, Washington and 'We the People'* (2020).

a television commentator, and speaker on the circuit, before peaking as a central member of Trump's transition team and Deputy National Security Adviser. Throughout the book she offers genuine insight to the new Presidential administration and exceptional glimpses into the mode of operation of key figures of the administration. She highlights some of the flaws in Flynn's personality that may have contributed to his downfall, and identifies the particular demands of Trump's briefing style that left Tillerson and McMaster as too proud grandees unable to adapt their communication style to the needs of their new boss. She is no naive Trump admirer, and is clearly an astute and balanced observer of the private theatre of power.

McFarland also gives an account of the intellectual transition of this former protégé of Henry Kissinger to become a believer in Trump's populist revolution and, although this point is less explicitly acknowledged by McFarland, nationalist cause. She devotes one chapter to Washington's failed economic and foreign policies, and presents a convincing diagnosis that this elite failure is behind the populist resurgence:

> for nearly twenty years we have pursued economic and foreign policies that worked well for some of our people but failed miserably for others. It didn't matter whether the Republicans or Democrats were in charge in Washington. The average, hardworking 'commoners' turned to Trump because they felt ignored or ill-treated by everybody else.

The latter part of her book is a statement of faith in democratic populism – the "we the people" of her title. I found this section less compelling since it suffered from the peculiar American blindness to their own belligerent nationalist reinterpretation of their empire of democracy. It becomes ultimately a restatement of American exceptionalism.

> America is a great nation for many reasons. But we are an exceptional nation for only one – that we have within our hands the power of regeneration. We can reinvent ourselves as a nation, just as we can reinvent ourselves as individuals.

In this view, America's empire of democracy is immune to decline. This view reads American history as the eternal youth, who can miraculously reinvent its fate an to repeat eternally recurring, 'new birth of freedom'.

Ultimately, this statement is merely a profession of faith, complete with the invocation of the sacred words of the democratic rites. But this profession of faith cannot insulate yet another grandiose, otiose empire from over-reach, cultural decay and decline. America does not have an exclusive claim to democracy, populism or national regeneration. It is not the fount of democracy in the world, but one deep stream of those political traditions. It is not exceptional, and not immune from the forces of history, conflict and disorder. It cannot stand outside Tamerlane's shadow, as the great historian of empires, John Darwin, described it. Many nations and many empires have the power to regenerate. But no other nation claims to be the sole and exclusive beacon of the world. As Darwin writes at the end of *After Tamerlane*:

> if there is one continuity that we should be able to glean from a long view of the past, it is Eurasia's resistance to a uniform system, a single great ruler, or one set of rules. In that sense, we still live in Tamerlane's shadow – or, perhaps more precisely, in the shadow of his failure.[163]

Reflections on America in Flames
1 June 2020

The descent of the American Republic into one of the outer circles

---

[163] Darwin, *After Tamerlane*, p. 506.

of hell is occurring before our eyes. Within a week an outrageous case of police brutality has spiraled into violence, looting, and despair across dozens of cities. The fire was ignited by a police force controlled by a city government that has been immune to practical reform and run by Democrats for years. Rarely has the United States of America seemed more ironically named. It is now a state of disorder, interspersed by occasional spasms of eloquence when people face choices that may define their moral lives.

I am a long way away from the imperial centre, where I live in quiet, if locked down, streets. Still, the events that I have seen are distressing, all of them: the original murder; the pain and grief of the family of George Floyd; the evasions of the local prosecutor and authorities; the peaceful protesters losing their platform to agitators with another goal; the absurd mainstream media reporters play acting as an Iraqi Information Minister telling their audience "everything is fine", while in the background of their shot the city is burning or a passing protester in a merry caravan throws a bottle at the reporter; the looting, so much looting that cannot be described as protest; the burning of businesses, libraries, shops, cars, police stations; the white kids intoxicated with ideology who threw Molotov cocktails into a police car with four of their fellows, and who were only saved from death by the naive terrorists' incompetence; the cynical white Antifa hipster in a beard and turned up jeans paying black kids on bikes to go and fight his battles for him; the black woman from the Minnesota housing estate crying in despair that she has nowhere to shop for basic supplies and no bus service to go anywhere else because of the rioters, and she was afraid, since the riots had made her wish she was in the same better place that George Floyd was. This is how history flows - an impossibly complex stage drama.

There have been moments of inspiration, of course. The Atlanta Mayor Keisha Lance Bottoms who spoke with true courage that "this is not a protest... this is chaos," urged all the rioters to go home and stop disgracing the life of George Floyd and every other person killed in

America.[164] Killer Mike and her courageous white female police chief backed her up. There have been black protesters protecting shops from rampaging Valley kids radicals. There has been a white security guard who quickly disarmed some dumb white radical pretender who had taken an assault rifle from a burnt-out police car and was trying it out for size, as if he were on the set of a movie about a PLO training camp.

But this virus of violence has spread in circles of crisis. The response to the coronavirus has led to a truly unprecedented economic crisis, with huge numbers of people locked out of their businesses and locked into their homes. The coronavirus crisis ran at the heels of the impeachment crisis that together exposed a political crisis, in which political actors acted with ex-officials of the security state and the Big Tech/Media oligarchs to subvert an elected, if erratic, President. And that political crisis was in turn provoked by the overturning in the 2016 election of a protected befuddled elite, who had grown too cozy with endless wars and billion-dollar bailouts of financialized elites to bear witness to the social crisis unfolding outside of their limousines and gated communities. The economic, political and social crises are nested within a cultural crisis – the decay of the infinite conversation that the *Burning Archive* laments. For America specifically, there is another crisis again: a late empire that is overextended and unwinding, but still believes it has an exceptional ability to stare down the tide of history, to ignore the tragedy of its sins, and to march forever in the arms of progress towards its manifest destiny.

So many crises, and so many temptations to believe that the pace of human affairs may quicken in these dark days. But, perhaps these are just riots, the return of the disorderly mob, a feature of society from time immemorial? Sometimes celebrated. Sometimes feared. Sometimes mythologised. It may not be the Second Coming. There may not be any beast slouching toward Bethlehem to be born. It may just be one small brick falling from a solid wall.

---

[164] *Fox News*, 29 May 2020.

Jeff Rich

Is America reliving the 1917 revolution?
5 June 2020

Over the last week I have been chilled by some resemblances between the current American political, social and cultural crises and the great people's tragedy that unfolded in Russia from 1917.

An intoxicated radicalism has taken hold in this ancient constitutional republic, and disordered its institutions of politics, culture, law and justice. A carnival of protest, rebellion, unrest and even talk of revolution and civil war has broken out. It has broken the shackles of the lockdown, and danced in the streets. Like a Russian imperial guard on a wild vodka-drinking bender, the crowds – or parts of the crowd – have extinguished their grief in intoxication, and in a wild frenzy are acting out their anger by smashing every glass, every dish, every bottle in the house.

The frenzy has been stimulated by many true grievances, not just the alleged murder of George Floyd, but many years of failures of many kinds. I say alleged murder, let me add, not to doubt what happened, but to respect the rule of law and to ensure justice is done [*later note, as indeed it was at the trial*]. The grievance is stark; no-one can watch the act without condemnation. Importantly, no-one did. It has been universally damned – by left and right, by true and false, by the President and the people on the streets. Nor is the grievance alone – there have been other killings, over many years. The statistics do not bear out some extravagant claims of the grieving protesters – genocide, being hunted, and so on – but grief howls its own truths, embellished with both delusion and deeper truth, embroidered with fragments of all the failures: past murders, past riots from Baltimore and Ferguson, 1992 and 1968, the mistakes of the lockdown, the transfer of wealth to Wall Street by the betrayer of hope, Barack Obama, the Crime Act of the Clinton era, excessive imprisonment, feral cities, drugs, failed drugs programs, poverty, failed poverty programs, broken families, endless wars, corruption of Congress by special interests and lobbying, and the plantation-owner attitude towards black voters of the Democratic Party. The last grievance is surely relevant since for decades the Democrats have run Minneapolis and most of the cities burning and rioting in America over the last week. This same plantation-owner attitude, expressed very recently by the alternative President, Joe Biden, to one of the leading African American radio/podcasting hosts – "If you have a problem figuring out whether you're for me or Trump, then *you ain't Black*."

Many of the governing elites perpetrated many of these failures in person, by themselves, with their own hands, eyes and minds, not behind the anonymous mask of "systemic racism". Now they conceal their guilt in acts of abasement. At the moment when cities are burning, the looters are breaking through windows, and the unprotected are abandoned, authority crumbles at the knees, and many of the cosseted elites reveal themselves as the 'cowards, liars and executioners' they truly are. They do not stand up to or suppress the insurrection. They pander to plain, ordinary crime. They call it sweet names, such as "largely peaceful protests". They try to ride the dragon in their own intoxication. The bad actors who pretend to be journalists – like Chris Cuomo, Don Lemon, the ridiculous Nikole Hannah-Jones (who claims property destruction, smashing windows, burning churches, looting family businesses is "not violence") and many more – imagine themselves the righteous intellectual patrons of the Revolution, like Maxim Gorky. Gorky was the cultural grandee of the Bolsheviks. Lenin described Gorky as "calflike" in his political naiveté: donating to the riots, inviting the thugs into their homes, providing succour to evil. As a recent study of Gorky by Anita Kondoyanidi has written:

> Gorky's personal experiences with violence at the hands of the Russian petit bourgeoisie and peasantry generated his strong and tenacious desire to recast Man and heal Russia and Russians from their innate pessimism and laziness. Once Gorky accepted selective use of violence in building an ideal Soviet society and

offered Russia a utopian project – the creation of a new, improved human being—he contributed to the horrifying reality of the 1930s, making himself an unintentional accomplice in the Soviet revolutionary and repressive experiment.[165]

They will fail, just as the degraded and demoralised elites of Russia failed to control the ruthless agitators and shadowy conspirators who saw them in the end as useful idiots.

I am not sure I quite ended the post the way I imagined when I began it. I am very troubled by the events, and especially the handling of the story by the mass media and so many intellectuals deranged by Donald Trump. They have become the Union of Soviet Writers protecting a shadow government they wish to reinstall. I am genuinely concerned about a coup of sorts, the involvement of the estranged and discredited deep state actors, under investigation for the RussiaGate hoax, and a fundamental breakdown in law and order in America. I feel betrayed by nearly all sides. One does not need to succumb to Trump Derangement Syndrome to have doubts whether Donald Trump can ride this storm. Even Steve Bannon says, he is an imperfect instrument. We all are. That is why we need institutions. But the corrupt faction of the American Empire is not to be trusted with the institutions of law, justice, security and democracy.

I am rereading Orlando Figes, *A People's Tragedy: the Russian Revolution 1891-1924* to refamiliarise myself with the events of Russia in 1917 that led to the breakdown of order, culture, and civilisation in a riot of agitprop, violence and terror that sought to remake humanity in a new normal. Another day, I may extend the comparison.

---

[165] Kondoyanidi, The Prophet Disillusioned: Maxim Gorky And The Russian Revolutions, PhD Thesis, Georgetown University 2019.

Jeff Rich

A Very Modern Charge of the Light Brigade
18 July 2020

The Crimean War of 1853 to 1856 is now a forgotten and neglected conflict, hidden in the century of peace in the nineteenth century. Yet it was a surprisingly fertile conflict in its unintended consequences. Moreover, this war has an uncanny resemblance to the events of our time. It involved a contest for Europe between two titans, the Russian and British Empires. It involved catastrophic failures by the aristocratic elites of both empires. The coronavirus pandemic in 2020 has also exposed dramatic, if earnest, failures among today's governing elites, who have been enthused with an ecstasy of errant epidemiology, and to a very modern *Charge of the Light Brigade*.

Tennyson made of these failures an immortal poem, but the more prosaic story of the Charge of the Light Brigade goes like this. On 25 October 1854 the Commander of the British forces in the Crimean War, Lord Raglan, ordered an attack on an artillery battery as part of the wider Battle of Balaclava. Orders were misunderstood or ill-conceived or poorly communicated: whichever reason, a light cavalry force, an agile and adaptive shock force, was sent along adverse terrain to attack supremely well-defended guns. They were mown down from three sides. The secondary commander of the British insouciantly refused to defend or protect or abort this mission. The Light Brigade soon retreated, but most of the officers died. They died going hard and going fast – against an enemy they did not understand, and to achieve an objective that, with brief reflection, would be exposed as unattainable. As William Howard Russell, war correspondent and witness to this battle, wrote: "Our Light Brigade was annihilated by their own rashness, and by the brutality of a ferocious enemy."[166]

Anglophone Empires continue to this day to blame those damned Russians for the folly of imperial generals. But Russell's condemnation

---

[166] *The Times*, 14 November 1854.

of the rashness of the command had more reverberations. The Crimean War was indeed one of the first to be extensively documented in newspapers and photographs. As the Vietnam War is known to the American Empire as the 'first television war', so Crimea was for the European empires the first mass newspaper war. Perhaps COVID-19 is social media's first pandemic? In any case, the media of the day took this rash failure and translated it into a worthy cause, celebrated powerfully in Alfred Tennyson's poem. "Into the Valley of Death," Tennyson sung, "Rode the six hundred... Theirs not to reason why,/ Theirs but to do and die." No-one remembers anymore the Noble Six Hundred. They are forgotten and lost in that better known line – *Into the Valley of Death*. And the folk line of every subordinate in a *Flight 93* bureaucracy – 'ours is not to reason why, ours is but to do and die', has become unmoored from its pretext: *'Someone had blundered'*.

The blunders of the Crimean War would become legendary and would ultimately be the fertile soil of its greater consequence. Tennyson's plangent urging to "honour the wild charge they made" would endure in literature, but not in policy. Poets are, after all is said and done, not the unacknowledged legislators of the world, but the ineffectual leaders of endless wars with the real. As history slowly papered over Tennyson's dreamy chant, the Crimean War became a watchword for mismanagement and elite failure. It provoked a late nineteenth century reconstruction of the state. In Russia, the failures of the war convinced the educated elites of the need to replace ruling values of patronage and honour with governing habits of law and competence. It catalysed changes to many social institutions – serfdom, justice, local self-government, education, and military service. These were profound changes, even if they could not save the dynasty from overwhelming events. In Britain, the Crimean War accelerated a shift from aristocratic patronage to professional common sense. It was the key event that drove the administrative reforms and establishment of a merit-based professional bureaucracy, as envisioned in the Northcote-Trevelyan report of 1854. Florence Nightingale became famous during the war, and was part of the same movement to practical, scientific and professional administration as the civil service reforms. Crimea midwived modern nursing and, in some ways, modern public health.

We can only hope that the blunders of today's elites, most especially our public health leaders in response to coronavirus, will provide the fertile soil for a similar counter-reformation. The political and cultural decay has gone too far. Our political, bureaucratic and commercial elites have become parasitic raiders on institutions they cannot cherish, cannot lead and cannot protect for the generations to come. Their incompetence, patronage, corruption and intellectual poverty have been exposed by this pandemic and the world crisis it has generated. There lies the hope in this locked down world. Their glory has faded, and we, who defy them by not living in lies, will make our way back from the mouth of hell.

America's Coming Century of Humiliation
21 March 2021

A tragic sense of history does not limit the depth of the fall of the mighty and flawed, nor does it pretend that prevailing orders degrade in a slow, controlled and managed decline. Collapse of political orders, institutions, empires and cultures as often comes quickly, almost suddenly, and rarely with expert forecasts pre-loaded. So it would seem. The accelerating disrespect of America, which has emerged in recent diplomatic exchanges, suggests a rapid fall may be the fate of the American Empire and its political and cultural order.

Last August I wrote the post below, teasing a comparison between the prospect of American decline and the "century of humiliation" experienced by China between the First Opium Wars in the 1840's and the 1949 Revolution. Though American elites often entertain the thought of decline, they rarely visualise it fully. A tragic sense of history would instruct these elites that empires really do collapse, and that elites rarely can control events. The deep flaws in culture and political order drive them to their death.

America's elites are yet to learn this lesson. They feel challenged, but they respond with a complacent or combative American supremacist idea: America is the indispensable nation. The idea has variations. America is the city on the hill showing the way to the world. America is the freedom loving rebel. The 'Leader of the Free World' overthrows the evil empires of the world, and makes them bend to the 'rules-based order' of the great republic, invented by the American mind.

This mindset is expressed in the intellectual pretence of the 'Longer Telegram' published by the Atlantic Council, and thought to reflect the thinking, or even the writing, of the Biden Administration's National Security Adviser, Jake Sullivan or its Secretary of State, Anthony Blinken.[167] This "telegram" sets out a strategy for China that assumes containment, not a multi-polar world. It imagines China will kow-tow to the dreams of the Yankee mandate of heaven. There it is written:

> the major problem facing the United States in confronting Xi's China is not one of military, economic, or technological capabilities. It is one of self-belief.

But the shrouded authors claim there is no reason to doubt American. Any doubters are 'corrosive forces' and counsellors of despair. The 'Longer Telegram' sings, America is forever young. It is constant in trumpeting the blazing triumph of its manifest destiny.

> The United States, as a country, is young, and the capacity for innovation is unsurpassed. The values for which it stands have stood the test of time. This is where the nation's leadership must once again step up to the challenge—not just to provide the

---

[167] Atlantic Council, *The Longer Telegram: Toward A New American China Strategy* (2021).

nation with vision, mission, and purpose; not just to frame the strategy and give it effect; but to cause the American people to once again believe in the nation and its capacity to provide effective global leadership for the century ahead. In doing so, the nation must also lead its friends and allies to once again believe in the United States as well.

But the problem is the world no longer believes in America. Its Capitol is surrounded by troops and razor wire to protect its elite from the fears generated by an event, which some call an insurrection and some call a false flag event. It runs its elections like a chook lottery in a pub. Its leadership is an infirm gerontocracy. Its wars are endless and futile, except for the corporations and oligarchs who profit from them. Its media and Big Tech tyrannize the minds of the world, and silence the voices of the parallel polis. Its institutions have failed. Its republic is exposed as a bankrupt, post-democratic media state.

Joe Biden boasts, like an aging mountain of a triad, that 'America is back'. The problem is the world leaders know exactly the emptiness of this self-deluding boast. Recent diplomatic events show the world's leaders no longer care to conceal their contempt for the mad old king. Joe Biden staged an interview with ABC news in which he called Russia's President, Vladimir Putin a 'killer'. Biden blustered that Putin would 'pay a price' and that he 'had no soul'. Biden must have assumed the whole world sat in the same echo chamber of compliant conformists that the American press gaggle has become. Perhaps he was building himself up as a "tough guy" for a domestic audience. Perhaps he was creating a diversion from his weakness towards China by displaying his toughness against Russia. Perhaps he was preparing the ground for another intervention in Ukraine by the neo-conservative war machine. But he clearly did not think it through. Vladimir Putin called him out as projecting. He read back America's shameful record of violence to itself. He wished Biden health, 'without irony'. Then he challenged Biden to a dialogue, live and without editing or prompts, on global policy and national security issues. Biden was exposed to the entire world as the "tough guy" emperor with no clothes, no authority, no teleprompter and no crown.

Then, perhaps even in a coordinated response, China's key diplomats responded to Blinken's over-long telegram with sharp rebukes, and a defiant tone. In part-quoted remarks Yang responded with defiance to the claims of rules-based order, serving democracy, and pursuing an ever-greater union:

> Well, isn't this the intention of the United States — judging from what, or the way that you have made your opening remarks — that it wants to speak to China in a condescending way from a position of strength? So was this carefully all planned and was it carefully orchestrated with all the preparations in place? Is that the way that you had hoped to conduct this dialogue? Well, I think we thought too well of the United States. We thought that the U.S. side will follow the necessary diplomatic protocols. So for China it was necessary that we made our position clear. So let me say here that, in front of the Chinese side, the United States does not have the qualification to say that it wants to speak to China from a position of strength. The U.S. side was not even qualified to say such things even 20 years or 30 years back, because this is not the way to deal with the Chinese people. If the United States wants to deal properly with the Chinese side, then let's follow the necessary protocols and do things the right way.[168]

But perhaps more tellingly, the Chinese diplomats (of far greater experience and stature than Blinken and Sullivan) said:

> The United States itself does not represent international public opinion, and neither does the Western world. Whether judged by population scale or the trend of the world, the Western world does not represent the global public opinion. So we hope that when talking about universal values or international public opinion on the part of the United States, we hope the U.S. side will think about whether it feels reassured in saying those things, because the U.S. does not represent the world. It only represents the government of the United States. I don't think the overwhelming majority of countries in the world would

---

[168] As reported in *Nikkei*.

recognize that the universal values advocated by the United States or that the opinion of the United States could represent international public opinion, and those countries would not recognize that the rules made by a small number of people would serve as the basis for the international order.

The chorus of international opinion puncturing these absurd fantasies of the American imperial elite will grow ever stronger in years to come. The citizens of the world will switch off Netflix, close down Twitter, and lead their lives by other values. America is no longer the city on a hill laying a foundation of a new world. The world has broken the spell, and can resist the incessant force-fed delusions of American culture that this enchantment was ever real, rather than a grand sermon of Winthrop and his successors. America is a decaying empire in denial, led by "an old, mad, blind, despised and dying King" (Shelley, "England in 1819"), and it is about to experience a rapid descent into a looming century of humiliation.

2 August 2020

Could it be that the current unrest in America and the disintegration of its political, social and cultural institutions are the beginning of its own 21st century version of the Chinese Qing Empire's Century of Humiliation – 百年耻辱?

Could it even be that the leaders of China are pursuing a hundred year marathon to supplant America as the global super-power? That is the hypothesis of Michael Pillsbury, a longtime China expert in America's security state. Pillsbury and his party of China Hawks tell a story that China plans to exacting a symmetrical revenge on the Empire that rose on the back of China's humiliation. They claim China plans to induce a similar sequence of institutional collapse through elite betrayals, commercial treachery, social decay, ethno-nationalism, political decay, and even covert armed rebellion.[169]

---

[169] Pillsbury, *The Hundred-Year Marathon: China's Secret Strategy to Replace America as the Global Superpower* (2016).

The comparison has been made by some American security analysts, although made at a superficial level that does not identify the full scale of the collapse of an imperial order that occurred in China in the nineteenth century.[170] So, comparisons are drawn between British importers of opium in 1840's and the flood of fentanyl from China into the United States of America over the last decade. The hawkish analysts highlight the malfeasance or immorality of China trafficking in addiction, but do not question the weakness of American society that led so many Americans to want to use the drug and to partake in its trade.

Other comparisons can be made between elements of the Century of Humiliation. The American commercial elite resembles the Hong Kong merchants of the 1840's, who sought to unlock commercial advantages with a complacent confidence that their imperial authority would never be weakened. Is #BlackLivesMatter at its source a millenarian movement of ethno-nationalism in conflict with a dominant ethnic group, similar to the Miao rebellion against the Han between 1854 and 1873? Is the unrest and insurrection the beginning of a widespread, devastating civil war – a full spectrum civil war, not only fought as a kinetic war – similar to the Taiping rebellion of 1850-64, driven by radical objectives of social change, a reborn form of religious faith and a charismatic, if delusional, spurned youthful leader in Alexandra Ocasio-Cortez? Is Hilary Clinton the Dowager Empress, never formally in power, and yet through plots, schemes and favourites presiding over an institutional sclerosis of the American Empire?

These hypotheses are only suggestive. However, it does seem clear that the American Empire and the idea of American Greatness are collapsing. The collapse is engineered by the exploitation of the weaknesses of its elites and institutions by its internal imperial rivals. The ball has been released from the top of the spiral, and nothing can stop it now.

---

[170] "Is China Inflicting a 'Century of Humiliation' on the World?", *The Diplomat*, 4 Feb 2018.

Jeff Rich

Obsession and Trump's Derangement of the Elites
11 October 2020

Byron York's *Obsession: Inside the Washington Establishment's Never-Ending War on Trump* (2020) provides some insight into one of the most poisonous patterns in today's cultural decay: the derangement by Donald Trump of the elites, especially the broadcast performers who pretend to be journalists.

York's book describes the long campaign of the Washington establishment – that includes politics, media, their oligarchical funders, the security and foreign policy institutions, and the parasitic institutions of commentary – to take revenge on Donald Trump for beating them at their own game – democratic politics. Not only that, he beat these dynastic leaders and their professionals – this gang of the smartest guys in the room – as a first-timer. They could never forgive him for that.

Nor could the media forgive Trump for using them as click-magnets, rather than, as they falsely believed, the media using Trump as a clownish, popular sock puppet. They had spent a year mocking his ridiculousness, and exposing their own blindness. They had signed up to the Democratic machinery to manipulate democracy, and had exposed themselves as ham-fisted fools.

So, as Byron York recounts, the march to impeachment began. Indeed as more declassified documents suggest each day, the psyop counter-intelligence operation against a Trump Presidency may have been initiated by Clinton one week after Trump received the Republican nomination. That was when the Russian collusion hoax began, and it has continued ever since.

Byron York provides a compelling and well-sourced account of the saga of Trump impeachment. The campaign to impeach Trump began the night he was elected, and was incited all along by scions of the Democratic establishment, the security state and media and financial oligarchs. He recounts how Nancy Pelosi's defensive disclosure in late 2019 that impeachment was not being rushed – no, it had been proceeding for two and a half years – revealed finally to Republicans that all the scandals, investigations and fact-checking nonsense were not the pursuit of truth and justice, but a conspiracy to get Trump and restore the establishment to power.

> Now, with the perspective of time, the Democratic effort to remove Trump, and the president's struggle to defend himself, appear less a rushed impeachment than a long and agonizing political civil war: The presidential campaign and transition were a prelude, a time of growing tension; 2017 saw the formal start of the war, with the appointment of a special counsel, and a sense of hope – at least on the president's side – that hostilities might be wrapped up quickly; 2018 was a stalemate, as each side, optimism gone, dug in for a long battle; 2019 saw what at first appeared to be the end of action – Mueller's last stand – only to see the conflict flare up again in one more desperate Democratic attack as the 2020 elections approached.

York's book is as pacy and reliable an account of these troubling events as you are likely to get. Also worth reading is Lee Smith's *The Plot against the President*, that has now been made into a film. It is deeply disturbing that America's institutions may have been poisoned by anti-democratic operatives of oligarchs and the security state who appear determined to orchestrate a restoration of power. One can only hope that these operatives of the American Empire will fail, and one day be exposed.

While York's book implies an explanation of the revenge of the Washington power elite (they feared being displaced by a President who saw through them and was not owned by them), his book does not really give an explanation of the derangement of so many in the media and political commentary class.

American readers of this blog may not appreciate how contagious this derangement is. Since 2016, the world indeed has experienced a pandemic of media and political commentary folly – a pandemic of Trump Derangement Syndrome. Media organisations around the world have excitedly, breathlessly and endlessly repeated every rushed fabrication about Trump and the RussiaGate hoax. They almost never report the resounding crescendo of facts that debunk their stories and expose their failure to meet basic standards of editorial judgment.

Take, for example, the Australian Broadcasting Corporation. Nightly it serves up biased reports from its American correspondents, who all seem to be auditioning for a gig on CNN and MSNBC. For a couple of years it published a podcast – "Russia if you're listening" – that spewed out every fabrication about Russian collusion. As the house of cards fell – after the Mueller report – the program pivoted to telling porkies about Vladimir Putin. Now it pretends to provide a retrospective on the Trump Presidency. Yet it has never published a correction of any of the errors of its reporting. Nor has the ABC more generally ever corrected and apologised for its widespread and systemic misreporting of the Russian collusion hoax. All the revelations in declassified documents over the last six to twelve months go unreported. Truth and fairness never come out.

What explains this bizarre obsession? There appears to be some kind of cultural power in attacking Trump, but why does it release people of all balance and critical judgment? Is it the echo chamber of media organisations – the ultimate social media pile-on? Is it protecting institutions and beliefs? Is it a collective madness? Trump does appear to function as a scapegoat in the culture, even here in the antipodes where it matters no whit. Mocking Trump is an ice-breaker to conversations with colleagues or friends. There is strong social disapproval if you query the facts behind the memes and claims that push these conversations on.

I simply do not understand it. It is the strangest obsession, and one that may require more invasive treatment, if as I expect, Joe Biden's incapacity and shilly-shallying with anti-democratic forces undo his presidency.

From the Burning Archive

The fall of the American Empire's Potemkin Province
15 August 2021

A "Potemkin village" is a construction that is a façade to give an illusory appearance to the powerful and the remote that a village, a society, a country or other province is thriving, peaceful and happy. The term derives from the propaganda exercise organised by Grigori Potemkin when Empress Catherine the Great made a visit to the Crimea in 1787. The recently conquered province still simmered with discontent and resistance, and yet, while Empress Catherine traveled on a river boat down the Dnieper River, Potemkin had arranged theatrical stage props that resembled thriving, peaceful, grateful villages to be erected by the river side. It gave the visiting Empire an illusion of achieving its objectives – projecting power and developing the country.

Today, we are learning that this old propaganda trick, more an art of self-delusion than mass deceit, has been used by the United States of America for twenty years in Afghanistan. The United States, NATO and even Australian forces have occupied their own command centres, Green Zones, high-tech military bases, civilian contractors, warlord palaces and occasional surges to create a Potemkin Province that assured the leaders they could believe in the illusion of geo-strategic control at the summit of Central Asia.

Now, the Taliban surround Kabul and control the country's borders, most of its territory, and most of its provincial capitals. They have seized a treasure trove of American military equipment, left behind like Potemkin's used stage props on the Dnieper. There are even reports this morning that the Taliban have seized American Black Hawk helicopters and can take to the skies in Kabul. This may cause some problems for the evacuation of the American Empire's personnel from Kabul Airport. Thus, in a few *blitzkrieg* weeks, after the Americans declared – in a euphemism that will surely go down in the books like "collateral damage" and being "economical with the truth – they would "draw down their civilian footprint" to meet a publicity deadline of the 20th anniversary of 9/11, the Taliban have exposed American power and control in Afghanistan as a projection of illusion, a Potemkin Province of an anxious empire in decline.

This dénouement will bring shock, shame and, less certainly, some chance to reconsider America's role in the world. What was it all for, this 20 years of war – or 40 plus years of war, if you count the arming of the *mujahideen* to sabotage the Soviet Empire? A striking and constructive response is provided by Maajid Nawaz, a former Afghani who moved to the United Kingdom. He even points out that the ostensible noble purpose of America's War in Afghanistan – to take revenge on Osama Bin Laden – was based on an illusion or a self-deceit. The strategist of 9/11 was in a Pakistani garrison town. Another intelligence failure?

But shame, humiliation and betrayal can do strange things to the mind, especially to the power-hungering mind of imperial strategists. The American airwaves are full with cries of shame. The search for scapegoats has begun, as has invention of legends of the 'stab in the back' that deprived the generals, like General McMaster, of their meticulously planned war.[171] The quality of reflection is poor. The generals look like they will walk scot-free for their incompetence and corruption, despite calls for accountability. Tucker Carlson in a remarkable monologue puts the acid on the American military, national security and political leadership.[172] He concludes:

> The Pentagon was supposed to build a functional national army in Afghanistan to protect the government, which we installed. But they didn't do that. So people didn't do their jobs and then lied about not doing their jobs. But they're still wearing the uniform of our country. Why is that? Good question. So for the first time in a long time, maybe we could hold our own leaders to account for the calamities they have caused. That's not simply a matter of justice, though. It definitely is that it is the only way to prevent disasters like this from happening again.

---

[171] https://www.bbc.com/news/av/world-asia-58191964
[172] https://www.foxnews.com/opinion/tucker-carlsonhold-someone-accountable-afghanistan

What are the odds of America's leaders being held account for these calamities? Pretty low, I fear. More likely, the manipulators of the post-democratic society of America will create some new mirage and more failure. Corruption and cultural viruses will bring this decadent empire of lies to its knees.

The World Island vs The Atlantic
20 August 2021

This year, 2021, may be remembered as a pivot year in world history. Not because of the pandemic. Not only because of the protracted crisis of the American republic. But because of the changed balance of power in international relations brought about by the decrepitude of the American Atlanticist Alliance and the strengthening of the Eurasian Alliance of China, Russia and the Central Asian States. The Fall of Kabul may be remembered as the American Empire's Suez Crisis moment, when a declining empire's authority at last collapsed, and the world's diplomatic, economic and geo-strategic institutions began to reassemble to meet newly revealed realities.

It is not only an empire's authority that has collapsed, but its ideas of itself in the world. It is no longer the beacon of democracy, but besieged by domestic enemies within; no longer the land of the brave and the home of the free, but the echo-chamber of the woke and refuge of the oligarchs; no longer the hyper-power that can create its own reality, but an expelled occupying power that cannot organise a safe airlift from Kabul airport; no longer the CENTCOM of all the seas, skies and lands of the world, but the self-aggrandising fantasist staring at a TV screen topped by clocks of the world's capital, which the most over-resourced intelligence agencies of the world cannot even set to the correct time. America no longer occupies the geographic pivot of history, but is crumbling back to its place in the outer or insular crescent.

These terms – "geographic pivot of history" and the "outer or insular crescent" – come from the essay by Halford Mackinder, "The Geographical Pivot of History," originally read at the Royal Geographical Society of London in January 1904 and later published in *The Geographical Journal* and as a book. Mackinder was a geographer, who later became a British Liberal Unionist politician who associated with the Fabians (a kind of early twentieth century progressive). He was also an early example of the poisoning of that progressive tradition by Anglo-American Russophobia – born in the rivalries of the nineteenth century, including the paranoid Great Game in Afghanistan, heightened by World War One and the Civil War in Russia (which Mackinder participated in on behalf of the Whites as British High Commissioner to Russia), bequeathed to America in the Cold War, and lately descended into Lear-like senile madness in the Russia Gate hoax. As an early entrepreneur of ideas, Mackinder is credited as one of the founding fathers of geostrategy and geopolitics.

In his 1904 essay, Mackinder gave voice to one of the enduring ideas of geo-strategy in the Anglo-American Empires, with all the tragic grandiosity of the "realist" school in international relations – to control the Eurasian continent was possible for the Anglo-American Empires through hemming in the pivot area of Russia. The idea was seeded in "The Geographical Pivot of History". Mackinder developed the idea in the wake of World War One and his own participation in the resistance to the early Soviet Union in the Russian Civil War. His vision was expressed in the book, *Democratic Ideals and Reality: A Study in the Politics of Reconstruction* (1919). His famous aphorism from this book, memorised by all geo-strategists of the American Empire, was:

> Who rules East Europe commands the Heartland; Who rules the Heartland commands the World Island; Who rules the World Island commands the World.

The Heartland was Russia and Central Asia. The World Island was Eurasia. And the vain ambition to command the World has at long last been exposed as a folly in Afghanistan today.

Towards the end of his life in 1943, Mackinder adapted his Heartland theory to the post-war, Atlantic world, with the fond hope that Britain could still clutch the knees of its new imperial master. The Atlantic Ocean would become the new command centre of the world, tying together North America and Britain as a "moated aerodrome". The rest of the world was confined to the "girdle of deserts and wilderness", and the "Monsoon lands" of the Indo-Pacific. But the determination to weaken Russia and play a Great Game in Central Asia endured. His successors in the American security state stripped these ideas of British imperial nostalgia and turned Mackinder's will to command the World into the Atlanticist worldview.

The Grand Master of this geostrategic worldview was Zbigniew Brzezinski, who advocated in *The Grand Chessboard*, an aggressive American global hegemony regardless of any doubts that might arise from the weak pusillanimous democratic temper. In 1997 Brzezinski expressed his essential concept of how America could command the world through an eagle's nest in the Hindu Kush:

> Eurasia is the world's axial supercontinent. A power that dominated Eurasia would exercise decisive influence over two of the world's three most economically productive regions, Western Europe and East Asia. A glance at the map also suggests that a country dominant in Eurasia would almost automatically control the Middle East and Africa. With Eurasia now serving as the decisive geopolitical chessboard, it no longer suffices to fashion one policy for Europe and another for Asia. What happens with the distribution of power on the Eurasian landmass will be of decisive importance to America's global primacy and historical legacy ... In a volatile Eurasia, the immediate task is to ensure that no state or combination of states gains the ability to expel the United States or even diminish its decisive role.[173]

---

[173] Zbigniew Brzezinski, *The Grand Chessboard: American Primacy and its Geostrategic Imperatives* (1998).

Jeff Rich

In the late 1970's Brzezinski was the National Security Adviser to the President Jimmy Carter. He wrote a memo to the President insisting America command the World by controlling Afghanistan, and its routes to the Persian Gulf, Iran, Southern Russia and Western China. It was Brzezinski, moreover, who armed the Mujahideen in Afghanistan, prior to the Soviet intervention in 1979. You can view on YouTube the staged news report of Brzezinski arriving by helicopter at the Afghan-Pakistan border to incite the start of the American-Afghan wars that ended this week in the capitulation of the global hegemon.

His thinking was a high-class version of Mackinder's heartland theory. Later George W. Bush would give it a common touch – we fight them over there, so we don't have to fight them over here. The same thinking justified the self-rationalising endless war strategies of a gaggle of generals including Mattis, McMaster and, most pathetically, the humbled Milley. This same thinking has now collapsed in Kabul.

And the collapse of this thinking will be a good thing for the world, assuming we can recover from and adapt to the shock. America should no longer dream of commanding the World, the World Island, and its Eurasian Heartland from its insular Atlantic coastline. The scales have fallen from the eyes of the world after its incompetence in Kabul. A former Italian Minister, Michele Geraci, wrote in the *Global Times* (the English-language unofficial mouthpiece of the Chinese Government):

> In a few hours, the West has not only lost Afghanistan, which it had never owned, but has thrown away years, decades, centuries of moral standing, defender of the rights of the weak, of human rights, of women's rights, of a democracy promoter. However, the betrayal that the West perpetrated against Afghan citizens, who are the ones who will pay the price for the West's political choices, cracks, in fact, destroys even the last ethical bulwark that the West boasted about: being the champions of international justice and protector of the oppressed of the world.[174]

---

[174] Geraci, "For Afghanistan The Silk Road Is Better Than The Tank Road," *Global Times*, August 2021.

China, Russia, Pakistan, Iran and the Central Asian States are now working actively to establish stable economic, diplomatic and political institutions that can include a stable, developing Afghan state. While the leaders of the Atlantic Alliance blame the Afghans, cry on television, gnash their teeth and throw out gratuitous insults about "stone-age" or "medieval" Afghani tribesmen, the Foreign Ministers of China and Russia are working together to establish a diplomatic solution that provides for regional security. They may not succeed, but at least they do not delude themselves.

It is worth quoting the recent remarks of Sergei Lavrov, the Russian Foreign Minister, from a press conference on 19 August at length:

> The Taliban does not yet control the entire territory of Afghanistan. There are reports about the situation in the Panjshir Gorge, where the resistance forces led by Vice President Amrullah Saleh and Ahmad Massoud are now concentrated. This makes our position even more consistent. In a situation where the entire nation of Afghanistan was in the grips of a civil war, we advocated the need for an urgent transition to a nationwide dialogue with the participation of all opposing Afghan forces and ethnic and religious groups in that country. Likewise, now that the Taliban have in fact taken power in Kabul and most other cities and provinces, we advocate a national dialogue that will make it possible to form a representative government which, with the support of the Afghan public, will proceed to develop the final arrangements for this multi-ethnic country.

Lavrov then discusses the Russian interpretation of these events.

> What's our take on this? In recent years, within the framework of the "expanded troika" (Russia, the United States, China and Pakistan) and in the Moscow format, which is generally recognised as the most effective mechanism for promoting external support for an Afghan settlement, we pushed for an early start to these talks. The government and the president of Afghanistan, who were bound by corresponding agreements, were not in a hurry to act on them. What happened, happened.

> When politicians are unable to work effectively, the temptation to resort to a military solution mounts. In any case, what we are now faced with absolutely confirms our consistent policy for creating the right external conditions and providing every support for a nationwide dialogue in Afghanistan.

Finally, Lavrov discusses the Russian protocol for diplomatic dialogue that could present a means to respond to these events.

> I'm convinced that the Moscow format has the best chance to succeed since the situation has already taken on a region-wide dimension, and neighbouring countries and countries located further away from Afghanistan are responding to it. As a reminder, all five Central Asian states (China, Pakistan, Iran, India, Russia and the United States) and the conflicting parties are participating in the Moscow format. No official proposals have been made so far. However, the effectiveness of this "backup group" behind the Afghan talks has invariably been recognised by everyone. We stand ready to resume the Moscow format, if needed. We welcomed the Taliban saying they want to start a dialogue with other political forces in Afghanistan. A meeting with the participation of Chairman of the High Council for National Reconciliation Abdullah Abdullah, former President Hamid Karzai and leader of the Islamic Party of Afghanistan Gulbuddin Hekmatyar has been announced. We operate on the premise that all members of this group said they were willing to meet and negotiate in the interests of the Afghan people. We will encourage these processes in every possible way and strive to translate these intentions into concrete actions.

Let us hope it works. But for it to work the Atlantic Alliance must adjust to a diminished status in the world, and give way to the emerging Eurasian Alliance that appears now to control the World Island, but without the Anglo-American ambition to Command the World. Two days before these remarks by Sergei Lavrov, he spoke by phone to Minister of Foreign Affairs of the People's Republic of China Wang Yi. The read-out of the discussion states:

> During the conversation, the ministers stressed the importance of the Treaty of Good-Neighbourliness, Friendship and

Cooperation in terms of developing comprehensive partnership and strategic cooperation between Russia and China in all spheres and elevating their relations to an all-time high, as the two countries mark the 20th anniversary of signing the treaty this year. On the subject of the approaching anniversary of the end of WWII, they paid special attention to stepping up coordinated efforts to counter any attempts to falsify the history of this war or to revise its outcomes. The ministers agreed on holding joint events devoted to the struggle of the two peoples against Nazis and militarists. They went on to exchange views on expanding coordination on foreign policy matters, including within the UN, as well as in light of the recent developments in Afghanistan and their regional implications.

The World Island has reemerged. The tide is receding on the Atlantic coast.

The Looming War of the American Succession
29 August 2021

In 1700 Charles II, King of Spain and Emperor, who presided over a vast global empire, died without a child and without a clear successor. His death triggered a great war for the geostrategic control of the possessions of the declining Spanish Empire by rival dynasties and rival great states. France and Spain were diminished, and the groundwork was laid for what turned out to be 300 years of Anglo-American ascendancy.

In 2020 Joe Biden was elected President of the United States of America, and began to indulge five decades of frustrated foreign policy schemes built on misunderstood security briefings. He was the perfect representative of an incompetent, self-deluded and corrupted elite. He initiated what he thought was a master stratagem in the Great Game of the Eurasian pivot area, replaying Brzezinski's Soviet Afghan trap for China and Russia. But Joe and his think tank boys, Blinken and Sullivan, were no Nixon and Kissinger. The Iberian diplomat and writer on geopolitics, Bruno Maçães, said of the performance:

> I have never seen such a monumental display of incompetence by a Western democracy as the American evacuation from Afghanistan.[175]

So, in 2021 the indispensable nation died without child or its esteemed mind or democracy. Its death triggered a great war for control of Eurasia, the oceans and the new spaces of information and culture. Mackinder plus Mahan plus McLuhan. So began the War of the American Succession.

---

[175] Bruno Maçães, *New Statesman*, 27 August 2021.

From the Burning Archive

Jeff Rich

www.ingramcontent.com/pod-product-compliance
Lightning Source LLC
Chambersburg PA
CBHW071952290426
44109CB00018B/1998